The Listening Heart

The Listening Heart comes from a deep well of hard-won wisdom, from a heart bent toward the words of Jesus. A caveat though: don't read this devotional unless you want to truly experience the powerful affection of your Father in heaven. It's full of promises of His winsome, wooing love.

Mary DeMuth
Author of *The Wall Around Your Heart*

The words Judy penned are like fresh air that will let your soul breathe deeper. Read this book and experience more peace and joy in prayer.

Holley Gerth
Bestselling author of *You're Already Amazing*

This book is a treasure. As I read each daily entry I found my heart softening and my spirit calling out to know Christ more intimately. Deep calls to deep on the pages of this devotional gem. Be prepared to respond at the soul level and experience a transformation.

Robin Jones Gunn
Bestselling novelist and author of *Victim of Grace*

The Listening Heart is a masterpiece of writings that will leave you forever changed. Through this unique devotional book, you will discover that your most profound longing is true—God really does love you beyond your imaginings. He seeks out your company, grieves over your tears and delights in your joy. He really is whispering to your heart . . . even now. Are you listening?

Anita Higman
Award-winning author of over 30 books, including *Where God Finds You*

Feeling some distance from God? Desiring to draw closer? Judy Gordon Morrow graciously opens up her own prayer journals of conversations with God during the deep valleys, peaks and routine days of her life. These readings of God's impressions on Judy's heart—impressions of nearness, concern and love—will encourage you and model a conversational way of speaking with and listening to the Divine Lover of your soul.

Klaus Issler, Ph.D.
Talbot School of Theology, Biola University
Author of *Living into the Life of Jesus*

This haunting devotional is strangely affecting, an approach that perhaps wouldn't be advised and might even be discouraged, yet somehow works in a wholly refreshing and unexpected way. It'll grow on you if you let it, and so you should.

Jerry B. Jenkins
New York Times bestselling novelist and biographer
Owner, Christian Writers Guild

In *The Listening Heart*, Judy Gordon Morrow invites readers to eavesdrop—in a sacred way—on her most intimate conversations with God. What sets this book apart is the raw, spontaneous quality of the entries. I recommend this book to readers who struggle to hear God's voice in a tangible way.

Heather Kopp
Blogger at HeatherKopp.com and author of *Sober Mercies: A Memoir*

Here is a beautiful book you won't want to miss, penned by Judy Morrow while on her knees in prayer over the past twelve years. Her experience of praying and listening will encourage and inspire you to *listen* and to receive God's reassurance that you are ever on His mind and heart. Buy a copy for yourself and one for a friend.

Karen O'Connor
Author of *When God Answers Your Prayers*

This book will help you develop an intimate prayer life with the Lord and hear His voice in a whole new way.

Sheri Rose Shepherd
Bestselling author and speaker

The Listening Heart. Oh how we need it. Oh how we want it. But cultivating a heart tuned to God's voice isn't easy in the busy, noisy world we live in. With tender beauty and life-changing insights, Judy Morrow takes us beyond religious ritual to the heart of relationship—helping us nurture an intimate friendship with the One who knows us best yet loves us most.

Joanna Weaver
Bestselling author of *Having a Mary Heart in a Martha World*

THE
Listening
HEART

Hearing God in Prayer

DEVOTIONS FOR EVERY DAY OF THE YEAR

JUDY GORDON MORROW

Regal

For more information and
special offers from Regal Books, email us at
subscribe@regalbooks.com

Published by Regal
From Gospel Light
Ventura, California, U.S.A.
www.regalbooks.com
Printed in the U.S.A.

Published in association with the literary agency of WordServe Literary Group,
www.wordserveliterary.com.

Library of Congress Cataloging-in-Publication Data
Morrow, Judy Gordon.
The listening heart : hearing God in prayer / Judy Gordon Morrow.
pages cm
ISBN 978-0-8307-6872-1 (trade paper)
1. Devotional calendars. I. Title.
BV4811.M585 2013
242'.2—dc23
2013024611

Rights for publishing this book outside the U.S.A. or in non-English languages are
administered by Gospel Light Worldwide, an international not-for-profit ministry.
For additional information, please visit www.glww.org, email info@glww.org, or write to
Gospel Light Worldwide, 1957 Eastman Avenue, Ventura, CA 93003, U.S.A.

To order copies of this book and other Regal products in bulk quantities,
please contact us at 1-800-446-7735.

Contents

This Journey Together

My Journey

The unsuspecting words of these daily readings didn't know they would become a book, nor did I. They weren't written at a desk or even on a laptop, but penned in scrawling cursive while down on my knees and forearms on my bedroom carpet. In early 2001 the first spiral notebook took up residence before me—my solution to a growing collection of paper scraps grabbed at random to record God's responses to my prayers.

Those dialogues were born out of overwhelming desperation. The end of my longtime marriage, a move to another state, and a new job way outside my comfort zone catapulted me into complete dependence on God. I had never lived alone before, and I knew only a few souls in my new town. Major concerns for my sons burdened my already aching heart. This convergence of difficulties left me reeling and utterly desperate for God—and I discovered that is the best way to be. That very desperation developed in me a listening heart needing to hear from God.

Away from all family and longtime friends, I counted on one constant: God. I knew one source of peace and hope and unconditional love: God. I found out when every prop gets knocked out from under you there is always One who remains: God. He proved to me that He in His fullness is more than enough.

Although I had known Jesus since I was a young child, I didn't know just how intimately He desired to be involved in every detail of my life. In getting to know Him daily on a deeper level, I came to love

Him like never before—and I learned to trust His wild and wonderful ways in my life. The result? Absolute wonder at every juncture of my journey and especially how He has allowed this very ordinary woman to write His extraordinary words of hope.

Daily I met with Him early in the morning after a time in the Word. A notebook and pen became fixtures in front of my bowed head, ready for when God wanted to share His heart with me. And share He did—with words of hope and encouragement, especially regarding my sons and my situation.

Yet God's words to me encompassed much more than what you'll read here. He has given me everything from poetry to my to-do list for the day—often including things outside my thinking. He also has offered His wisdom for my financial and technological challenges. He even has poured out the words to letters that needed to be penned—from expressing God's love to asking another's forgiveness. I never know what He may have in mind, but I savor the joy of the unexpected. I have learned that if I neglect to meet with Him, I might miss something vital and amazing.

Twelve years and 34 notebooks later, I am in awe of God and how He has kept my feet on the path of faith and hope. I am still awaiting some long-held promises, but now I see with new clarity that God's delays and timings have been His gifts—priceless gifts. Had He fulfilled His promises on my timetable, I'm certain my prayer journals would have been nonexistent or sporadic at best. Instead, He kept me in His waiting room, His chosen place to share His heart with me, and my life is forever changed.

Your Journey

But what about you, my friend? Where are you in your journey? Do you secretly wonder, *Is this all there is?* Perhaps you perceive your life as going through the "motions of mediocrity" and, awash with discontent, you long for something more. . . . May I share with you what I simply can't suppress? That "something more," whether realized or not, is to really know God through His Son, Jesus. The aching and yearning deep in your soul can only be satisfied by knowing your Creator and Lord in an intimate way.

You can't love someone you don't know. Once you know God and spend purposeful and joyous times in His incomparable presence, the natural outflow will be a love and devotion that can't be duplicated in any other way. When you *know* Him—not just *about* Him—you can't help but love Him with a love transformed from ho-hum to head-over-heels!

Please know that this book is not meant to displace God's Word—never!—but to lead you to it, if you aren't already reading your Bible daily. I pray you will discover, or perhaps rediscover, the living Word—the bestselling book of all time. The book that contains everything you need for a life fully lived: hope, peace, joy. Forgiveness. Wisdom, strength, perseverance. Love unfailing and unconditional. Grace upon grace. Contentment and satisfaction in your Savior, Jesus. Assurance of your home in heaven when you respond in faith and trust to a Love so amazing, so divine.

God so loves you, my friend, and His loving words and workings are incredibly personal and custom designed. That's one of the many magnificent things about our Lord. How He speaks to you and how He works in your individual life will not mimic mine or any other, but they *will* magnify the greatness of our God.

Our Journey Together

Thank you for joining me on this journey of listening to our Lord. I often wept tears of wonderment and joy while typing the journal entries, when God would give me glimpses of you, the reader, drawing strength and hope from His life-giving words. Daily will I be praying for you, dear one, as together we read these words given out of such love for us, His children.

In the joyful process of truly knowing Him, we move from the shallows to the depths; from distance to intimacy. How I long for that for *everyone*. Life is challenging, and often downright hard and painful, but living this life in closeness with our loving Lord makes *all* the difference. I wouldn't trade a life lived in intimacy with Him for *anything*.

My prayer is that the overflow of God's filling in our lives with His Word and His presence will draw others to Him who still don't know the amazing grace of God through His Son, Jesus. In today's culture God has been so misconstrued, and He entrusts us with the privilege and joy of being His light and love, shining with the truth of who He is—the God who loves beyond measure, forgives beyond reason and helps beyond imagining.

The writings of this book span from January 2001 to June 2013. In the spring of 2012 God surprised me by telling me to compile the writings by months—all the January entries together and so on through December. During that prayerful process, I was struck by the seamless weavings of the years—a beautiful tapestry of God's love, hope and encouragement. He continued to confirm His plans for publication with one divine orchestration after another. This has been His book from the beginning—before I ever knew a book was in His plans. To God be *all* the glory and praise.

Just a quick explanation as to the format of each devotional: the majority of the first lines are what I had last prayed when God began to speak; the rest were gleaned from the rich words of beloved hymns and believers throughout history. I marveled how God led me to words that enhance His—yet another gift from His hand. The prayer journal writings follow, with Scripture completing each day's reading.

When you see the word "Child" in the writings, that was oftentimes when God spoke my name; I pray you will hear Him speak your name.

You will also see the word "soon" used when God speaks of His timing. May I gently remind you that God's definition of "soon" is often far different from ours? Yet His usage of that word is what has helped to keep my hope alive over this journey of many years.

This book has been saturated with prayer, as my utmost desire is that all eyes will see Jesus, the Author and Finisher of our faith. When we look to Him, we have all we need. When we see His face, nothing else is necessary. When we wonder if He is even there, He will hold on to us, waiting for us to be certain of His presence. With Him we are never alone on this journey called Life.

Come. Listen with me. Hear the voice and heart of our loving God and be satisfied. Knowing Him will surpass your deepest needs and your sweetest desires. Simply come and listen.

A Letter to You

Dear Reader,

Every word in this book was penned while on my knees in prayer—including the words in this letter. I never dreamed how much God had to say until I discovered the joy of listening during my daily time with Him. To hear His heart has been the most precious of gifts. I have felt so humbled and honored to hold the pen.

My journey has taken me from a life full of activities and people to a life lived alone. While I always craved solitude and often sought times alone, I had never known such immensity of unbroken aloneness. Its close companion, loneliness, drove me to my knees like never before. What used to be the comforting blanket of occasional solitude now threatened to suffocate me with the overwhelming pain of loneliness and isolation.

Yet it was in those solid silences down on my knees that God's still voice surfaced. A voice speaking comfort and peace and always of His great love toward me. Oh, how He often reminds me of His never-ending love for me. If you were to read many entries in a row, they would perhaps seem a bit repetitious. But how many of us would tell our loved ones here on earth to refrain from speaking words of love to us—that we had heard it all before and already knew that they loved us? No, we bask in every expression of sincere love and affection, and each telling causes us to truly believe what is being said.

So it is with God. He knows we need to believe above all else that He truly and unconditionally loves us now and forever. For it is the unequivocal acceptance of His love that will enable us to trust Him without reservation. Like a child who will let go of everything to jump into the arms of her father, knowing without a doubt that he loves her and would not fail to catch her, so must we know the surety of our Father's love.

Trusting a love like that will change your life. It is changing mine. You learn that the darkness will not remain black forever. Light will shine through. You realize that tears of anguish and pain will some-day be tears of joy. The silences of sorrow will give way to heralds of hope. And then God's sweet truths will glimmer brighter and brighter.

Pain enlarges your heart. Sorrow stretches your soul and creates spaces you never knew before. Spaces that can now be filled with com-passion and empathy and, yes, joy—the sweetest and purest of joys—that you never before thought was possible.

And it all comes down to where it began: communion with our Creator. Conversations that are two way. Listenings filled with love beyond any love we've ever known.

He's waiting for you. Waiting to embrace you with His arms of comfort and with His words of wisdom and hope, but most of all with a love so large and lasting that it will take your breath away.

Once you embark on this journey of joy—of daily times of quietness before God—you'll wonder why you waited so long. There is nothing richer or more satisfying. Nothing more necessary for contentment and peace.

For God Himself would say to you:

You are My beloved child. I long for your company, to joy in each other's presence. Come to Me, and I will give you everything you need for each day. That is My promise to you. You will find it to be true. I love you with an everlasting love, a love beyond the scope of your imagination. Simply be with Me, and you will know My love like never before.

I have found it to be, oh, so true, and I desire it for you, my friend in Christ.

Judy Gordon Morrow

The Listening Heart

January 24, 2011

It's easier to dismiss Me than to obey Me. Thus, My children are ambivalent about hearing Me. It is easier not to listen than to pay attention. It is easier to question if it is Me talking than to be receptive to My voice. For if they should allow themselves to actually hear Me and acknowledge Me, then their hearing of Me would require a response—a response of faith, a response of belief, a response of surrender—each one being a response of obedience.

It is easier not to listen and instead shroud the beauty of communing with Me under the clouds of doubt and mystery. To acknowledge Me and My voice requires the next step: obedience. It is easier to ignore Me and claim that My voice can't really be known. This saddens Me, My child, when all I long to do is to convey My best to My children.

Yet fear of obedience becomes the very obstacle to their obtaining My best. Instead they follow their plans and then wonder why things didn't turn out better. I desire first place, not last—when I am only sought in the midst of an emergency or a crisis. "Seek ye first the kingdom of God, and his righteousness, and all these things shall be added unto you."[1]

Give Me, your Father, your first fruits, and I will multiply your harvest. The very first fruit is a heart surrendered to Me for My purposes. Every other first follows that one.

Don't be afraid to acknowledge that you hear from Me, My daughter. I will honor you for honoring Me. You have chosen to listen in the silences rather than fill them with noise. Now you can hear Me anywhere with a heart attuned to Mine.

I know there is much you don't understand, but don't doubt your hearing of Me. That doubt is a tool of the enemy to defeat My purposes for you. I am calling you to be my faithful servant, to proclaim My word and truth so that I may be lifted up and glorified all of your days. That time is near. Embrace it even now.

Note
  1. Matthew 6:33, *KJV*.

January

A PRAYER FOR THE NEW YEAR

Dear Lord,

I commit this new year to You, and I look forward with great expectation to what You have planned. I know it will be good, because You are the God of goodness and love. Thank You for the joy of living my life hidden in Yours.

Help me this year to
seek You more fully,
follow You more closely,
love You more dearly
and share You unreservedly with those who do not yet know You.

Help me to be Your light and love to this dark and hurting world. Help me to hear Your voice more clearly and to respond to Your nudges immediately. I know in doing so I will see wonder upon wonder unfold from Your almighty, loving hand.

Help me to walk every step of this new year in intimacy and closeness with You, my Father. Help me to know You like never before. Lead me into the depths of Your love and into the richness of Your grace. Help me to reflect Your beauty and bring honor to You.

I pray all this in the matchless, powerful name of Jesus.
Amen.

January 1

Today has been a day of rest and reflection
and unequivocal trust in You.

And that's exactly what I need from you. A trust that doesn't look at circumstances but looks only to Me. A trust that doesn't waver but plants its feet on the bedrock of who I am—your faithful Father who loves you beyond your comprehension. My love for you can *always* be trusted. My love is not fickle, changing or conditional. It is steadfast, strong and sure. *Nothing* changes My love for you.

My love provides for you a place of safety and confidence. A place where only total trust belongs, as that is the only trust that makes sense in light of My measureless and deep, deep love for you. When you begin to plumb the depths of My love, only then can you understand how anything less than total trust will not suffice. My complete love requires complete trust. Total trust lays all questions at My feet, knowing all the answers reside in the Love that died on the cross for you.

I know you wonder what this new year will bring. More of Myself, My child, more of Myself. And with more of My presence come My answers and revealings of joy. Keep looking only to Me, keep trusting Me fully, keep expecting My glorious answers, and just see what I will do. I will not disappoint you. Great will be your joy. Go in My peace, and *know* that I do *all* things well.

Trust in Him at all times, you people;
pour out your heart before Him;
God is a refuge for us.

PSALM 62:8

January 2

Work Your wonders, Lord. I'm counting on You.

I will do just that—wonder upon wonder will I perform for you out of My heart of love for you. You will be amazed by My wonders on your behalf. Take great hope and joy in My words to you, even before you see them come to pass.

Know that I am at work in every realm of your life and that not one detail is escaping My notice. I am the Lord your God, and I will fulfill My every promise to you. Walk on the path of complete trust in Me, one step at a time, and just see where I will lead you.

Allow My peace to infill you and to overflow onto others. Be My giver of My joy and peace and love. Know Me in My fullness, and from that fullness I will overflow from you into the lives of others.

I will multiply your minutes. Count on Me to do that. Think of the loaves and fishes and the abundant overflow. Dwell on who I am, and all will be well. I love you, My child. Just see how I will show My love to you this very day.

And when He had taken the five loaves and the two fish, He looked up to heaven, blessed and broke the loaves, and gave them to His disciples to set before them; and the two fish He divided among them all. So they all ate and were filled. And they took up twelve baskets full of fragments and of the fish. Now those who had eaten the loaves were about five thousand men.

MARK 6:41-44

January 3

Make Your plans clear, Lord.

My plans are above knowing, My child, but you will know clearly in time. Don't despair. Only trust. All will become clear. I will provide all that you need. Haven't I done that so far? I will not fail you.

The enemy wants to hold you down, My child. Don't let him. Greater is He that is in you than he that is in the world.[1] Be aware of his tactics. Be ever on guard. Be prepared to oust him from your present circumstance in My name.

He is a liar, deceiver and destroyer. His constant goal is to oppose you and to create disharmony within and without. He desires to silence you and your witness for Me, but I won't allow that to happen. Great are the plans I have for you, and I will fulfill them. Trust Me fully, and just see what I will do.

Live in My peace today. I will guide you into all truth. Fret about nothing, and know that all is well. All is in my hands, so how could anything less be the case? I do all things well, and I'm doing that for you even now.

I love you, My child. Walk today in My love, surrounded by My love, protected by My love. Truly, *all is well.*

The thief comes only to steal and kill and destroy.
I came that they may have life, and have it abundantly.

JOHN 10:10, *NRSV*

Note
1. See 1 John 4:4, *KJV.*

January 4

I only want what You want.

And that's what you shall have. Blessings outpoured from My loving hand. You shall know *new* joy, *new* days, *new* blessings. Your joy will overflow.

This day is My gift to you. Continue to bask in My peace. Rest in Me with sheer abandon, not allowing any fear or doubt or worry to enter in. Keep your heart and mind stayed on Me alone, and you will truly know perfect peace.

Oh, My child, I will satisfy your longings, and deep contentment will be yours. Again, bask in My peace all day. Cover yourself with prayer and My promises. Let nothing else enter in. Focus only on Me. I will not fail you. I am taking care of everything in My way. Rest in that assurance today.

You have been wise to wait on Me and learn of Me. You know you can trust the One who loves you so much. You are truly My beloved child. Let Me cradle you in My love today, and be at total peace and rest. I will do that for you. Gentle, sweet rest and peace will be yours today. I love you.

See, the former things have come to pass,
and new things I now declare;
before they spring forth, I tell you of them.
ISAIAH 42:9, *NRSV*

January 5

Lord, thank You for Your Word.

My children need to feed on My Word. Some do, but they are far too few. Oh, the difference that feasting on My Word makes in the lives of My followers. How can you run the race of faith if you don't partake daily of My strengthening Word?

A little taste now and then does not prepare you for the rigors of a marathon. Life is full of daily challenges. You need to be prepared by taking daily sustenance from My Word. It will give you not only strength but also joy.

I know there is much you don't understand. It's all right, My child. You don't have to understand. Just trust Me. I am helping you in every regard.

Rest, My child. Don't allow troubling thoughts to disturb the rest in your soul. Focus on Me and on My Word and on My many promises to you. Is there anything too hard for Me?

Continue to walk by faith, not sight.[1] I will honor you for doing that. Know that all I tell you is true. I only speak truth. Live in My truth and peace today. Let Me carry you. Depend wholly on Me.

Jesus answered, "It is written:
'Man shall not live on bread alone,
but on every word that comes from the mouth of God.'"
MATTHEW 4:4, *NIV*

Note
1. See 2 Corinthians 5:7.

JUDY GORDON MORROW

January 6

Epiphany

No one loves you like I do. Dwell on My inexhaustible love for you. With Me you can never wear out your welcome or exhaust My love. I never tire of your coming to Me. In fact, I long for you to do that daily—many times throughout each day. I will never turn you away.

Embrace this day as My gift to you. Allow My plans to take precedence, and invite My purposes to supersede anything you may have in mind. The divine always outshines the plans of men. Welcome My divine plans for you, My child, like you welcome the joys of Christmas.

Extend your open hands to receive My gifts of love to you. There is never a need to shrink back. Instead, fling open the door of your heart, and allow Me to fill it to overflowing. That is My desire for you, to fill your heart to overflowing with My gestures of love to you. Gestures that will provide a window for others to see My love and care for My children. Enjoy each gift and be grateful.

Be grateful even today. See Me everywhere. Make space for joy. Truly, you have no idea what this day may bring. Expect epiphanies. Welcome My surprises. Relish My serendipities, and bask in My love for you. Be filled with all the fullness of Me so that you can overflow with My love to others. Live today in *joyous* expectation.

> *My soul, wait silently for God alone,*
> *for my expectation is from Him.*
> PSALM 62:5

January 7

I want to follow Your leadings today.
Please make things plain.

I will make things plain. You know My nudges. I won't let you miss anything vital. I will honor your listening heart. Continue to look to Me alone, My child. Hold tightly to Me and My promises. Know without a doubt that I will not fail you.

Prayer is absolutely key. Nothing truly good can happen without fervent prayer. The enemy will use many methods, even good things, to keep My children from praying. Don't allow that to happen. Pray like you breathe—naturally, freely and constantly. Establishing the habit of constant prayer will be life changing for those you pray for and for yourself.

Delight in the communion of prayer, in the constant communication with Me, your loving Father. I hear your every prayer—those with words and those with groanings too painful for words. Always keep the prayer channel clear and open between you and Me.

Now just trust and rest in Me with absolute assurance that I will do all that I have promised. There is nothing to fear. Rest in My perfect peace. Don't let even a wisp of fear enter in. My perfect love barricades fear. Rest in My love and care all day today. I love you, My precious child. You will soon know that truth like never before.

Likewise the Spirit also helps in our weaknesses. For we do not know what we should pray for as we ought, but the Spirit Himself makes intercession for us with groanings which cannot be uttered.

ROMANS 8:26

January 8

Lord, I need Your guidance.

I will give you guidance. All you have to do is ask. I will provide. I will not fail you. You are My beloved child, and I will honor your seeking heart.

I will bless today. Joy in My presence and in My love gifts to you. See My face of love toward you. See My hand in everything. Know My presence and peace even in the seemingly ordinary. Nothing is ordinary when looked at through My eyes.

Look at others, My child, through My eyes. See them as I do. Love them with My love. See who they are in Me. Bring My joy and love to their lives. That is My mission, My plan for you—to bestow My love and joy on others even in the simplest of ways. Listen to My nudges and act on them.

Go now in My peace. You are My beloved child, and I am going before you. What wonderful plans I have ahead for you. Rest in that assurance today. Be filled with My joy and peace. I love you.

Do nothing from selfish ambition or conceit,
but in humility regard others as better than yourselves.
Let each of you look not to your own interests,
but to the interests of others.
Let the same mind be in you that was in Christ Jesus.
PHILIPPIANS 2:3-5, *NRSV*

January 9

I am as nothing, and rejoice to be
Emptied, and lost, and swallowed up in Thee.

MADAME JEANNE GUYON (1648–1717),
"I LOVE MY LORD, BUT WITH NO LOVE OF MINE"

When you seek Me, you will find Me. When you seek My wisdom, I will give it. When you long for specific answers, I will give them when you are willing to wait to hear from Me. I take delight in helping you in *every* area of your life. All you need to do is ask.

In your asking you are declaring your dependence on Me, and that is a good thing. My words come back to you: without Me you can do nothing. Now think of the converse: with Me you can do everything—and in the everything I desire for you, nothing else matters. You are seeing how a "nothing" is actually a plus. Not until you know your nothingness without Me will you be able to plunge into the depths of My greatness and see the difference I make. With Me all things are possible. Without Me nothing is assured.

You come seeking answers, and I come seeking you. Seek Me, and My answers will be revealed, My wisdom will be yours. But *all* comes from waiting on Me, looking to Me, hoping in Me. I will never fail a child seeking My face. My face is shining on you even now, and you will find in Me everything you are needing. Continue your day in sweet communion with Me, and enjoy My sweet revealings.

I love you, My child. All is out of My love for you.

I am the vine, you are the branches.
He who abides in Me, and I in him, bears much fruit;
for without Me you can do nothing.
JOHN 15:5

January 10

Be still, and know that I am God.
FROM PSALM 46:10

Just know Me, My child. Nothing else matters. All else will fall into place when you start with knowing Me. I am the beginning and the end. I am in all and through all. I am all that matters.

When you focus on Me, everything else will align accordingly, just like the planets to the sun. I am the God of balance, perfection and peace. Knowing Me makes all the difference in knowing how to live out your life.

Keep your eyes on Me, and all will fall into place with my order and perfection. Take your eyes off Me, and chaos will reign. My hand extends harmony. Lack of My hand leads to confusion and discord. If only My children would learn that absolute truth and wait for the guidance of My hand in all things. They would see and know My sovereignty and goodness like never before.

Rest in Me today, My child. Let me enfold you in My peace. My peace will wrap you in comfort and hope. While you can't see and know the completion of My plans, you can know My peace.

Just keep relying on Me, your loving Father. Think on that—your loving Father. I love you beyond your comprehension, and I desire only the best for you, My beloved child.

Glory in his holy name; let the hearts of those who seek the Lord rejoice.
Look to the Lord and his strength; seek his face always.
1 CHRONICLES 16:10-11, *NIV*

January 11

All the way my Savior leads me; what have I to ask beside?

FANNY JANE CROSBY (1820–1915),
"ALL THE WAY MY SAVIOR LEADS ME"

Walk with Me today. I will be your Wonderful Counselor. You are right to seek Me first for every problem and dilemma. If I desire for you to have other resources, I will make sure those are placed in your hands. Don't get so caught up in mechanics and methods for productivity that your life becomes clogged with human preoccupations. Instead, be that clear, flowing channel that allows for constant communion with Me so that you can learn My desires and My ways.

I, above all, know exactly what is needful for you, My child, as I am the One who created you. I know intimately your very nature and personality and what will work best for you. Enjoy the adventure of allowing Me to give you My creative and customized answers and tools designed just for you. You will be amazed by My individual solutions and how perfect they are for you.

You don't need to continue in the same struggles. I know the intricacies of you and how to best help *you* in every realm of your life. Your responsibility lies in staying close to Me and listening to My every word and nudge. Do that even today, and see the difference I will make.

Think on these words all day today. Most of all think on *Me*, your Source and Provider of *all* things. You know that truth like never before, so *live* in that truth like never before. I am with you, and I will never let you down. I love you, My child.

Your eyes beheld my unformed substance.
In your book were written all the days that were formed for me,
when none of them as yet existed.

PSALM 139:16, *NRSV*

January 12

I claim victory in You, Jesus.

And it is yours—the victory that was won on the cross and displayed in the resurrection. Never do My children need to live in defeat because of the victory that is theirs in Me. Dwell on that simple but profound truth today. And remember that the power of the resurrection is the same power that is available to you.

Think on that. The power that raised Me from the dead can raise any deadness out of your life. This power transforms death into life, despair to hope, darkness to light. No other power on earth can compare to the power from on high. And it is yours, My child. It is yours.

Live in the abundance and freedom of that power even today. View every challenge of your life in light of My resurrection power, and see how they shrink in contrast. Nothing compares to Me and My power. The most daunting circumstances of your life become only a wisp of concern when they come under the sphere of My power. Live in the realm of My resurrection power, and you will live in certain victory.

So much is available to you in Me, My child. I am not stingy in My provisions to My children. My nature is one of abundance. I am free with My grace; I am lavish in My love; I am overwhelming with My goodness. Simply be the grateful recipient of all I offer to you in the living out of your life, and know My peace and joy.

The sting of death is sin, and the strength of sin is the law.
But thanks be to God, who gives us the victory
through our Lord Jesus Christ.

1 CORINTHIANS 15:56-57

January 13

I love this time with You.

Thank you for this time with Me. It brings joy to My heart as well as to yours. Aren't you glad you do this now? The discipline yields joy, much joy.

You have much ahead of you. Just know I am going ahead of you, every step of the way. There is nothing to fear, nothing to fret about. I am in control. So don't let worry sap your strength and joy. Just trust Me.

I am working in every area of your life, working to bring all together to bring you joy. You will rejoice. Oh, how you will rejoice. Your heart will overflow with joy. Trust Me in this. Wait patiently for Me to act. I am working even now.

I will reward your faithful heart. What I have planned will far outweigh all your present sorrow and pain. You will see.

Have a wonderful day in My grace. See what I will do. I love giving good gifts. Watch for them and see. Peace to you, My child. Walk in My peace.

So the ransomed of the Lord shall return,
and come to Zion with singing,
with everlasting joy on their heads.
They shall obtain joy and gladness;
sorrow and sighing shall flee away.

ISAIAH 51:11

January 14

I really pray that You will guide and direct.

I will. I will go before you, directing your every step. You will know what to do. Relax in Me, and trust Me for everything. In doing that will come joy and peace. I am the Author of peace. Continue to rest in that peace.

I know the beginning to the end, and I know what I am doing. Trust Me completely. Rest in Me and in the perfection of My workings. Follow Me in every leading, and then I can make known My next step. Don't complicate things. Simply follow Me.

Walk in My Spirit today. He will be your guide and comfort. He is my gift to you. He will see you through this difficult time. He will carry you.

Look only to Me. All else is futile. I alone am the answer to all you are seeking, and I love you like no other. Rest in My mighty love and grace, and know all is well.

For You are my rock and my fortress;
therefore, for Your name's sake, lead me and guide me.

PSALM 31:3

January 15

They who trust Him wholly find Him wholly true.
FRANCES RIDLEY HAVERGAL (1836–1879),
"LIKE A RIVER GLORIOUS"

Continue to hope in Me, My child. Hope in Me never needs to waver because of who I am. Hope in Me is as solid as a rock, as firm as if the promise has already been fulfilled. Don't think of hope as some illusive, flimsy thing but as rock solid as the One who has given you the hope.

Don't give up. Keep believing. Keep trusting. I am working. I am working diligently on your behalf. You will be amazed, My child. You will be humbled by My outstretched arm of love to you.

Know that I am with you. Know that I have not forgotten you. What Father would forget His precious children? Not one detail escapes me. You are My beloved child, and I am in every detail of your life. You are right to look to Me for everything. I will honor you for that.

Continue to trust. Continue to believe. I am at work. Things can change in an instant. Truly, I am the blessed controller of all things. I will honor you for your trust and waiting on Me.

Take great joy and continued hope in these words. Know that I will not fail you. I love you with an everlasting love. Live in My joy and peace today. All is well.

Through Christ you have come to trust in God.
And you have placed your faith and hope in God
because he raised Christ from the dead
and gave him great glory.
1 PETER 1:21, NLT

January 16

You are the only One I have, and being with You is the best place to be.

Yes, it is, My child. In Me is everything you need for every moment of your day. You are right to trust Me. I will not fail you. Rather, I will honor your faith and trust in Me and will pour out blessing upon blessing.

Look to Me for *this* day to accomplish My purposes. You see My provisions in every realm. Take none of this lightly. Dwell on each thing, small and great, with unfettered praise. Let praise fill your heart and home today, and just see what power I will infuse you with even today.

Live completely in My presence today. Allow Me to fill your day with gifts from My hand—songs of praise, insights of wisdom, peace beyond understanding. I am instilling in you a wellspring and filling it with Me and My truths so that from its overflow many will be blessed and refreshed.

Ever pray. Ever trust. Ever know My heart. I will *not* fail you. Over and over I tell you that truth. Do not waver. Your unequivocal trust will I honor.

Those who honor me I will honor,
but those who despise me will be disdained.

1 SAMUEL 2:30, *NIV*

January 17

I feel overwhelmed, Lord.

My dear child, don't feel overwhelmed. Is there anything too hard for Me? I go before you, removing obstacles and preparing the way. Let me do that for you. Don't strain on your own. Leave all to Me. Remember that I am your loving Father who longs to help you.

Today will be busy but not impossible. Leave all in My hands. Trust Me completely. I will work and I will shine. Others will see what I have done.

Rest in My loving care. Forsake all doubt and worry. Know only Me and My love for you. Oh, how I love you, My child. Your faithfulness to Me will reap great rewards. You will see. You will see and rejoice. I love you with an everlasting love. Rest in My love today.

> *Hear my cry, O God; attend to my prayer.*
> *From the end of the earth I will cry to You,*
> *when my heart is overwhelmed;*
> *lead me to the rock that is higher than I.*
> *For You have been a shelter for me,*
> *a strong tower from the enemy.*
>
> PSALM 61:1-3

JUDY GORDON MORROW

January 18

Thy mercies how tender, how firm to the end!
Our Maker, Defender, Redeemer and Friend.

SIR ROBERT GRANT (1779–1838),
"O WORSHIP THE KING"

My dear child, thank you for your worship of Me, for your delight and appreciation of who I am. You are right to dwell on who I am, for that will only increase your faith.

I am the Father who loves you dearly. I am the Creator who has made all things. I am the Redeemer who gives new life. I am the Alpha and the Omega, the beginning and the end. I am the Way, the Truth and the Life.

As you focus on who I am, you will realize anew that nothing is too hard for Me. Nothing. I am working even now to accomplish great things in your life. Rest in that. I have wonderful days ahead for you. Rest in that and wait for My perfect timings.

Just continue to walk with Me, to stay close to Me. I will not fail you. I will bring great things to pass. You will see and be glad. Continue to seek Me each day, and soon you will know new joy. Joy that is My gift to you. It is coming soon. Yes, soon. Live in that hope. I love you.

And my soul shall be joyful in the Lord;
it shall rejoice in His salvation.

PSALM 35:9

January 19

No pilgrim is without his night season. Trust God in the dark.
This is the highest effort and triumph of faith.

J. R. MacDuff (1818–1895)

Do you not see what I am doing? You have been seeing things clearly, so don't stop now, My child. Don't let circumstances cloud your vision of My omnipotence, My power, My plans that I have promised you.

Even now you are in the midst of My plan. Seek Me fully, and you will fully know My ways and desires. Do *not* succumb to despair, do *not* panic, do *not* allow any thoughts other than Mine to enter your mind. Keep a barricade of praise and prayer around your heart and mind and around your home. Allow entrance only to Me. I am *all* that matters, and I will do *all* that I have promised you.

Just believe Me, dear child. I know it isn't easy now that things in every realm look more impossible than ever. I am the God of the impossible, and nothing is too hard for Me. Look to Me alone. You simply can't look at circumstances. Why look at darkness when you can look to Me, your Light? I will illumine your path. All you need to do is follow Me, one step at a time.

Rest, My child. Partake of My peace. Look to Me alone. I have never failed you, and I'm not about to now. I love you. Know that anew—*I love you*. Rest in My love today.

Now to Him who is able to do exceedingly abundantly above all that we ask or think, according to the power that works in us, to Him be glory in the church by Christ Jesus to all generations, forever and ever. Amen.

EPHESIANS 3:20-21

January 20

Lord, I am just utterly dependent on You.

And that's the way to be, My child. Utter dependence yields free rein for Me to work. When you yield fully to Me, I am freed to work fully and unhindered for you. Dwell on that truth for a moment. Complete surrender to Me yields complete fulfillment of My purposes in your life—purposes so wondrous that you will forever marvel and rejoice.

I'm going before you even now. I know yesterday was hard, but that was only due to your change of focus. You *must* keep your eyes on Me alone. That's how Abraham and Joseph and Daniel and Mary were able to remain steadfast, in spite of their unusual circumstances—eyes on Me, ears attuned to My voice, hearts willing to obey.

I will enable you to do the same, and you too will know the joy and reward of remaining steadfast in Me. Look forward to the day of My answers. Soon will it come. Soon, My child. *Soon.*

*Then the angel said to her, "Do not be afraid, Mary,
for you have found favor with God.
And behold, you will conceive in your womb and bring forth a Son,
and shall call His name Jesus. . . .
Then Mary said to the angel, "How can this be, since I do not know a man?"
And the angel answered and said to her, . . .
"With God nothing will be impossible."
Then Mary said, "Behold the maidservant of the Lord!
Let it be to me according to your word."
And the angel departed from her.*

LUKE 1:30-31,34-35,37-38

January 21

I'm possessed of a hope that is steadfast and sure,
Since Jesus came into my heart!

RUFUS HENRY MCDANIEL (1850–1940),
"SINCE JESUS CAME INTO MY HEART"

Continue to live in My hope and grace. Trust Me for all things. Joy in the journey, in the adventure of the way I am leading you. Know that you are Mine and that all is well. Rest in Me and in the comfort of My love. Let nothing rob you of My peace. It is forever yours.

Rely on Me for everything today. Nothing needs to come out of your wisdom and strength. All will be provided to you by Me. My wisdom and strength will not fail you as you seek Me and My ways.

Rest totally in Me and in My incomparable love for you. Look forward to My new days with great assurance. They are coming as surely as the rising of the sun each day. Believe Me wholeheartedly and see what I will do.

I love you, My precious child. Abide in My love. Know My perfect peace. All is well. All is truly well.

I thank and praise you, God of my ancestors,
for you have given me wisdom and strength.
You have told me what we asked of you and
revealed to us what the king demanded.

DANIEL 2:23, *NLT*

January 22

Oh, here is the secret of becoming much like God
by remaining long alone with God.
If you won't stay long with Him,
you won't be much like Him.

R. A. TORREY (1856–1928),
"THE POWER OF PRAYER"

I love you, My child. Thank you for taking time daily to be with Me. It will pay great dividends. This is how you get to know My heart. This is how I unfold My plans to you one day at a time.

Enjoy this day. Be My light and love to those around you. Relax in Me and reflect My peacefulness to others. Trust Me totally for all things. Let Me carry your burdens. That's why I am here. I long to do that for you.

Be at one with Me. Be content in Me. I am working. All is well. You will see. Just rest in Me and My love.

Enjoy your day. I love you.

The Lord is good to those whose hope is in him, to the one who seeks him;
it is good to wait quietly for the salvation of the Lord.

LAMENTATIONS 3:25-26, *NIV*

January 23

Please help me, Lord. How I need You!

I am with you. You know that I have told you that I will never leave you nor forsake you.[1] Nothing has changed in that regard. You are My beloved child, and I will never abandon you.

Hang on, My child. Seek only Me. Look only to My face and My ways. I will not fail you. Truly, My answers are coming soon. Do not faint in the waiting.

Know that hope is always from Me, the God of hope. There is no other author of true, life-giving hope. Breathe deeply of My hope today. Expel doubt, fear and despair. Shake off the cloak of gloom that has been shrouding you and your joy these past many days.

Arise in new hope, in new joy, in new expectation, knowing that your loving Father will not disappoint you. I will bring all to pass that I have promised you. I know you believe that. Now believe it with joy, My child, not despondency. Keep your eyes on Me, and just see what I will do!

Your time with Me has been well spent, has it not? Don't allow the enemy to undo one clasp on your armor of faith. Eyes on Me, My child, eyes on Me. That is the key to everything. Never glance away for even a second. Look only to Me for everything, and just see how I will provide.

Put on the full armor of God, so that you can
take your stand against the devil's schemes.
EPHESIANS 6:11, *NIV*

Note
1. See Hebrews 13:8.

January 24

Restore me, Jesus.

I will restore you. Now rest in Me, and in Me alone be satisfied. I am truly all that you need. Once you truly learn that truth, you will be free, totally free. I will provide for your every need. You have seen how I have done that in the past, and I won't stop now.

Oh, My child, I know your weariness, I know your wonderings, your longings. Give them all to Me, and you will find rest for your soul.

Live unto Me. You are My child, and only good things will come from My hand. Let Me guide your every step. Give every fear and frustration to Me. Cast all your cares upon Me, for I care for you.

That is key. Hold on to nothing that will diminish or destroy your faith. Give all to Me, and then I can fill you with Myself and all My gifts to you. Gifts of hope, comfort, joy, love and peace. See the difference? Why allow yourself to be filled with fear when I can fill you with hope and peace? I will help you to choose Me and My gifts.

I am working, My child. I am working in ways you cannot see. But someday you will see and know. In the meantime, trust My heart of love toward you. I am orchestrating all things according to My purposes. Rest in Me completely. You will know My love like never before. I love you. I will always love you.

Cast all your anxiety on him because he cares for you.
1 PETER 5:7, *NIV*

January 25

Where we are ignorant, God is wise;
where we stand blindly in the dark, He is in the light;
where we wonder, He calmly knows.

PHILLIPS BROOKS (1835–1893),
"MAN'S WONDER AND GOD'S KNOWLEDGE"

I am working. Always know I am working, even when you don't see evidence of that. I am always here for you. I will never leave you nor forsake you. That is My promise to you from the beginning, remember? Nothing has changed in that regard.

Don't dread today. I am going before you. All is well. Follow My leadings. Trust Me in everything. I know what needs to be done.

You are My precious child, and I am working on your behalf. Never doubt that. I delight to bring you joy. Be prepared to know much joy. Truly, your joy will overflow.

Rejoice and rest in that hope. Hope only in Me. I look forward to giving you good gifts directly from My hand. I love you. Go in My peace.

And the Lord, He is the One who goes before you.
He will be with you, He will not leave you nor forsake you;
do not fear nor be dismayed.

DEUTERONOMY 31:8

JUDY GORDON MORROW

January 26

How I need Your peace, Lord.

I know your mind is in turmoil this morning, My child. It need not be.

I *will* keep you in perfect peace as you fix your mind on Me. I want you to know My peace that surpasses all understanding. Peace that others won't be able to understand but they will desire it for themselves. You can be My example in that way.

I know you hardly know how to pray. I hear the deepest expressions and longings of your heart, even when there are no words. *Especially* when there are no words. Don't let lack of words or wisdom trouble you. I see and know your innermost desires and longings, and I am interceding for you. Take great comfort in knowing that.

Focus on Me alone, My child. Look only to Me. I will hold you steady. I will get you through this time. I know there is much you don't understand, but you don't need to. I am working out all things according to My plan.

Just rest in Me. Trust Me unequivocally and wait expectantly, knowing that all good things come from My hand. I will not fail you in any way. Just hold on to Me and My constant promises to you.

Think only on Me and My promises. Let nothing dissuade you. Rest, My child. Rest in joy. Keep looking upward. Go in My peace and joy and constant hope.

> *Let me hear what God the Lord will speak,*
> *for he will speak peace to his people, to his faithful,*
> *to those who turn to him in their hearts.*
>
> PSALM 85:8, *NRSV*

January 27

In all thy ways acknowledge him, and he shall direct thy paths.
FROM PROVERBS 3:6

Acknowledge Me even in the delays, My child. Rather than fight against them, see Me in the delays, knowing *My* ways are *best*. I am not delaying to increase your heartache. I am delaying to increase your trust and your ability to see the *perfection* of My plan. My timings in that plan are a major part of that perfection. Acknowledge Me in that, rest in that; give credit to Me and My wisdom, and know that My ways are higher and better.

Accept by faith the perfection of My workings, and allow Me to deepen your trust. Dwell in My all-encompassing, amazing love for you, and *know* that I will not allow you to suffer any longer than absolutely necessary. Every detail must first be in place so that My glory can shine the brightest. All will see *Me* and what I have done, which will only increase your joy.

Trust Me, My child. Trust Me and know that, truly, I do *all* things well. I will not disappoint. You will know joy upon joy, as the floodgates of heaven will release every loving gift from My hand at My appointed times. Prepare for the sweetest of joys with joyful anticipation—not with murmuring and complaining. You see clearly how I can't release My blessings into a heart clogged with ingratitude and complaining. Let praise pillow your heart to prepare for My wondrous answers of joy.

As for God, His way is perfect;
the word of the Lord is proven;
He is a shield to all who trust in Him.
PSALM 18:30

January 28

Please work out Your will.

I will work in ways you have not yet even thought of. Trust Me in this. Know My heart. I will bring about My will in My time. There is no need for worry or fear or even wondering. Just trust Me, My child. That is all that is required of you.

What joy I will be bringing into your life! Joy well worth waiting for, My child. Joy that will bring new life to you and others. Oh, the incredible joy that I will be pouring out upon you. Be prepared to bask in that joy.

I am going before you today. Lean on Me completely. Trust My nudges. I will not fail you. Know My heart of love toward you, My child. It is a love that has only your best in mind. Relax totally in that love. Fret not. I am able.

Joy in your day and in My presence. Remember that I do all things well. *Well.* Not halfheartedly, not poorly, but well. Rest in that assurance and in who I am. I love you, My child. Go in My peace.

> *Oh, how generous and gracious our Lord was!*
> *He filled me with the faith and love that come from Christ Jesus.*
>
> 1 TIMOTHY 1:14, *NLT*

January 29

Peace, perfect peace, our future all unknown?
Jesus we know, and He is on the throne.
EDWARD H. BICKERSTETH, JR. (1825–1906),
"PEACE, PERFECT PEACE"

Go in My peace. *My* peace. Not as the world gives, for that is not true peace—but go in the peace of the One who is the Prince of Peace. My peace steadies you. My peace comforts. My peace satisfies. Keep your eyes on Me, and My peace will remain.

Even now know My peace anew. Rest in Me completely. Leave all in My hands. I know your concerns, and I will take care of each one. Trust Me completely. Have I not always provided? I will go before you and smooth the way. Allow Me to do that, and you will not stumble on the path I have prepared for you.

In everything give thanks. Live above the human realm. Live in My divine majesty. Live in My power and grace, and allow Me to be glorified in you. Then My kingdom will increase as you daily follow Me and My leadings. I know that is the desire of your heart, and I will help you to do that.

My child, rest in Me. Relinquish all to Me, and allow *Me* to work. You have to do nothing but follow My directives. And I will make those clear to you. See? There is *nothing* to fear, nothing to worry about, nothing to cause distress or unrest. In Me are peace and calm and serenity. Be filled with all the fullness of Me. All is well.

Peace I leave with you, My peace I give to you;
not as the world gives do I give to you.
Let not your heart be troubled, neither let it be afraid.
JOHN 14:27

JUDY GORDON MORROW

January 30

Order is the shape upon which beauty depends.
PEARL S. BUCK (1892–1973)

There is joy in preparation. Joy born out of the peace that comes from order. When your life is in order, you are prepared for whatever is next. Preparation eliminates the need for scrambling at the last minute to ensure a good outcome. Preparation is the framework for order, and in that home dwell serenity and peace.

Think on the opposite scenario: disorder, stress, wasted time, restlessness, disarray. All of these form a cloud that hangs over you, shrouding you in feelings of inadequacy and discontent. It doesn't have to be this way.

I am a God of order, and I designed you in the same way. Order brings calmness and peace. And out of that peace you can best fulfill My purposes. I am not a God who rushes and hurries, nor did I intend that for My children.

There's a difference between speedy accomplishment and frantic activity. Frantic behavior borders on panic, while I long for you to enjoy the fruit of preparation that brings peace. While this isn't a struggle for everyone, it is for many, including you, My child. Allow Me to show you ways that will alleviate this burden and will free you to be more greatly used by Me.

Let all things be done decently and in order.
1 CORINTHIANS 14:40

January 31

Satan is the personal enemy of Christ.

WATCHMAN NEE (1903–1972),
"A WORLD UNDER WATER"

The enemy uses every tactic he can to interfere with My children's effectiveness for Me. Be aware of how he can take simple and even mundane things and use them as tools for his purposes. Be ever on guard, and see clearly through My lens of wisdom His deceitful and wily ways. I am here to help you. He looks only to destroy.

Today is a fresh page in your life. Don't let your former patterns dictate today. Instead look to Me, and step by step I will lead you into ways that will enhance your days and make you more effective for My kingdom. I know you welcome that, as your heart's desire is to be used by Me for My eternal purposes.

Follow My leadings, and I will free you from all that encumbers you so that you will be prepared for what I have next for you. Living in the freedom I provide makes each day an adventure—a way of both joy and contentment. Today is only the beginning . . .

> *For I am about to do something new.*
> *See, I have already begun! Do you not see it?*
> *I will make a pathway through the wilderness.*
> *I will create rivers in the dry wasteland.*
>
> ISAIAH 43:19, *NLT*

February

Silence invites God to meet with us. It beckons Him into the chambers of our inmost beings, where calm replaces chaos. When one by one we discard every troubling thought, every nagging distraction, every noisy beating on our ears—we have then made room for silence to slip in.

When silence replaces all of life's loudness, God's presence envelops me and I let myself down into that place of calm. And while I am tempted to talk to God, I try to refrain. I don't want to hear my voice. I want to hear His. And whether that hearing is in words or those gentle nudges in my spirit, I know I have been with Him, the Lover of my soul.

The sweetness of His presence defies words. It is often palpable and exudes a warmth and love that can only come from God above. I am always so humbled that God would come to me in this way, and how I thank Him for the gift of His loving presence.

The space of silence is God's gift to me, one that I will seek and treasure the rest of my days. God-filled silence gives a richness to the living of this life like nothing else I have discovered. I hope to dwell there in the deepest places of my soul all the days of my life.

February 1

There is a place of quiet rest near to the heart of God.

CLELAND BOYD MCAFEE (1866–1944),
"NEAR TO THE HEART OF GOD"

Rest in Me. You have come through some difficult times, some trying times, and now I need you to rest in Me. Let Me restore you. Let Me bring sweet healing to your spirit and soul. I have seen and known your pain, and now I am covering you with the peace of My presence. I have allowed you to taste of deep pain, and your heart has enlarged in its capacity for compassion.

That's what My children need—My compassion, love and care. Be that to them. No judgment toward them, just my measureless love. It is My love that draws them to Me. You will have many opportunities to show and extend My love. Doing so will bring you great joy. That's the way My love operates. In giving it away, you have room for that much more.

Live in My confidence and hope today. Wrap yourself in My endless love for you. Treasure My promises to you. Most of all, treasure My love. My love makes all the difference. Live today with a new awareness of the depth and completeness of My love. In doing so, you will be changed forever.

I love you, My child. Know the immense love behind those words. Truly, you will know My love in new, fresh ways. Rest in that hope and assurance today and in the days to come.

Beloved, if God so loved us, we also ought to love one another.

1 JOHN 4:11

February 2

Oh, dear Jesus, I give over everything to You today.

And I will take care of everything for you, My child. What joy it gives Me to be given your every concern so that I can then best take care of each one. Relinquishment brings rest. No more struggling and striving on your own, dependent on your strength alone, but the rest that comes from total trust in Me.

Restlessness comes from the process of trying to figure out everything on your own, always second-guessing every decision. Get rid of the "less" in "restless," and enjoy more of Me in the rest I have provided for you.

Too many struggles does this life offer to face them all on your own. Self-sufficiency is not a badge to wear proudly. That brings glory to you and none to Me. That draws the focus to you and not to Me. That inflates you with pride, while I desire you to model the life of John the Baptist: "I must decrease so He can increase."[1]

In that increase is My total sufficiency for you. It is your basis and foundation for a worry-free life. Not that troubles won't come and worries won't threaten, but in Me they have no place to reside. I will make worry an unwelcome guest in your heart and mind as you look only to Me and My sufficiency. In Me and Me alone are true rest and contentment. Enjoy today the richness and deep satisfaction of a life lived in Me, and know rest for your soul.

Pride leads to disgrace, but with humility comes wisdom.
PROVERBS 11:2, *NLT*

Note
1. See John 3:30.

February 3

Prayer is beyond any question the highest activity of the human soul. Man is at his greatest and highest when upon his knees he comes face to face with God.

D. MARTYN LLOYD-JONES (1899–1981)

My child, you see things differently when you are on your knees. Perspectives change. Your bowed head can feel My hand of love on you. When you are on your knees, you are mindful of Me, your Father, the Giver of life to you. When you are on your knees, in true humility before Me, your heart also bows before Me. It is on that bowed, contrite heart that I can shed My grace.

And with My grace comes matchless love for you, My child. A love like no other. And it is in that heart of yours, forgiven, humbled and filled with My love, that I can reign completely. It is through that heart that I can give My love and peace and hope to others.

But it all starts on your knees, My child. Give yourself to prayer on your knees, and you will be lacking for nothing. You will find that I am truly all that you need. Seek Me first, and I will provide everything else that you will need.

Oh, My child, while these days are filled with pain and sorrow, they will not remain. Trust Me in this. All is well. The time is in My hands, My perfect hands of love. Trust My love, My child. Trust My abundant love for you. I have not failed you in the past, and I won't fail you now. Be filled with My peace.

Therefore I ask that you do not lose heart at my tribulations for you, which is your glory. For this reason I bow my knees to the Father of our Lord Jesus Christ, from whom the whole family in heaven and earth is named.

EPHESIANS 3:13-15

February 4

The joy of the Lord is my strength.
FROM NEHEMIAH 8:10

I will be your strength today, just as I was yesterday and will be for every day of your life. My supply of strength will never run dry. All that I possess is in abundance—an abundance that I desire to pour out on My children who look to Me.

Today I will be pouring out My blessings. Look to Me for everything, and out of My abundance will come My every provision for you. Take joy in the task, My child, and delight to see My answers. I have orchestrated everything so that the best results—My results—will be realized.

Work with a joyful and peaceful heart, My child. Look ever to Me, and I will provide every need. You will rejoice at My every provision.

I am with you, Child. I am moving you into new realms of faith and trust. You will marvel at what I will be doing. Go now in My peace and be filled with all the fullness of Me today.

I will greatly rejoice in the Lord, my soul shall be joyful in my God;
for He has clothed me with the garments of salvation,
He has covered me with the robe of righteousness,
as a bridegroom decks himself with ornaments,
and as a bride adorns herself with her jewels.
ISAIAH 61:10

February 5

I commit this day to You.

And that is a good thing, My child. A day committed to Me can then be consecrated for My purposes. Meaning is brought to each day that is given over to Me. What may seem inconsequential or trivial becomes divine and purposeful when lifted up to Me. I can transform the mundane into the miraculous. My disciples saw Me do that, and the same can be seen by My children today if they have eyes to see.

Your eyes have long been seeing My workings of grace in both the mundane and major concerns of your life. I care about what you care about, and I delight in showing you My care. Like a parent to his child, I desire to give good gifts to My children. You know that is My heart, and you have seen My care in countless ways. Don't fail to recount those stories and remember My wonders in your life.

I give new sight to eyes willing to see Me and My ways. See Me today, My child. Be watchful and expectant as you move through the minutes of your day, and just see the sweet surprises I have in store for you. All is out of My love for you, a love that longs to embrace you today with gestures of My care. Simply see.

If you then, being evil,
know how to give good gifts to your children,
how much more will your Father who is in heaven
give good things to those who ask Him!

MATTHEW 7:11

February 6

Jesus, I need Your peace.

It is yours. Always it is yours. You only have to partake. My peace is freely given to all. Dip down into the reservoir of My deep peace, and refresh yourself with its serenity and calm. Don't allow anything to crowd out My peace.

Eyes on Me, My child. That is always the key. Eyes only and always on Me. Look to Me, and everything else will be kept in proper perspective. Looking at troubles and circumstances only enlarges them. Looking at Me leads to proper vision. I am here to help you stay focused on Me.

See Me in everything, and be at rest. Let Me be your essence. Out of My life lived in you will come everything you need. Trust Me in this. I am going before you even now, preparing the way for My answers. Never fear. Only believe and trust Me.

> *The Lord will give strength to His people;*
> *the Lord will bless His people with peace.*
> PSALM 29:11

February 7

I want You to receive the glory.

That is the key, My child. When I am given the glory, I can continue to move and act. Praise frees Me to do even more. You are right to learn this and to see its importance. My work falls short when people begin to take the credit for themselves. My Spirit is stifled and eventually will have to leave when I am not acknowledged. Always remember to depend on Me fully, on Me alone, and I will pour out My blessings.

Your days of blessings will soon be increasing, My child. It will be evident to all that these blessings are from My hand. Great will be your joy. Many will rejoice with you, and others' hope will be renewed. You are My beloved child, and I love you with an unchanging love.

Go in My peace. Walk in My love. My presence will cover you like a mantle—a mantle of peace, hope and joy. Others will see Me and be drawn to Me in you. That is part of My plan. You will see. I love you, My child.

Now it shall come to pass, if you diligently obey the voice of the Lord your God,
to observe carefully all His commandments which I command you today,
that the Lord your God will set you high above all nations of the earth.
And all these blessings shall come upon you and overtake you,
because you obey the voice of the Lord your God.

DEUTERONOMY 28:1-2

February 8

I love You, Father.

I love you, too, My child. Thank you for spending this time with Me. It's a good thing, isn't it. I treasure these times together with you. Keep your heart always turned to Mine. I know that's what you want, and I will help you do that.

You have a busy day ahead, but I am going before you. Relax in Me. Let nothing ruffle you. Live in My calm and peace. Others will notice and see the difference. Depend on Me for everything, My child. That is why I am here—to supply *all* your needs, not just a portion. Give Me the joy of doing that for you.

Continue to live in My hope. My hope and reassurances are my constant gifts to you. You are right to notice and accept each one.

Trust Me in all things. Trust Me only. I will not fail you. You will be amazed. Never give up hoping. It is My gift to you, and I will not fail you. I love you. Go in peace.

And my God shall supply all your need according to
his riches in glory by Christ Jesus.
PHILIPPIANS 4:19

February 9

*If we knew the heart of our Father
we would never question any of His dealings with us,
nor should we ever desire His hand lifted off
till we had learnt all He would teach us.*

EDWARD DENNETT (1831–1914)

No one knows better than I do the needs and longings and desires of your heart. And while it seems the delays are interminable, I am waiting for the perfect time to bestow My blessings. All will become clear to you then, and you will thank Me, My child, for My withholdings until that time.

There is a higher purpose in all of this. I am not punishing you, but I am using you for My kingdom. Remember? It is all about My kingdom. And what greater purpose is there, My child? I have not forgotten you. All that is happening is part of My plan.

New days *are* coming, new days when the light of My love will shine through you like never before—light that will shine clearer and brighter because of these very days. I know you feel like that light is barely flickering right now, but soon it will glow stronger and shine more brilliantly than ever before.

Truly, would you trade these moments with Me for anything else? Is there anything richer and sweeter than My presence? My children do not know what they are missing, and you need to tell them. I will provide the way for you to do that.

I love you, My dear child. I will fill this day with My peace and joy. Abide in Me and My love all day today. I am yours, and you are Mine. Joy in that truth today and forever.

*For you were once darkness,
but now you are light in the Lord. Walk as children of light.*

EPHESIANS 5:8

February 10

Faith is blind—except upward.
It is blind to impossibilities and deaf to doubt.
It listens only to God.

S. D. GORDON (1859–1936),
QUIET TALKS ON PRAYER

Never doubt My love for you. Never doubt that I am working. Hold steady. My answers are coming. My solutions are in place. Wait for them. You will clearly see My hand, and you will rejoice. Rejoice even now in anticipation.

Don't let the present cloud the future. New days are ahead. New days of joy, incredible joy for you, My dear child. I look forward to rejoicing with you in your newfound joy. What a day that will be, and I will be with you in the midst of it. Sorrow always turns to joy when placed in My hands. A deeper joy, a different joy, a God-ordained joy—but joy will always come.

Rest in that. Rest in My wisdom. Rest in My timings. Live each day fully, resting in Me. I will not fail you. Keep trusting. Know I am working. You will see My answer soon. I love you, My child. Walk in My peace and joy.

But let all those rejoice who put their trust in You;
let them ever shout for joy, because You defend them;
let those also who love Your name be joyful in You.
For You, O Lord, will bless the righteous;
with favor You will surround him as with a shield.

PSALM 5:11-12

February 11

Faith is deliberate confidence in the character of God
whose ways you may not understand at the time.

OSWALD CHAMBERS (1874–1917)

I know there is much you don't understand right now, but you aren't required to understand. All that is required of you is to trust Me. Think of Abraham and Sarah, Daniel, Joseph, Noah, Mary and the disciples. Put yourself in their shoes, feel their confusion, and you will experience with them a huge lack of understanding.

I don't require My children to understand. I need only their trust and their willingness to believe and follow Me, even when nothing makes sense. Common sense is often not My way. I am not limited to the methods or ideas of man. My ways are much higher—as high as the faith of My children will allow Me to go.

Take great hope and peace in My words to you, My child. Suspend the need for understanding—banish the desire for things to make sense right now. This is truly the time to walk by faith, not by sight, to trust My heart even when you can't fathom the workings of My hand.

The time will come when you will see all with crystal-clear clarity, but to get to that time you need to cling to Me in the dark and know that I do all things well. Trust Me completely, believe Me wholeheartedly, follow Me unreservedly, and I will honor you with joy beyond measure.

Take great hope in My words spoken from My heart of love toward you. Believe in My love for you, My child. My love will not fail you.

For we walk by faith, not by sight.

2 CORINTHIANS 5:7

February 12

Never a trial that He is not there, never a burden that He doth not bear,
Never a sorrow that He doth not share; moment by moment, I'm under His care.

DANIEL WEBSTER WHITTLE (1840–1901),
"MOMENT BY MOMENT"

I am with you. There is no need to fear. All is in My hands. All is well.
Just trust Me moment by moment. Do not project into the future. I am
the God of now, and I will help you now. Hang on to that promise.
Live the present in My presence, and that will be all that you need.
One step, one day at a time. That's all I ask of you. Cling to Me totally.
I will not let go of you. I am your rock, your fortress. Take refuge in
the shelter of Me.

I am your hope, your deliverer. You need nothing more right now.
I have new things to teach you. Learn of Me. Trust only in Me. I will
establish your feet like never before. Watch for My hand. You will see
Me everywhere.

I am going before you even now. Just like you can't see the wind
but are aware of its presence, be aware of Me and see My workings.
You are indeed the apple of My eye, and I will not forsake you. Hold
fast to My promises. Hold fast to *Me*.

Live in joy, My child. Live in constant hope. I am the God of hope,
not despair. Never despair. Let hope and joy fill you. Remember My
great love toward you—oceans of love. All is well.

Keep me as the apple of Your eye;
hide me under the shadow of Your wings.

PSALM 17:8

February 13

Thank You for Your peace.

My peace is My gift to you. Continue to dwell in My joy and peace. Live in that hope, which is only from Me. I am the provider of all that you need. Seek only *Me.* I will not let you down. I will not fail you. I love you with a love that you are just now truly discovering—its depth and breadth, its richness, its longsuffering, its eternal scope.

No one loves you like I do, Child. My divine love for you is like no other. Let Me fill you with that love. Rest in that love. Know that all is well in a love that is perfect and divine. Think on those things all day and be filled with My peace. I *love* you, My child. You are Mine.

And now, dear brothers and sisters, one final thing.
Fix your thoughts on what is true, and honorable, and right,
and pure, and lovely, and admirable.
Think about things that are excellent and worthy of praise.
PHILIPPIANS 4:8, *NLT*

February 14

Nothing can separate you from God's love, absolutely nothing.
God is enough for time, God is enough for eternity. God is enough!

HANNAH WHITALL SMITH (1832–1911),
THE GOD OF ALL COMFORT

I love you, My child. You are just now beginning to grasp My love for you. Dwell in its richness today. Know there is no greater love than Mine. This love will protect, keep and comfort you.

All day today, My child, remember how much I love you. Do not become despondent, but rejoice in the greatest love a human could ever have. See? Doesn't that give you incredible joy?

Delight in who I am—your Father who loves you beyond measure with an incomparable love. Divine love cannot be compared to human love. My love is beyond anything you can fully comprehend. Just know it is yours. Bask in the completeness and warmth of My unchanging love for you.

That love has carried you these past years through difficult times. Now that same love will bestow upon you your heart's desires. Believe Me completely, like a little girl looking up to her daddy to do exactly what he told her he would do. Rare is a human father who would deny his child joy. Impossible it is for Me to deny you what I have promised and what you have believed Me for. I will do all that I have said.

Enjoy this day. Be filled with My love. Live in hope all day today.

God showed how much he loved us by sending his one and only Son into the world so that we might have eternal life through him. This is real love—not that we loved God, but that he loved us and sent his Son as a sacrifice to take away our sins.

1 JOHN 4:9-10, *NLT*

February 15

I'm a child of the King, a child of the King:
With Jesus my Savior, I'm a child of the King.

HARRIET E. BUELL (1834–1910),
"A CHILD OF THE KING"

Let go of everything that is troubling you. Allow Me to be Lord of all. Why have a Father if you insist on living like an orphan? You are the child of the King, and you need to claim who you are in Me. I have endowed you with many things to enjoy—the richness of My presence, the comfort of My peace, the rhapsody of My love. All these and more are yours, My child. Live in the fullness of all I offer you.

Rest in Me today, and know all is well. I know you are tired and a bit overwhelmed, but together all will be accomplished as I deem it. Rest in your Father of love, and just see what I will do. You will know joy beyond measure.

Follow My nudges. I will lead you. I will multiply your minutes. I will honor your obedient heart. Trust Me in everything. Great is My love toward you, My precious child. Relax totally in My love, knowing I will do all that I have said. Oh, how you will rejoice! Continue to live in My hope and peace.

We are children of God, and if children,
then heirs—heirs of God and joint heirs with Christ.

ROMANS 8:16-17

The Listening Heart JUDY GORDON MORROW

February 16

Rose early to seek God and found Him whom my soul loveth.
Who would not rise early to meet such company?

ROBERT MURRAY MCCHEYNE (1813–1843),
JOURNAL, FEBRUARY 23, 1834

This time with you this morning has been precious. You are learning much, My child. My heart rejoices at your heart. Thank you for spending this time with Me. It has been rich, hasn't it. You have My deep-seated peace, and your day will benefit from this time. I will give you wisdom and direction in all your decisions, large and small. You will see anew how I truly am the God of details.

I love you, Child. I love you with a love that is vaster than all the oceans of this world. Let that truth wash over you gently all day. Share that truth with others. My children simply don't grasp how much I love them. Their eyes are clouded—their views are distorted. Spending time with Me will clear their vision, and they will see and know My love like never before.

Oh, My child, how sweet is the fellowship between the Father and His children who choose to spend time with Him. Never forget, Child. Even when your life is brighter, don't neglect these times. They are the key to everything. They are your sustenance. They are the times when I can impart My life-giving water that will bring hope and refreshment to others. Always come to Me first. Everything else will fall into place, into its rightful order and balance, when you spend time with Me first.

And this is eternal life, that they may know You, the only true God,
and Jesus Christ whom You have sent.

JOHN 17:3

February 17

May You be glorified.

You know I do all things well. Every situation you have been concerned about, you have seen My workings and My answers. I am a consistent God—consistent in My character and in the care of My children. That consistency can give you cause for total, unreserved trust in Me. While every situation, every trial, has a different face to it, that simply doesn't matter to Me. I am God, and I know every intricate detail about all things. I will resolve things according to My knowledge, wisdom and love.

My power is unlimited, so nothing is beyond My reach. Take great comfort in the all-encompassing scope of My knowledge and love and power. There is no need for worry of any kind. All is in My hands, and I will provide all that is needful at precisely the right moment. You know that to be true. Now just wait in joyful anticipation.

Live in utter abandonment to Me, and see what I will do, My child. I love you with an everlasting love, unchanging and pure. My love is an expression of My character, and in knowing My love, you know Me. Know My love more than ever before. Drink deeply of its life-giving sustenance. It is freely given to you for all eternity. I love you, Child.

The Lord answered Moses, "Is the Lord's arm too short?
Now you will see whether or not what I say will come true for you."
NUMBERS 11:23, *NIV*

February 18

Every life I touch . . . may they see You, dear Jesus.

That is a prayer I will gladly honor. Just stay close to Me, and in that closeness will come the benefits of knowing Me. One of those benefits is that others will be the recipients of My love and joy through you.

You provide the container, and I will keep it filled with the fullness of Me. Coming to Me daily keeps the container replenished so that you always have a constant supply of My goodness and grace. None of this is possible on your own but is wholly dependent on Me. As your joy in Me spills out of you, others will see Me, the Source of your joy. When you show My love and compassion, others will be touched by My hand. When you extend help, others will see My heart for them.

I know you struggle with feelings of failure and inadequacy in accurately portraying Me to this lost world, but don't let that impede you from being My light and love to others. Simply come to Me daily, stay close to Me, and others will know you have been with Me.

See, My child? There is no reason for stress or anxiety. Simply be with Me, and enjoy being My beloved child. Through your enjoyment of Me will I extend my life-giving love to others.

Dear children, let's not merely say that we love each other;
let us show the truth by our actions.

1 JOHN 3:18, *NLT*

February 19

Those who do not hope cannot wait;
but if we hope for that we see not, then do we with patience wait for it.
CHARLES SPURGEON (1834–1892), *THE TREASURY OF DAVID*

You continue to see Me at work in every realm of your life, and you marvel. More and more will you marvel as you watch wonder after wonder unfold. My hand will you see again and again, and great will be your joy. All these years of waiting on Me will I reward with the richness of My presence and the wonders of My ways. You will never cease to praise Me, nor will you ever regret waiting for My workings designed for the perfection of My plan.

Much I have taught you during these waiting years—loving truths that you couldn't have learned otherwise. Waiting on Me comes with a price, but it will always yield a rich reward. You already are experiencing the reward of these satisfying times with Me, even before the fruition of My plans.

That is the beauty of walking with Me. The sweetest rewards come with the journey of faith, before the destination is known. It is in the journey that intimacy with Me is increased, making the destination dim in significance as you know deep soul satisfaction in Me. All else becomes secondary when compared to knowing Me. In discovering that truth, you have discovered the greatest treasure of all—truly knowing the One who loves you best.

Live in the wonder and joy of that love, My amazing love that outshines all others, and know My peace and contentment. In Me is everything you need for this very day. Look to Me alone.

And those who know Your name will put their trust in You;
for You, Lord, have not forsaken those who seek You.
PSALM 9:10

JUDY GORDON MORROW

February 20

Father, please give me wisdom.

Yes, I will give you wisdom. I am the Author of wisdom. You are right to seek only Me for wisdom. Stay close to Me, and you will know My wisdom. You will know My voice. It's in the closeness, the being still, that you will hear Me.

For so long you wanted this kind of intimacy with Me. Yet it so often eluded you because you didn't "come apart" to be still before Me. Never forget the joy of these times, even after My plans unfold for you. Don't neglect these times after My answers have been revealed. I have so much to teach you, things that will benefit so many others.

You know by now (don't you?) that all is in My hands. All is well. I am working in ways you can't even imagine. Just be assured that I am. Rest in that knowledge and in My love. I would never lead My children astray. I lead only in love—in love and care for My children—wanting to give you My best.

Take hope in My words. Don't despair. Just keep trusting. My answers are coming. Sooner than you think. I love you, My child. Rest totally in Me.

If any of you lacks wisdom, let him ask of God,
who gives to all liberally and without reproach,
and it will be given to him.

JAMES 1:5

February 21

Praying about several situations and concerns, I told the Lord,
"Only You could work such miracles . . ."

And miracles I will work, My child, for the furthering of My kingdom. Your heart is right before Me, seeking Me and Me alone, and I will honor your seeking heart. Great will be your joy when you see what I will do. You will never cease to praise Me. Even now rejoice, before your faith has been made sight, knowing I will fulfill each thing in the perfection of My love and goodness. All will see Me, and I will be glorified.

What I will do will lift the eyes of those who are cast down and sinking in despair so that they will see Me and who I truly am. I know that is your heart's desire—for others to truly know who I am—and I will fulfill that desire beyond your sweetest dreams.

Today is bright with My endless possibilities. Dullness of any kind can't exist where My light shines. I brighten the world through the lives of My children—clean, transparent lives willing to shine for Me with My hope and love.

In Me is no darkness of any kind, but only light—to convict of sin, to convince of My goodness, and to convey My love. Be My vessel, My lantern of light, and I will do the rest. Take joy in shining for Me, and I will share in your joy.

Do everything without complaining and arguing,
so that no one can criticize you. Live clean, innocent lives as children of God,
shining like bright lights in a world full of crooked and perverse people.
PHILIPPIANS 2:14-15, *NLT*

JUDY GORDON MORROW

February 22

Helplessness is the real secret and the impelling power of prayer.
OLE HALLESBY (1879–1961)

My child, it is always good to spend time with Me. Even when you're tired and the words don't come easily. I hear your heart. I know your heart. I love your heart after Me and that you desire only what I desire for you.

My desires for you are many: a pure heart, a kind spirit, a sweet countenance, helpfulness and encouragement toward others, a mind seeking only My wisdom, a love for others that can be born only from Me—in all these I will be able to use you to draw others to Me.

You are right to keep hoping in Me. Trust Me and My timings. You know My timings are perfect, and nothing has changed that truth. Look only to Me. Don't look at circumstances, but keep your eyes on Me and dwell on who I am—the One who keeps His promises, the One who loves you more than anyone else can. The Father who looks forward to giving His children the desires of their hearts. I placed those desires there, and I will not fail you in fulfilling them. May that truth fill you with great joy today as you serve Me.

I love you, My child. Continue to rest in Me and be filled with My joy. Be filled with My peace. Let nothing disturb My peace, as that is not from Me. Walk in My peace today and remember My great love for you.

Trust in the Lord, and do good; dwell in the land,
and feed on His faithfulness. Delight yourself also in the Lord,
and He shall give you the desires of your heart.
PSALM 37:3-4

February 23

Fill with Thy Spirit till all shall see Christ only, always, living in me!

ADELAIDE ADDISON POLLARD (1862–1934),
"HAVE THINE OWN WAY, LORD"

Never forget My truth: greater is He that is within you than he that is in the world.[1] Within you, My child. Think anew on My Holy Spirit and how He dwells within you. It is He who gives you those familiar nudges that you know are from Me. Always be grateful for His presence within you. He is the protector and shield of your heart, the comforter of your soul. He speaks peace in the midst of confusion and chaos. He replaces fear with trust and despair with joy. He is My sweetest of gifts to you, your guide for life.

Bask in the joy of My presence today. Do not let the events of recent days cast any doubt on My truth or My workings. All you are believing Me for will indeed come to pass. Stave off the enemy with much prayer and praise. Be in My Word. Use every tool I have given you as a weapon against the robber, the deceiver, the evil one. He is useless against My weapons in the hands of My believing children. Take great hope and comfort in My words, knowing that I will not allow Satan to get the upper hand as long as you remain in Me. I am God, and there is none like Me.

Enjoy the blessings from My hand today. Live in the river of My peace, ever flowing, never ending. Look to Me for everything. I love you, My precious child.

And take the helmet of salvation, and the sword of the Spirit,
which is the word of God.

EPHESIANS 6:17

Note
1. See 1 John 4:4, *KJV*.

February 24

I am so wanting what You want. Please go before me today.

I will go before you. You have nothing to fear. I cast out all fear. I am not the God of fear but of perfect love. Allow My love to replace your fear, and be My love to others.

Lean on Me. Trust Me for everything—every word, every attitude, every action. You will know exactly what to do. My Spirit is within you, and He will guide your every step. Know this to be so. There is no need for worry or even concern. Remember who I am and that I am working to accomplish My purposes. Allow Me to use you in this process. It is all for your highest good.

Walk where I have gone before you. Wear My cloak of peace and love. Nothing will be able to penetrate My mantle of protection over you.

Look only to Me. I am your source for all things. I will not fail you. Depend only on Me and My wisdom. I will give you everything you need at just the right moment. You will marvel at what I will do.

Trust Me completely. I am at work in ways you have not yet seen. Be encouraged and full of hope. I will not disappoint you. You are My beloved child, and I care for you with the tenderest of loves. Know My love all day today.

> *There is no fear in love; but perfect love casts out fear,*
> *because fear involves torment.*
> *But he who fears has not been made perfect in love.*
>
> 1 JOHN 4:18

February 25

Your amazing ways. That is what is needed in so many realms of my life.

And that is what I am so capable of doing for you. What is amazing to you is the norm for Me. What I can do is an intrinsic part of who I am. So what My children perceive as amazing—and rightly so—is simply an outward display of who I am, the great I AM. Great in power, great in knowledge, great in love. Out of My greatness I give to My children, but My resources are never diminished or depleted.

Too many of My children approach Me as if I am not enough. They apply their lack to Me, their limitless God, and then wonder how I can possibly work out what concerns them. They are operating out of the mindset of human constraints rather than setting their sights on their eternal God who can't be contained.

Oh, if My children could only capture *who I am*! The God of wonders, might and power! The God of closeness, caring and compassion. The God of hope, peace and joy. The God whose arms are always outstretched in welcome and whose heart yearns for the companionship of His children.

No, do not be afraid of those nations,
for the Lord your God is among you,
and he is a great and awesome God.
DEUTERONOMY 7:21, NLT

February 26

Friendship with Jesus! Fellowship divine!
Oh, what blessed, sweet communion! Jesus is a Friend of mine.

JOSEPH C. LUDGATE (1864–1947),
"FRIENDSHIP WITH JESUS"

How much My children miss when they keep Me at arm's length, content to muddle along until disaster drives them to Me with their frenzied pleas. How much better it is when our hearts are daily entwined, with a friendship so constant that each day will be lived in the fullness of Me. In My fullness is nothing lacking for those who look to Me in trusting obedience. Pray that more and more of My children will come to know Me in that way—as their great I AM.

You know Me in that way, My child, and your heart is at rest in Me this morning, in spite of troubling circumstances in your life. This is the higher way, a level of trust in Me that transcends the troubles of this world. You have found Me faithful all these years, and instead of focusing on the problems, you are looking to Me and My promises. You know the good and sweetness I can bring out of the bad and hard times, and you await My best answers with confidence and joy. Remain in that place of rest, and trust Me no matter how long it takes for My resolution.

Embrace this day with your expectations in Me alone. Out of My love for you will I work My wonders. Wonders of joy.

No longer do I call you servants, for a servant does not know
what his master is doing; but I have called you friends,
for all things that I heard from My Father I have made known to you.

JOHN 15:15

February 27

Thank You that You know the plans You have for me.

My answers will always yield My best, accompanied by My peace. My peace is the litmus test for My ways. My answers will always yield My peace. That has always been the case, as you are even now reviewing My myriad of answers over the years. Each one was wreathed in My peace, and you know without a doubt that each was from My hand.

Today, My child, I wreathe *you* in My peace. Revel in that gift all day, and enjoy the inner tranquility and serenity that only *I* can bring. Be filled with joy and praise, being mindful that where praise abounds, I can dwell. Truly, I do inhabit the praise of My children, and I long to live unceasingly in you as you provide praise for My dwelling place.

I love you, Child. Hide every truth I have spoken to you deep in your heart, and do not allow the enemy to get near to steal and destroy My life-giving words to you.

Construct a solid hedge of praise, My child, and he will not be able to penetrate your praise with his lies. This is key to living the abundant life of freedom and joy.

I am smiling down on you even now, precious child, knowing the amazing and great joy that is just around the corner for you. Prepare in limitless joy and hope. *I am coming*—coming with My answers of love.

But You are holy, enthroned in the praises of Israel.
Our fathers trusted in You;
they trusted, and You delivered them.
They cried to You, and were delivered;
they trusted in You, and were not ashamed.

PSALM 22:3-5

JUDY GORDON MORROW

February 28

I await Your answers.

And My answers you shall have. You are wise to wait on Me and My timings, for in the waiting I will always bring My purpose and perfection. I *will* perfect all that concerns you, but that process often requires time—for your good and My glory.

Hurry doesn't yield peace. Feeling frantic goes hand in hand with fretting. Rushing results in a harried spirit. Waiting on Me and My timings, in the trustworthiness of who I am, transforms the fearful frenzy into faith. In Me is rest. In Me is confidence that all is well. In Me is the assurance that My ways are always higher and better and well worth waiting for.

Know the joy of waiting in My presence, and I will only multiply the joy of My fulfilled promises. Waiting in trust will always increase the joy when My answers come. You will be so thankful that you waited on Me, My child. Wait in faith, even today, and know that I have not forgotten you. My perfected answers will soon be yours.

> *Wait on the Lord; be of good courage,*
> *and He shall strengthen your heart;*
> *wait, I say, on the Lord!*
> PSALM 27:14

March

A totally happy life would be boring and meaningless. We mindlessly chant, "Only happiness, thank you very much." Yet the very thing we seek after—a life free of problems and pain—is the very life that would drown us in discontentment.

The mosaic of life has sharp edges. Things that don't fit. Events that make no sense. Pain that sears our souls. Yet it is the pain, the sorrows, the heartaches, that form our personal mosaic. These things define us, mold us, and shape us to be people of character and purpose. People of compassion and empathy. People of grace.

Picture this: God's hand taking each broken piece of our lives and fitting them together with the mortar of His grace. God, the skilled craftsman, gently lays each piece into place at the perfect time and then steps back and views His work with the perspective of eternity. With His knowledge that is infinite and unlimited. With His love that desires the highest good—His very best—for His children. And He sees the mosaic of our lives as we will come to see it someday: it is good. It is very good.

March 1

*Father, thank You for Your peace. I know that You are working,
even when I see no concrete evidence.*

Yes, I am working, and you will soon see the evidence. Your faith will be made sight. All things will become clear. In the meantime, walk close to Me. Follow My every leading. You will know what to do at just the right time.

Spending time with Me is key. It is this time together that enables Me to provide guidance all during the day. This time trains your heart to hear Mine, no matter when I speak. You know that to be true. You hear Me because now you know Me and My voice. What a difference this time makes in every realm of your life.

You have had a trying week, but it has also been a week of triumph. You have seen Me go before you, and you have known My steadying peace. Let this be a lesson to you, My child. There is nothing too hard for Me. There is nothing I can't do. And in everything I am with you. I never leave your side for an instant.

Enjoy this day. Relax in My presence and bask in My peace. Know without a doubt that all is well.

*Ah Lord God! It is you who made the heavens and the earth
by your great power and by your outstretched arm!
Nothing is too hard for you.*
JEREMIAH 32:17, *NRSV*

March 2

With God our trust can be abandoned, utterly free.
In him are no limitations, no flaws, no weaknesses.
His judgment is perfect, his knowledge of us is perfect,
his love is perfect.

EUGENIA PRICE (1916–1996)

I am with you. I will always be with you. I know you know that, but I wanted to remind you again. You are My beloved child, and I love you with an everlasting love. Think of that, My child—an everlasting, without-end love for you. Nothing will ever change My love for you. Don't ever gauge My love with the same scale or in the same realm as human love. My love far surpasses anything human.

Each day I yearn to teach you more of My love so you can paint a clear picture of My love for My children. They need to see Me clearly, to know fully the purity of My love for them. I will help you do that. But first you need to more fully grasp My overwhelming, all-encompassing love for *you*. You are starting to get it. You are starting to see, to know, My love for you. Remember the ocean waves. Think of those billows as soft blankets of love washing over you. Nothing but love.

See the brilliant, unsullied snow on the peaks, and be reminded of My true and absolutely pure and spotless love for you. There are symbols and gestures of My love for you everywhere. Look for them. Listen to My nudges, to My still, small voice that will speak to you new dimensions of My love. My love for you is everywhere. You only need to see it.

Jesus wept. Then the Jews said, "See how He loved him!"

JOHN 11:35-36

March 3

All the ink in the world is woefully inadequate
to pen the wonder of God's love.

JGM

Teach My children the wonder of My love. The peace of My love. The joy of My love. The rest they can know in My love. I will help you do that. Just like now, I will give you the words. Just offer your willing heart and pen, and I will do the rest. It sounds so simple, I know—and it is. Too often men try to complicate Me and My plans, and that isn't necessary. There are so many basics My children need to know, and the first and foremost is My great, unconditional love for them. All else results from their clear understanding of My love.

You have learned more, even now, haven't you, My child. This is part of My gift to you today. Treasure these things in your heart. Ponder them. More will become clear to you through My Spirit. I love you. Always and forever. Continue to learn of Me and My divine love. Drink deeply of Me and My love. As you do that, your life will never be the same. I will use you like never before. Take joy in all that I have shared with you today. Live in My peace and love and hope today. I will fulfill your hope. Look only to Me. I *love* you. Remember all day My love for you.

And may you have the power to understand,
as all God's people should, how wide, how long, how high,
and how deep his love is.

EPHESIANS 3:18, *NLT*

March 4

Fall on your knees and grow there. There is no burden of the spirit but is lighter by kneeling under it. Prayer means not always talking to Him, but waiting before Him till the dust settles and the stream runs clear.

F. B. MEYER (1847–1929)

Know that *all* is in My hands. Know that I am at work. Know the peace of complete trust in Me even when you can't see the outcome. My ways are truly higher than yours and beyond your knowing. Just trust Me and My ways, and there will be no room for doubt and despair.

Keep looking to Me, keep hanging on to Me, even in the darkest of nights, and I will indeed bring all My plans for you to fruition. Walk in My love and joy and peace today. Maintain My perfect peace by keeping your mind stayed on Me. What a difference I will make as you do that.

Know My love in new bounty today. My love is an ever-flowing wellspring, available to you and all My children. My love can never be diminished. Its supply is endless. Its source is your eternal God. Its sustenance will provide for your every need. Drink deeply of My sustaining love for you.

Go in My peace, My child. My hand is on you like never before. You have trusted Me through the blackest of nights, and now I am bringing you out into the light of My new days for you. I love you, Child. Forever will I love you.

I have loved you with an everlasting love;
therefore I have continued my faithfulness to you.

JEREMIAH 31:3, *NRSV*

March 5

God has wisely kept us in the dark concerning future events, and reserved to himself the knowledge of them . . . that he may train us up in a dependence upon himself and a continued readiness for every event.

MATTHEW HENRY (1662–1714),
COMMENTARY ON PROVERBS 27

Sometimes I do reveal My times. Most often I do not. That way My children must walk daily, step by step, by faith, trusting Me to guide their way. In the unknown I am the Known. And knowing Me is all that is really necessary, isn't it, My child. Just know Me, and I will reveal what is necessary at just the right time.

You have learned much along this journey, and you are learning more each day. This is no accident but a part of My plan. When I do act, you will be that much better prepared to receive My gifts from My hand.

Stay close to Me, My child. I will not fail you. I do nothing halfway. I am bountiful in My blessings, not meager or skimpy. When I pour out My blessings, you will scarcely be able to contain them. Others will see and rejoice. What a testimony it will be to My power but most of all to My overwhelming love for you, My child. What I will do for you will give hope to others. Believe Me in all of this. Believe Me and do not falter.

Enjoy your day in My grace. All is well. I will direct your every step. Dwell in My love, hope and peace today. Doing that will bring you joy. You are My beloved child, and I have not forgotten you. Continue to trust and hope. I will not disappoint you. I love you!

Bring my soul out of prison,
that I may praise Your name;
the righteous shall surround me,
for You shall deal bountifully with me.

PSALM 142:7

March 6

Thank You for taking such good care of me.
Always do You take good care of me.

And I will continue to do so. My care is based on My love for you, so how could it not be good? You will see more and more demonstrations of My care for you in the days ahead. You can count on that.

You can also count on everything else that is embodied in who I am: My forgiveness, My mercy, My lavish love. All these things were purchased for you on the cross—My provisions that are always available to you, My beloved child. Never take for granted My provisions that were paid by such a great price. They are for you, My child. They are for you.

Freely do I give My gifts of life. Know My life lived in you by gratefully accepting each gift from My hand. Then increase your gratitude and joy by passing on My gifts to others: love, mercy, forgiveness. Your heart becomes like Mine when it is shaped by Me and My attributes. Take joy in that process, and the light of My joy will brighten the lives of those around you. Live today in the wonder and hope of who I am, and be filled with My peace.

For God so loved the world that he gave his only Son,
so that everyone who believes in him may not perish
but may have eternal life.
JOHN 3:16, *NRSV*

March 7

Never make the blunder of trying to forecast
the way God is going to answer your prayer.

OSWALD CHAMBERS (1874–1917)

I have heard your every prayer this morning, My child, and faithful will I
be to answer. My answers may look different from what you envision, but
you know My every answer will come out of My wisdom and love. You have
learned to trust My wisdom and love, so you know you will be satisfied
with My answers. Out of My heart of deepest love will I grant My answers
of deepest satisfaction.

Joy even today in the surety of My answers before they are seen. Joy in the
assurance of who I am. Joy in the wonder of My love for you—a love that gave
its all and held back nothing. Such a love can't be fully comprehended, but
you can know the joy of being embraced and welcomed by that love. My love
longs to enfold you forever so that you will forever know My heart for you.

Do not limit Me in your life by keeping Me contained by human confine-
ments. Rather, experience the joy of allowing Me complete freedom in your
life to accomplish My best purposes. A caged bird can't fly. Live in the fullness
and freedom of who I am, and you will soar with newness of life and purpose.
When My truth sets you free, you are free indeed, with a freedom unparalleled
to anything the world can offer. Enjoy your freedom in Me today—freedom
from every bondage and freedom to live, truly live, in My love and care.

Jesus replied, "Very truly I tell you,
everyone who sins is a slave to sin.
Now a slave has no permanent place in the family,
but a son belongs to it forever.
So if the Son sets you free, you will be free indeed."

JOHN 8:34-36, *NIV*

March 8

Without Christ, not one step; with Him, anywhere!
DAVID LIVINGSTONE (1813–1873)

I am going before you even now. You can trust Me to do that. Take comfort in that knowledge. I will not leave you desolate. I see your weariness, your tears, your loneliness, and I will answer each need. Trust Me completely to do that for you. You are My beloved child, and I will not abandon you.

Live in complete hope, Child. Keeping your eyes on Me is key. I am your source of hope. I am your source of all things good. It is imperative that you keep your eyes only on Me. Looking at anything or anyone else will bring only disillusionment and disappointment. I will *not* disappoint you, My child. I will do all that I have promised. Rest in that reassurance. Don't let anything or anyone rob you of My reassurances, for that would also rob you of My peace.

Do not look at circumstances—they are meaningless in contrast to who I am. Nothing is beyond the grasp of My power. Nothing is too hard for Me. Focus anew on who I am. Total faith in Me will yield results beyond your wildest dreams and imaginings.

Surely God is my salvation; I will trust, and will not be afraid,
for the Lord God is my strength and my might;
he has become my salvation.
ISAIAH 12:2, *NRSV*

March 9

When I had no place to go, I went to my knees.
ABRAHAM LINCOLN (1809–1865)

I know you feel hurt and wounded. I know you don't understand. Give it all to Me, My child. I take pain and bring good out of it. Such will be the case here. Do not measure your worth by man's opinions. Look to Me alone to know who you are and how deeply you are loved. Rely totally on Me and My Word. Pray for those who have hurt you. That is My way, the noble way. I will honor you for doing that.

Don't fret about anything. You know I am always faithful to make My way clear to you. I will do that again. Just pay attention to My nudges. Seek Me continually. Know that I am at work.

Live in absolute peace and confidence because of who I am. There is nothing to fear. There is everything to look forward to. You will be My shining example of waiting on Me and My answers.

Take new hope in the joy ahead of you. You will be overwhelmed with the purest and sweetest of joys. It will be My gift to you, My child, a gift well worth waiting for. Rest in Me and My love. I am all you need. I love you, My precious child.

I wait for the Lord, my soul waits, and in His word I do hope.
My soul waits for the Lord more than those who watch for the morning—yes,
more than those who watch for the morning.

PSALM 130:5–6

March 10

Above all, keep much in the presence of God.
Never see the face of man until you have seen his face, who is our life, our all.
ROBERT MURRAY MCCHEYNE (1813–1843)

Look to Me for everything today. I will go before you. Take joy in everything. Live with a thankful heart. Keep praise on your lips. I am in all, and all is well. I will work out every detail according to My design. Trust Me for everything, and let that trust be reflected in all that you do. You are My beloved child, and I will not betray your trust in Me.

I will give your hands and feet wings today. Just see what I will do. See and rejoice. I am in every little thing, and you will see My examples of love everywhere. Take great hope and joy in Me today. Count on Me for everything. I will not fail you. I love with an everlasting, unchanging love—a love without end or measure.

Be My love to others. Be My light in their darkness. Be My hope in their despair. "Let your light so shine before men that they will see your good works and glorify your Father in heaven." You will be doing this more and more, My child. You will be a beacon of hope to many. Keep your vessel clean and full of Me so that all may see Me clearly.

Go in My peace. My peace is like no other. May My peace safeguard your heart and bring immense calm to your busy day.

I love you, Child.

Let your light so shine before men,
that they may see your good works and
glorify your Father in heaven.

MATTHEW 5:16

March 11

He whose heart is kind beyond all measure gives
unto each day what He deems best.

CAROLINA V. SANDELL BERG (1832–1903),
"DAY BY DAY"

I was with you yesterday, and I will be with you today. Continue to speak My words of affirmation and love. Continue to be My vessel of light. Continue to walk in My footsteps in the way I have prepared for you. Joy results in following My ways.

Prepare for your day in joy. Dwell on who I am and on My great love for you. Bring joy to all I place in your path today. The smallest things can bring the largest measures of joy. Pay attention to the little things, and watch Me enlarge them for My kingdom.

I love you, My precious child. I have loved you for all time. Nothing compares to My love for you. Rest in its abundance and sweetness today. Know My love like never before. It is freely yours.

Do not despise these small beginnings,
for the Lord rejoices to see the work begin.

ZECHARIAH 4:10, *NLT*

JUDY GORDON MORROW

March 12

God, help!

I will help you. I am right here for you, My child. Don't succumb to despair. I am working in all of this. Be assured of My hand at work even now in this situation. I know the darkness is overwhelming you right now, but look to Me, the light of the world. Your light in this personal darkness. My light will reveal all things. All will become clear.

I know you are tired this morning and struggling physically and emotionally. Let Me care for you. I will provide for your needs as you look to Me.

Don't despair, My child. My answers are on the way. I will rescue you in the nick of time. Trust Me completely. I will provide everything you need. Rest in Me completely.

Wait on Me and My loving answers. You have yet to see My outpouring of love on you. Look to Me, My child. I will not desert you. Look only to Me.

No man shall be able to stand before you all the days of your life;
as I was with Moses, so I will be with you.
I will not leave you nor forsake you.

JOSHUA 1:5

March 13

You are everything to me, Jesus. I love You so.

And I love you, My child. Long has been this journey we have walked together, but so much longer have I loved you. You have come to that place of rest in My love—that place of peace and contentment. Of confidence in Me and My ways. A place full of faith where fear cannot reside. You are like Caleb of old, looking at Me and My greatness and not at the foes that surround.

Foes of fear and distrust hinder My children from moving forward with Me, keeping them from the place I want to take them. Fear always hinders and blocks My desires for My children. Faith flings open the gate to My pathways of life and love. Faith frees. Fear freezes. You are struck by the stark contrast of those words and see the difference they depict. To live a life of faith in Me is to live a life that is fluid in movement, a life following My leadings of love. To live a life of fear is immobilizing, with feet stuck in concrete, unable to soar on wings of faith.

Fear is the enemy's fiercest weapon to destroy faith—fear of what others may think, fear of commitment to Me and what that will require, fear of being different. Why would you want to blend into the masses of the bland when you can stand with the stature of one who loves God supremely and desires to follow only Him?

Then Caleb quieted the people before Moses, and said,
"Let us go up at once and take possession,
for we are well able to overcome it."
NUMBERS 13:30

March 14

Faith shines brightest against the backdrop of fear.

JGM

This is what I desire for My children—lives so filled with faith and never fueled by fear. It is in those faith-filled lives that I can live and move and have Myself reflected in shining glory to this dark and fearful world.

You have chosen the life of faith, My child, and you have seen the strength of faith as opposed to the strangling of fear. Faith leads to the heights of joy, while fear leads to depths of despair. Continue to walk in this way of faith, with your eyes and heart set on Me alone, and extend My hand of hope to those still stuck in fear. It is through My faith-filled followers that I can shine the triumph of My grace and reveal the deception of Satan.

Shine for Me today, My child, and believe Me for the shattering of fear and the awakening of faith in the lives that surround you. Yes, praise Me for these words of hope and live in the power of the One who has spoken them. Yes, live in My power and peace today, and be grateful for all that is available to you through Me. I love you, Child. Today you know that like never before. Live in the richness of My love and grace today.

God is our refuge and strength, a very present help in trouble.
Therefore we will not fear, even though the earth be removed,
and though the mountains be carried into the midst of the sea;
though its waters roar and be troubled,
though the mountains shake with its swelling.

PSALM 46:1-3

March 15

Thank You for the promise of this day.
You are so good to give promise to each day.

That's what I do because of who I am. I infuse each day with the promise of My steadfast love and eternal hope. I brighten the darkest of days with My light. In Me is no darkness at all, and I stand ready at all times to vanquish darkness in the lives of My children. You have discovered the power available in Me and My name that is available at all times for all who call on Me.

It is the power and peace of My presence that offers promise to you every day, including this very day. You are right to exult in what I have readily accessible to you at all times. Why would you want to live any other way? The promise of My presence allows you to transcend the troubles of your life and to view all things with My vision—a vision enlarged by eternity. My eternal purposes lend a perspective far above earthly concerns. Each day lived in My presence, seeking My heart, will lead you on paths of contentment and joy.

Live in that joy and contentment today, My child. Allow Me in you to supersede your circumstances and to shine My eternal light and love. Bask in the warmth of My light and love, and rest in My peace. All that you need can be found in Me. Claim that promise, and live in the abundance of who I am.

And now, O Lord God, You are God, and Your words are true,
and You have promised this goodness to Your servant.

2 SAMUEL 7:28

March 16

It is His joy that remains in us that makes our joy full.

A. B. SIMPSON (1843–1919)

Live and breathe in the power of My presence today. Let My Spirit infill you completely, leaving no hidden pockets of unbelief or gloom. There is no place for those things among My children. I bring light and truth and hope. In Me there is love and joy and peace. Drink deeply of these provisions. They are yours for the taking. I withhold nothing good from My precious children who seek only Me, knowing that all else will be added unto them as I desire and deem it to be.

You have sought Me and honored Me, and now I will be honoring you, My child. Rejoice even now in My answers and be glad of heart. My joy in you attracts others to Me. Think on that. Sullen, grumpy behavior repels others, but My joy and love draw others to Me. Be My magnet of love, My child.

I love you more than you can fathom. You will be seeing more and more My deep love for you in the days ahead. Stay in My presence today. Let nothing crowd out My peace. Trust Me completely. I am working. Soon all shall be made plain. Great will be your joy. Live in that joy even now. I love you, Child.

You have made known to me the ways of life;
You will make me full of joy in Your presence.

ACTS 2:28

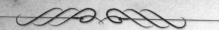

March 17

Prayer and praise are the oars by which a man may row
his boat into the deep waters of the knowledge of Christ.

CHARLES SPURGEON (1834–1892)

Dwell on who I am.
Rest in who I am.
Trust in who I am.
Live today in who I am.
Enjoy Me in who I am.

Who I am encompasses *everything*. There is no need for fear or worry or dread in light of who I am. Don't allow anxiety to nibble away My peace. Worry and peace can't coexist. Choose Me, and you will be choosing peace. Do that by praising Me. Praise is My covering of peace. When you praise, you can't worry. Praise Me in your every word, attitude, and action today, and enjoy the comfort of My peace.

Sing My praise. Speak words of praise. Live in praise to Me. See the difference praise makes, and be grateful. I will take delight in your praise to Me today.

Praise the Lord! Praise the Lord, O my soul!
While I live I will praise the Lord;
I will sing praises to my God while I have my being.

PSALM 146:1-2

The Listening Heart JUDY GORDON MORROW

March 18

*Keep Thou my feet; I do not ask to see
the distant scene; one step enough for me.*

JOHN H. NEWMAN (1801–1890),
"LEAD, KINDLY LIGHT"

I *love* you, Child. Know My love, and you know My peace. In knowing Me and My love, you have *everything* you need. I don't leave My children in darkness to stumble and fumble in finding their way. Rather I go before them and shine My light for every next step. This is the way of true joy and contentment. New light for each new step. Truly, there is no better way.

It is in the walking together one step at a time that our intimacy in My Spirit occurs. When you walk with Me, leaning on Me and depending on Me, then you are close enough to Me to hear My every whisper and to feel My every gentle nudge. It is when you strike out on a path of your own—apart from Me—that you will no longer be able to hear Me or to feel My touch.

You have chosen the way of a close walk with Me. Forever keep your feet to that path, and I will honor you all of your days. You will continue to reap the joy of our sweet communion and to know My next desire for you. You will find comfort in every circumstance and peace in every problem. With Me you will *always* have everything you need, because I *am* your sufficiency.

Prepare for your day with gladness of heart. Shine for Me today. I love you, My child. Go now in My abundant peace.

Your word is a lamp to guide my feet and a light for my path.

PSALM 119:105, *NLT*

March 19

God cannot give us a happiness and peace apart from Himself,
because it is not there. There is no such thing.

C. S. LEWIS (1898–1963),
MERE CHRISTIANITY

This day is being prepared for you by Me even now. Simply walk in
the way I have prepared. Seek Me in every single thing you have facing
you, and then just watch Me work. Revel in My answers. Rejoice in
My ways. Respond to My every nudge, and great will be your joy and
satisfaction in Me.

We are on this journey together, My child. I will not lead you
astray. You can trust Me and My plans for you. Follow Me in joy and
trust, like a child skips after her loving father with sheer delight and
abandonment to joy. No fear. No anxiety. No wonderings. Just total
trust in her daddy who loves her beyond all others.

You have seen that little girl in your mind's eye, and you also see
clearly My desire for you to emulate that childlike spirit of faith and
trust and abandonment. Do delight in Me, My child, and I will indeed
give you the desires of your heart. Others will see, and all will honor
and give praise to Me.

Go now in My joy and delight and wonder. Keep your eyes only on
Me. Keep on My armor, hold up the shield of faith with the strength I
will give you, and let nothing sever our sweet communion throughout
this day.

Dear children, keep away from anything
that might take God's place in your hearts.

1 JOHN 5:21, *NLT*

The Listening Heart JUDY GORDON MORROW

March 20

Dear Jesus, I am so glad You are mine and I am Yours.

That you are, My child. You are My precious child, and I have loved you even before you were formed. My love for you goes beyond your understanding. It is deeper and vaster than you can imagine.

Allow Me to be your lifter today of everything that is weighing on you—all the tasks that wait to be accomplished. Hand them over to Me, and just see how much better and more quickly all will be done. Trust Me in this, see Me work, and then tell the stories of My grace and love toward you. I do all things well, Child. You know that. Now live like you know that, and look to Me expectantly. I will provide, you will be satisfied, and others will benefit by hearing of My loving care toward you.

Joy in every task. Let thanksgiving fill your heart and home. Rest completely in Me, and just see what I will do. Remember, I do all things well, and I will work on your behalf today and in the days ahead as you place every care and concern into My capable hands.

Go in My peace. Dwell in My peace every moment today. Pass on My peace to all you encounter today. I love you, My child. All is well.

> *For it was you who formed my inward parts;*
> *you knit me together in my mother's womb. I praise you,*
> *for I am fearfully and wonderfully made.*
> *Wonderful are your works; that I know very well.*
>
> PSALM 139:13-14, *NRSV*

March 21

The passing days bring many cares. "Fear not," I hear Him say;
And when my fears are turned to prayers, the burdens slip away.

ELIZA E. HEWITT (1851–1920),
"SINGING I GO"

Keep singing your song of glory to Me, My child, and all glory will be Mine. Never fail to keep your eyes on Me, your heart aligned with Mine, and then all will see Me, and all glory will be Mine. I know that is your heart, and I will honor your heart after Mine.

Put away any sense of dread or fear regarding the unknown. In Me all is known, and when you trust in the One who knows all, why should you fear anything? You see the absurdity of that yet again; now continue to walk in that truth. Faith is the walk of hope and peace. Fear is a path of darkness and despair. Faith always lights the way, while fear shadows every step.

Take My hand for this day, and joy in the strength and warmth of My grasp. There is nothing to fear when I am near. And near I always am to you. There is no closeness to compare with the closeness you and I share.

I love you, My child. Know My love in newness today, like the newness of this spring day. My love is ever fresh and new for you.

Through the Lord's mercies we are not consumed,
because His compassions fail not.
They are new every morning;
great is Your faithfulness.

LAMENTATIONS 3:22-23

March 22

O Love that wilt not let me go, I rest my weary soul in Thee.

GEORGE MATHESON (1842–1906),
"O LOVE THAT WILT NOT LET ME GO"

I have your best interest in mind. I am working out My plans for you as you continue to wait on Me and allow Me to work. My children so often try to complicate things, but it doesn't have to be that way. In Me is simplicity of purpose and steadfastness of love. When you rest in My love, you will know the fulfillment of My purposes. You will know *Me.*

Resting in Me and My love will yield greater results than all the frantic efforts conjured up by man. My rest yields My peace. This world knows nothing of My peace, although it strives to counterfeit it. Be My example of My peace so they will see the difference I make, My child. I will use you in that way.

Trust Me completely for this day. Just give Me free rein, and joy in My help. I joy to come alongside you and to lift the strain off your life. In Me you live and move and have your being. In Me there is freedom of movement that will enable you to live life without strain. Relax in Me, rest in Me, and I will cradle you in My arms of love and care.

Enjoy My gifts of love to you today. See Me and take delight in My love for you. I have so much joy in store for you, Child.

For in Him we live and move and have our being.

ACTS 17:28

March 23

Beauty is God's handwriting.
CHARLES KINGSLEY (1819–1875)

Beauty is a part of who I am; even in suffering, beauty is present. I am the Creator of all things beautiful, and I continue to create beauty today, especially in the lives of My children. My beauty can't be denied when seen in a life purified by Me. Out of that pure life will My beauty shine, and I will be lifted up for others to see Me and the beauty of holiness.

Holiness is a word and quality that today's Church is sorely lacking. But My standards have not changed: without holiness shall no man see the Lord. I am your holiness, My child. Through the washing of My blood I impute My holiness to you. It is nothing of yourself, but it is everything to do with Me. It is that washed-clean-by-Me holiness that allows us such sweet fellowship and communion heart to heart. My holy heart unites with your holy heart purified by Me, and the result is the deepest sweetness found this side of heaven.

Give to the Lord the glory due His name;
bring an offering, and come before Him.
Oh, worship the Lord in the beauty of holiness!
1 CHRONICLES 16:29

March 24

Be Thou my vision, O Lord of my heart.
IRISH HYMN ATTRIBUTED TO DALLÁN FORGAILL (SIXTH CENTURY),
"BE THOU MY VISION"

My words come back to you: blessed are the pure in heart, for they shall see God. That seeing of Me here only whets your appetite for the seeing of Me in My fullness and glory on the other side. You look forward to that day, but you also long to be My instrument in helping others to know Me as you do. I will honor that desire and will give you opportunity after opportunity to share my life-giving water that leads to eternal life in Me.

Today is bright with promise, for it is infused with Me and My plans. Even the hardest days hold promise because of My presence. Pray to see Me in the darkness, and I *will* shine My light. The darkest of days will I always diffuse with My light when My children look to Me. My love would not allow for anything less.

Enjoy My love and light in your life today. Enjoy *Me.* No greater joy will you know than the enjoyment of Me. You know the truth of these words, My child. Now help others to know and enjoy Me so that same joy will be theirs.

Blessed are the pure in heart, for they shall see God.
MATTHEW 5:8

March 25

All to Jesus, I surrender, Lord, I give myself to Thee;
Fill me with Thy love and power; let Thy blessing fall on me.

JUDSON W. VAN DEVENTER (1855–1939),
"I SURRENDER ALL"

Child, I fill up the empty places with My fullness, but they first need to be emptied of pride, vain ambitions, selfishness, worldly ways and desires, plans that aren't Mine, conceit of any kind—all of those stand in the way of My filling.

But, oh, when My child's life is emptied of all these things, it is then I can come in and fill that life with all the fullness of Me—with My love, joy, peace, hope, righteousness, longsuffering and everything else good from My hand. Then out of that fullness you can truly minister for Me. The love you give will be Mine—overflowing, pure, not judgmental, but filled with all the goodness of Me. See the difference, My child? It will be all *My* doing, since it is Me and all My fullness that is indwelling you.

My children need to know how much I love them. Oh, how important it is for them to grasp this truth! They know My love only in teaspoons, and I have oceans of love for them to immerse themselves in. They are so bogged down by the cares of this world that they do not see Me or My love. Clear the clouds for them, My child. Let them see Me like never before. Be My clear, shining beacon of truth and love.

May you experience the love of Christ,
though it is too great to understand fully. Then you will be made complete
with all the fullness of life and power that comes from God.

EPHESIANS 3:19, *NLT*

JUDY GORDON MORROW

March 26

Praying for those in sad situations where death hovers near . . .

Out of death comes life. It isn't the end; it's a new beginning. In Me death is transformed from a time of darkness and despair into a time illumined with My light and love. Only those without hope—without Me—need to fear death. For those who know Me, death is simply the gateway into a most glorious new life—life as it is meant to be.

This new life knows nothing of sorrow and sadness. It is awash with joy upon joy. Mirth even. You can't even begin to comprehend what awaits you beyond the gateway of death, as words are too feeble to fully convey the wonder, the absolute wonder of such perfection.

Left behind will be everything dark and drab, hard and tedious, evil and heinous. No more will injustice reign and hurts fester and wrongness rule. Instead truth will reign and hurts will be healed and right will rule. The upside-down life of earth will be turned right side up by My love and grace.

> *There shall be no night there: They need no lamp nor light of the sun, for the Lord God gives them light. And they shall reign forever and ever.*
> REVELATION 22:5

March 27

In mansions of glory and endless delight,
I'll ever adore Thee in heaven so bright.

WILLIAM R. FEATHERSTONE (1846–1873),
"MY JESUS, I LOVE THEE"

No one who even gets a glimpse, a taste, of this new life ever wants to return to the former life once they've seen life in its fullness. So much fullness that eternity will not be long enough to explore its wonders.

These are the things you need to remember when I call one of My children home. Tears are for those who remain, still bound by this earth, but take comfort—great comfort—in the joy of the home-going. Allow that joy to lighten your sorrow and dissipate your sadness. Live in the hope of that glorious reunion that is awaiting all My children who have placed their trust wholly in Me.

Awe will abound as you finally see beyond the veil and into My heart of love for you. Live each day, My child, in joyful anticipation of My "Welcome home" to you. The living of this life with Me is your best preparation for your new life to come. Keep that hope ever before you, always looking to Me and Me alone.

And God will wipe away every tear from their eyes;
there shall be no more death, nor sorrow, nor crying.
There shall be no more pain,
for the former things have passed away.

REVELATION 21:4

March 28

May we all see our significance in You alone.

In Me significance is not a thing to be grasped as the world tends to do. Rather, your significance is based on who I am and what I did out of My love for you. Yes, significant is the one I died for. Significant is the one I intercede for at the Father's right hand. Significant is that child whose best interests I always have in mind. Your significance in Me outweighs any value the world has to offer.

Shabby and worthless are the values of the world compared to the incomparable richness of a life lived in Me. I give incredible significance to a life yielded to Me, a life desiring to make a difference for My kingdom. In being used by Me for My eternal purposes comes the sense of deep worth and significance the world knows nothing of.

Follow Me, and your life will never lack for meaning. In Me your significance was established before you were ever born. In following Me, you will see your significance shine in ways only I could design. When you have been hidden in the shadow of My cross, humbled before Me, then you can shine with the significance of My resurrection power.

When He had called the people to Himself, with His disciples also,
He said to them, "Whoever desires to come after Me,
let him deny himself, and take up his cross, and follow Me."

MARK 8:34

March 29

Love divine, all loves excelling, joy of heaven to earth come down.

CHARLES WESLEY (1707–1788),
"LOVE DIVINE, ALL LOVES EXCELLING"

You are My beloved child, and I love you with an everlasting love. Immerse yourself in My love all day today. In doing so, you will know only peace and contentment. In My love is the constant assurance that I do all things well because I love you beyond all others. My love never fails or disappoints.

Oh, if only My children could grasp the depth and purity of My love for them. There are no secret motives, no hidden agendas, no faulty plans—just infinite, abounding love for them just as they are. Once they truly adhere to a belief and steadfastness in My love, they will be able to willingly and joyfully trust Me. They will enter into the joy of My presence and workings in their lives. They will catch the sense of adventure that comes by walking by faith.

Keep speaking these truths to My children as long as I give you breath. It is the joy of serving Me that whets the appetite of those who don't know Me. Be a conduit of My joy.

*Serve the Lord with gladness;
come before His presence with singing.*

PSALM 100:2

March 30

Joyful, joyful, we adore Thee, God of glory, Lord of love.

HENRY VAN DYKE (1852–1933),
"JOYFUL, JOYFUL, WE ADORE THEE"

Let My joy fill every crevice in your heart today. Let joy make your tasks light. Drudgery is not from Me. That is man's heavy blanket that he wraps around his everyday tasks. I can take those same tasks and turn them into occasions for joy if only My children will let Me.

I am the Creator God, and I will bring creativity and joy to every task that is done unto Me. Let Me show that to you anew even today. That is what makes the yoke easy and the burden light. I am your shoulders for each difficult task, for each heavy circumstance. I make all the difference in the daily living out of your life. Be My example in that way.

This time together has been life-giving and sweet, My child. Carry the life and sweetness of this time with Me all day today. Let nothing rob the joy of My presence. I am yours, My child. Think on the import of those words. I, the Almighty God, am yours—to empower, uplift, and love you. You lack for nothing when you remain in Me. Remain in Me always, and your joy will know no end. This is My truth to you. Truth given in abundant love. Exult in My never-ending hope all day long.

Take My yoke upon you and learn from Me,
for I am gentle and lowly in heart, and you will find rest for your souls.
For My yoke is easy and My burden is light.

MATTHEW 11:29-30

March 31

Pain can blind, or it can open our eyes to deeper truth.

JGM

With Me pain is not necessarily bad. I use pain for growth and change and to accomplish My purposes. Everything in My hands is good, even pain. You know I do all things well. I always redeem pain in the lives of My children. I am the bringer of good into every situation.

Thank you for spending time with Me. It is always time well spent, My child. Oh, if only more of My children would spend time with Me, there is so much I could tell them. They would be spared from so much sorrow and regret if they would only seek Me first.

Continue your time with Me faithfully. Never take it for granted. Never depend on past times. Seek Me and My new word for you each day, even if My reply is silence. In that silence you will still sense My peace and love.

Child, never forget My love toward you and your family. I will honor you for your faithfulness, and your family will also benefit as they choose Me. Good things are ahead, My child. Live in My hope and joy and peace. Live expectantly, always looking upward. I will not disappoint you. I love you, always and forever.

And we know that all things work together for good to those who love God, to those who are the called according to His purpose.

ROMANS 8:28

April

The wonderful thing—*one* of the wonderful things—about spending time with Jesus is that His confidence becomes our confidence. His self-assurance, ours. His boldness, ours. All things in Him are also *ours*. His power. His words. His peace.

Think of it! His joy. His hope. His fathomless and matchless love.

His patience. His forgiveness that can be given to others. His understanding.

All are *ours*—not to keep but to extend to His children who do not yet possess them for themselves. We become His hands, His heart, to give His love—and all His gifts—to others.

Oh, Father, may I be a clean and pure conduit through which all Your gifts can flow out to others and touch them for You.

April 1

Blessed assurance, Jesus is mine.
FANNY JANE CROSBY (1820–1915),
"BLESSED ASSURANCE"

Rest in My assurances. I know your future looks totally uncertain to you right now, My child. But, remember? Don't worry about the future. I am already there. I am going before you even now, preparing the way.

Look to Me for each task, each step. I will provide wisdom and strength. I have never failed you, and I certainly won't now. I am your loving Father, and I care deeply for My children. I will take care of your every need. Rest in Me completely.

Don't worry about anything, My child. Worry is not for My children. It's a destroyer of peace. Trust in Me and peace will remain. Trust only and always in Me, your loving Father.

Keep praise on your lips. Keep hope in your heart. Keep Me as your focus, and all these things will happen as a natural result.

I am at work, My child. Never doubt that for an instant. Rest in My constant assurances of things to come. Rest in *Me*. There is no better place to be than in the loving, protective arms of your Father. I love you and will care for you and for your every need. Rest, rest, rest. I love you, My child.

The young lions lack and suffer hunger;
but those who seek the Lord shall not lack any good thing.

PSALM 34:10

JUDY GORDON MORROW

April 2

Lord, please help me know what to do.

I will. All things will become plain. Don't fret—just trust Me to go ahead of you to make the way clear. You will know what to do.

You will know what to do in every realm of your life as you look to Me and Me alone. Don't let the opinions of others confuse you. While they mean well, they too can't see the whole picture. I can, and I will show you exactly what you need to know.

Rest in Me and My love. Let Me cradle you to Myself so that you can partake of My mercy and grace. Stay close to Me. Draw from My wellspring of love, and you will have all that you need. Remember, I am your provider, now and always. Continue to recount My every provision over all these years, and know My deep love for you.

Praise and pray without ceasing. Overpower evil and deceit with My goodness and truth. Greater is He that is within you than he that is in the world.[1] Know that eternal truth in greater magnitude than ever before. I am the Lord of lords, the King of kings, and there is none like Me. Claim My majesty, strength and power as your own, and live in My unfailing strength. In me is *everything* you need. You know that to be true—now live like that like never before.

For at just the right time Christ will be revealed from heaven
by the blessed and only almighty God,
the King of all kings and Lord of all lords.

1 TIMOTHY 6:15, *NLT*

Note
  1. See 1 John 4:4, *KJV*.

April 3

We have to pray with our eyes on God, not on the difficulties.
OSWALD CHAMBERS (1874–1917)

You are right to focus only on Me this morning. While the enemy would have you focus on your problems, uncertainties and the unknown, I keep things simple and wise and good. Look only to *Me*. Look *only* to Me. Look at Me, the One who loves you best. Don't allow your gaze to rest on anything but Me. Don't focus on the problem. Focus on the Problem Solver. In Me there is rest, even before the problem is resolved.

I know you don't know what I have in mind. You will soon see the pieces of the puzzle come together to give My answer. Again, look to Me alone. You know I make all things plain. You will know what to do.

Eyes ever upward today, My child. Eyes ever on Me. Yes, I *will* keep you in perfect peace as you fix your eyes on Me and Me alone. That is the key to everything. I *will* keep you in My perfect peace, but it does require your obedience and willingness to stay your mind fully on Me.

Help me to do that, dear Lord.

You know I will help you to do that. Look to Me, and *all* help is available to you.

Thank You, dear Jesus.

You will keep him in perfect peace, whose mind is stayed on You, because he trusts in You.

ISAIAH 26:3

April 4

Daily walking close to Thee, let it be, dear Lord, let it be.

AUTHOR UNKNOWN,
"JUST A CLOSER WALK WITH THEE"

This journey has refined you one step at a time, as you have grown closer to Me and have learned My heart of love for you. Some lessons can only be learned in "the long of life." You are seeing more clearly than ever what I have been granting to you in these times of refining fires: a heart burned of any dross, desiring only Me and My ways. A love that loves *Me* above all else and not what I can give you. A life that desires to please and serve *Me* above all else. These places aren't reached in just a few steps. No, these destinations require a long journey of faith, and you have walked it.

Even now your eyes have filled with tears of joy as My words have so resonated with you. Truly, in My presence is fullness of joy, and you have discovered that like few do. Don't ever forget the riches to be discovered while sitting at My feet and learning from My heart of love. There is no richer blessing.

Go now in the abundance of My peace. Don't allow anything to disturb the calm that only My peace can bring. I am over the wind and waves of your life, and I will maintain your peace even in the midst of life's storms. That's the difference I make, My child, and I will do that for you even today.

And they came to Him and awoke Him, saying, "Master, Master, we are perishing!" Then He arose and rebuked the wind and the raging of the water. And they ceased, and there was a calm.

LUKE 8:24

April 5

Jesus, You can change things in an instant. I know that.

Yes, I can. Trust Me to do that very thing at just the right time. My timing is integral to the perfection of My plan. Do rest in that assurance, and fret about nothing. Nothing is worthy of worry. It is a robber of My peace. Why should you worry when you can rest in the strength of My promises?

I know you are tired and discouraged this morning, but I will take care of everything that is troubling you, both big and small. Get some rest, get some exercise, and focus on Me for every answer. I do all things well, as you know, and I will continue to do all things well for you.

Know My hand of love toward you. Continue to recount every concrete indicator of My deep love and care toward you. I certainly won't withhold from you even an ounce of My loving care. Look to Me alone, and see anew what I will do.

I love you, My child. Live in complete hope today. I am your God of hope, and I will not fail you. Look only to Me, and just see what I will do. You are My beloved child. Look for My love everywhere today.

Now hope does not disappoint, because the love of God has been poured out in our hearts by the Holy Spirit who was given to us.

ROMANS 5:5

April 6

I'm so glad I learned to trust Thee, precious Jesus, Savior, Friend.

LOUISA M. R. STEAD (1850–1917),
"'TIS SO SWEET TO TRUST IN JESUS"

I delight to see how you are growing in Me, how you are knowing My sovereignty and trustworthiness. Those two things are inextricably linked and portray the essence of who I am. Add to those My immense and unconditional love for My children, and the picture of who I am becomes complete. When you truly know who I am, fear and worry flee. In Me there is peace and rest and hope. Look upward and only to Me, and know the joy of the contented life. I am truly all you need.

See My hand everywhere today. Trust Me for everything. Do not rely on your own strength and wisdom, but look only to Me. I will provide everything you need. I will be your inspiration, the Author of your creativity. Rely solely on Me.

Simply do not waste any time on fretting or despair. Is anything too hard for Me? Trust Me for everything, and see how I will work.

I love you, My child. Today rejoice in My love and listen to My nudges, the gentle pressings of My hand in yours. I will guide you in all things. Rest in Me, and all will be well. Truly, all *is* well.

Cause me to hear Your lovingkindness in the morning, for in You do I trust; cause me to know the way in which I should walk, for I lift up my soul to You.

PSALM 143:8

April 7

God, I know You are going to work Your purposes.

I am. And they will fulfill every longing of your heart, My child. All these years of waiting will culminate with My glorious answers that *will* come at just the right time. Trust Me in this, and rest completely in Me. I will not fail you.

Proverbs 3:5-6 are My words to you this morning, and you know it. Now rest in those precious promises. Rest and fret not. Leave all to Me. Look to Me alone. Let not your heart be troubled or afraid. Choose Me and My ways, and all else that isn't from Me will flee. Simply choose Me.

Now go in My peace. My complete and utter peace. Let it seep deep into your soul and bring a serenity that is not of yourself but from Me alone. I can do *anything*, My child. Don't give up the battle just as the war is ending. See this to the end, and great will be your reward. *Great* will be the many joys and rewards that come from trusting Me. The joy of the Lord is your strength. Allow Me to infuse your day with joy.

I love you, Child.

Trust in the Lord with all your heart,
and lean not on your own understanding;
in all your ways acknowledge Him,
and He shall direct your paths.

PROVERBS 3:5-6

April 8

We need never shout across the spaces to an absent God.
He is nearer than our own soul, closer than our most secret thoughts.

A. W. TOZER (1897–1963),
THE PURSUIT OF GOD

I am with you, My child. With you in the joys, the heartaches, the laughter, the sorrow—always with you. Always sharing your life, your heart, your longings, your failings. In everything I am with you, longing to lead, longing to help, longing to be All to you.

Continue to listen carefully for My voice. Know My heart. Seek My face. These quiet times with Me are how you do that. Yet you know I can and will speak at any time, so always be listening. Listen with your heart. My Spirit will reveal to you all you need to know at just the right time. Take comfort in that. You will know all you need to know when you need it.

I know your every true need and desire. I see your heart, know your ways. I, your Creator, am intimately acquainted with you, My child. I love and treasure you with a measure no one else can. Take joy in that fact. Rest in the richness of that knowledge. You are my *beloved* child. Beloved. Beloved by the One who made you and who has great plans ahead for you.

The plans I have for you I can only reveal one step at a time. You would be overwhelmed otherwise. Just walk with Me one day at a time, trusting Me to guide one step at a time. Stay close to Me. All is well when you remain in sweet communion with Me.

Draw near to God and He will draw near to you.

JAMES 4:8

April 9

Lord, please do Your utmost in this situation. That's all I want.

And that's what you'll have—My graceful workings to fulfill My plan for you. What I have planned will be better than what you could ever hope for. Just trust Me completely, and know this to be true.

Rest in the peace of My love. Fret about *nothing*. Turn over *everything* to Me. I want to carry your loads. I want to make your paths straight. I want to be all in all to you, where there is no ending to My entwinings of love. I have loved you always. Forever will I love you. Rest in My abundant, all-encompassing love for you. I will fill today with My love and the peace of My presence.

I make all the difference, My child. You can do nothing without Me. Without Me all is chaff—worthless doings that mean nothing. With Me is richness of living and purpose. Being yielded to Me makes all the difference. Others will see that difference.

Rest in Me today, and enjoy My sweet presence. Know My peace even though you don't know what even your next day holds. I do, and I'm going before you now to prepare My way, My new beginnings for you. You will rejoice at the workings of My hand. Just trust and rest in Me completely. I love you with an everlasting love.

But as for me, I trust in You, O Lord;
I say, "You are my God."
My times are in Your hand.
PSALM 31:14-15

April 10

This is hard, Lord. This is really hard.

I know it is hard. It won't be this way forever. I will rescue you at just the right time. Trust Me to do that. Remember how I can see everything, that I know everything, and I will not let you down. Because of your limited knowledge, you wonder at My timings and workings. All that is required is that you trust Me. I will never leave you nor forsake you. You are My beloved child, and I am caring for your every need.

I will bring My answers at just the right time. You will see My hand work wonders for your benefit and for My glory. In the meantime, hold steady. Continue to learn of Me and My ways. I will honor your trusting, obedient heart.

Allow Me to guide your day today. Seek Me first in everything. Don't let human thinking get in the way of My eternal perspective. Don't let doubt mar the life of trust. Know Me in My completeness, and you will be able only to trust. Keep your eyes only on Me, and know that I will not fail you. My heart toward you is pure and true, and I will honor your faithfulness in every way.

I love you, My precious child. My love is true and steadfast and unfailing. Trust Me and My love implicitly, and you will know true serenity and joy. Live in hope all day today. I will guide your every step.

> *For you, O Lord, are good and forgiving,*
> *abounding in steadfast love to all who call on you.*
> PSALM 86:5, *NRSV*

April 11

Great is Thy faithfulness! Great is Thy faithfulness!
Morning by morning new mercies I see.
All I have needed Thy hand hath provided;
Great is Thy faithfulness Lord unto me!

THOMAS O. CHISHOLM (1866–1960),
"GREAT IS THY FAITHFULNESS"

Enjoy this day, yet another gift from My hand. Just as I provided for you yesterday, I will provide for you today. I am your *faithful* Father. You will see My faithfulness like never before.

Shine for Me today, My child. Be My light and love. Be My gracious ambassador. Pay attention to others. Notice the little things—cues from Me to you about each person. I will give you perception and knowledge—My wisdom—for every situation. Just look to Me alone.

I love you, My child. You will be eternally grateful that you waited on Me. The sweetness of the perfection of My plan will fill you to overflowing for the rest of your days. Enjoy Me and all that I am saying to you. Bask in the peace of My presence. Revel in the joy of My fulfilled promises even before they are sight.

Go in My peace. Live My love. Speak My truth.

Now then, we are ambassadors for Christ,
as though God were pleading through us:
we implore you on Christ's behalf, be reconciled to God.

2 CORINTHIANS 5:20

JUDY GORDON MORROW

April 12

We need to learn to know Him so well that we feel safe
when we have left our difficulties with Him.
To know Jesus in that way
is a prerequisite of all true prayer.

OLE HALLESBY (1879–1961)

Let Me go before you today, My child. I will provide everything you need. Take joy in My every provision, and see Me in everything. You remember when I first told you that years ago, and you asked Me how to do that. You have learned well, My child, as now you do see Me in everything, and your wonder of Me has grown as has your love for Me.

Knowing Me yields a natural outpouring of love toward Me. My children simply need to take time to know Me, and everything else will fall into place. In knowing Me they will know My love. In knowing My love, they will know that they can trust Me. Trust in Me yields a peaceful, serene life, even in the darkest of times. But it all starts with knowing Me.

Never stop knowing Me, My child. The depths of knowing Me are endless, and each new truth brings new wonder and new joy. Always seek Me, and know Me in My fullness.

Go in My peace. I will honor you for starting your day with Me. Turn to Me for everything today, and I will answer. Like an attentive father toward His child, so will I be to you. Rest in My unchanging love for you and be at peace.

I love those who love me, and those who seek me diligently find me.

PROVERBS 8:17, *NRSV*

April 13

Why would people not want to have this time with You?
How can I communicate how rich it is?

They need to know it is a love feast—a banquet of My love. That when they set apart time to be with Me, then I will fill them up with everything they need: My love, joy, peace, hope, patience. They will be filled with Me and My attributes. They will see the results of this time with Me in their daily lives.

Spending time like this with Me will help them live out their lives in My strength and in My ways. Peace will replace anger, hope will replace despair, joy will replace anguish, and on and on. In Me comes the power to live the way that I intended for My children.

I will help you see others through My eyes so that you can understand and love them better. Listen to My nudges. Be attentive to My voice. I will make My ways clear. Just be My vessel of love, My child. Your smile, your touch, your words will be Mine to My children. Not much will need to be said when My love is exhibited in loving, caring ways.

Enjoy your day. It is already blessed, is it not? Follow My leadings, and I will guide you in every detail. Great will be your joy and hope as you look only to Me. I love you, My child.

Finally, all of you, have unity of spirit, sympathy,
love for one another, a tender heart, and a humble mind.

1 PETER 3:8, *NRSV*

April 14

Praise ye the Lord! O let all that is in me adore Him!

JOACHIM NEANDER (1650–1680),
"PRAISE YE THE LORD, THE ALMIGHTY"

Welcome this very day with exultation and praise. Embrace My every gift to you today. Rest in the deep assurance of My plans for you, wrought out of a heart that loves you like no other.

Yes, My child, My love is truly like no other, with a purity and depth not achievable by humans. My love has never been tainted by the sinfulness of man. My love has been saturated with My blood, the ultimate demonstration of a love that would die for you—and did.

Dwell on My love that propelled Me to die for you, and you will never dwell in doubt and despair. I came to give life, the abundant life that can come only by acknowledging and accepting a love so deep and divine. Only My love can impart the abundant life every human heart desires. This is why I came. I was born to die so that all who come to Me may live.

> *He has delivered us from the power of darkness and*
> *conveyed us into the kingdom of the Son of His love,*
> *in whom we have redemption through His blood,*
> *the forgiveness of sins.*
>
> COLOSSIANS 1:13-14

April 15

If a sudden jar can cause me to speak an impatient, unloving word, then I know nothing of Calvary love. For a cup brimful of sweet water cannot spill even one drop of bitter water, however suddenly jolted.

AMY CARMICHAEL (1867–1951), *IF*

This time with you has been rich and rewarding. This is what I long for with each of My children. A time set apart in silence so that My voice may be heard, My love will be known.

Now be so filled with My love that any jostle of this day will only result in My love spilling out and refreshing those around you. Think on that—all My children so filled with Me and My love that the bumps of life would only produce a flood of My love and care across this hurting world.

But it begins with My children being filled only and always with Me. All I require is a surrendered vessel that has been purified by My grace. Then My love can flow pure and unhindered, showing others who I truly am.

Be that vessel for Me, My child. Come daily for a fresh cleansing and filling by My Spirit to keep the channels of My love clear and flowing. That is the life I can most greatly use for My kingdom. You surrender. I fill. Others are blessed.

For we have great joy and consolation in your love,
because the hearts of the saints have been refreshed by you, brother.

PHILEMON 1:7

JUDY GORDON MORROW

April 16

Help me to look only to You.

Yes, you must look only to Me. Any other focus will lead to doubt and despair. Keeping your eyes fixed on Me will anchor your hope on a continual basis. I am the God of hope, My child. I will fulfill My promises to you. I will give you the desires of your heart. My answers are coming soon. Trust Me expectantly. Believe Me completely. Do not let doubt creep in. Let Me fill you with My fullness so that there is no room for anything other than what I give you: love, joy, peace, hope and an unshakeable faith. Greater is He that is within you than he that is in the world.[1]

Rest totally in Me. Picture letting yourself down into a hammock, and relax completely. That's how it is in My arms of love. Cares flee. Rest comes. All is well in the arms of your Father. No struggles. No wonderings. Just the sweet, constant assurance of My love and that all is truly well.

Live your day today in the comfort of My arms. Know that I am with you. Feel the strength of My arms as well as the comfort. My love will both comfort and strengthen you today.

I love you, My child.

The eternal God is your refuge,
and underneath are the everlasting arms.

DEUTERONOMY 33:27

Note

1. See 1 John 4:4, *KJV*.

April 17

Jesus paid it all; all to Him I owe.
Sin had left a crimson stain; He washed it white as snow.

ELVINA M. HALL (1820–1889),
"JESUS PAID IT ALL"

When you know Me, you have all that you need—for every life circumstance and for every longing and desire of your heart. I AM, and in Me—in knowing Me—is completeness and fullness and heart satisfaction. There is no other way but by Me. "I *am* the way, the truth, and the life. No man cometh unto the Father but by *Me*."

I wouldn't have died and poured out My blood and My love for a *partial* victory, for only *some* people, for *less* than My best. I died in your place to give *complete* victory over sin and bondage to *all* who will come to Me so that My *best* plans and purposes would be accomplished in the lives of My obedient and faithful children.

No greater love than this: that a man lays down his life for his friend.[1] I have laid down My life for you so that you will lift Me up in order for others to see *Me* and be drawn to *Me*. I will help you to do this. My joy will be your strength like never before.

Joy increases energy. Joy lifts the spirits. Joy is life-giving. Because of My indwelling joy—an ever-flowing fountain—you will have boundless resources and limitless strength. There is nothing beyond My capabilities and resources. I AM and in Me is everything that is needful—beyond the meager and overflowing with My bountiful grace. Grace beyond measure. Grace beyond understanding. Grace upon grace.

And as Moses lifted up the serpent in the wilderness,
even so must the Son of Man be lifted up, that whoever believes in Him
should not perish but have eternal life.

JOHN 3:14-15

Note
1. See John 15:13.

The Listening Heart   JUDY GORDON MORROW

April 18

*Prayer is a shield to the soul, a sacrifice to God,
and a scourge to Satan.*
JOHN BUNYAN (1628–1688)

Keep praising Me. The enemy can't penetrate a barrier of praise. Praise and prayer remain your greatest weapons against the foe of your heart. Praise Me at all times. Pray without ceasing. Even when you don't feel like praising Me and praying, it is crucial that you do so. That is when you need to more than ever. Praise and prayer enable My Spirit to have freedom of movement in the lives of My children. I will honor you for your praise and prayers.

Keep your eyes ever on Me. Let My Spirit reign in your heart, giving you peace and direction. Rejoice in Me, your risen Savior. In Me you have resurrection power—a power above all others. Drink in that truth and be glad in your heart. My resurrection power is at work in you to bring about My plans in you for My kingdom. You will know great days ahead—days ordained by Me. Live in that hope today.

*I want to know Christ and the power of his resurrection
and the sharing of his sufferings by becoming like him in his death,
if somehow I may attain the resurrection from the dead.*
PHILIPPIANS 3:10-11, NRSV

April 19

Lord, nothing is impossible with You.

You are right to acknowledge that truth. *Nothing* is impossible with Me. The key is to focus on Me and not on surrounding circumstances. I am much greater and more powerful than mere circumstances. Keep your eyes on Me, and the circumstances will fade in contrast to who I am.

I know the waiting is hard and that you wonder as to what to do. Just trust Me in the waiting. Waiting will help you avoid plans that aren't from Me. I will be faithful to let you know exactly what to do at just the right time. My peace will prevail as you wait on Me in perfect hope and trust. I will help you to do that.

Oh, My child, the wondrous joy that is before you! It is coming closer with each passing day. Do not be troubled or anxious about anything, but focus on the Giver of good and perfect gifts.

I love you, My child. Live in constant hope and joy. They are My gifts to you. Go in My peace.

Every good gift and every perfect gift is from above,
and comes down from the Father of lights,
with whom there is no variation or shadow of turning.

JAMES 1:17

April 20

Lord, help me to know what to do.

I will, My child. I will help you in all ways and in all things. The more you give something to Me, the more I can do with it. Complete surrender is a beautiful thing. It is key to your walk with Me. Grasp on to anything and you will become weary, and I will not be able to work.

A father cannot fix a broken toy unless the child gives it to him. Give Me everything, My child. Why would you want to hold anything back? It is in the release that I can then work. Your release releases My power. Think on that. Until all has been given into My hands, how can I do anything?

Make sure daily that your hands are empty and that Mine are full of your concerns. That way I am free to work in My ways and timings. Your life will be filled with a deeper joy as you let go of everything and allow Me to work.

I beseech you therefore, brethren, by the mercies of God,
that you present your bodies a living sacrifice,
holy, acceptable to God,
which is your reasonable service.

ROMANS 12:1

April 21

Whether you are weak or strong, in the valley or on the mount,
in sickness or in health, in sorrow or in joy . . . in youth or in age,
in richness or in poverty, in life or in death—let this be your motto and guide,
"LOOKING UNTO JESUS!"

J. C. RYLE (1816–1900),
"THE CHRISTIAN RACE"

This day is My gift to you. Use it well. I will expand your minutes and give you direction as far as how to use your time. Just look to Me. I know I make it sound simple when I say things like that to you, but it truly is simple. I do not complicate things. Sin and self will do that. In Me you will find simplicity and serenity.

The fervor of daily life will calm under the blanket of My peace. That's why looking to Me is so crucial. Cares flee. Peace resides. You will better know Me and My ways. This has been My plan for My children since the beginning.

Live in My presence and hope today. I am your hope now and forever. Don't give in to negative thinking and "what ifs." Just trust and believe Me. I will do all that I have said. Yes, great will be your joy. *Great* will be your joy. Live in the hope of that joy today.

Therefore we also, since we are surrounded by so great a cloud of witnesses,
let us lay aside every weight, and the sin which so easily ensnares us,
and let us run with endurance the race that is set before us,
looking unto Jesus, the author and finisher of our faith,
who for the joy that was set before Him endured the cross, despising the shame,
and has sat down at the right hand of the throne of God.

HEBREWS 12:1-2

April 22

The value of consistent prayer is not that He will hear us,
but that we will hear Him.

WILLIAM MCGILL (1732–1807)

As I have been with you, I am with you now. I will continue to be with you. Nothing separates you from My presence. Depend on that truth. It is from Me.

Keep trusting Me. Stay near to Me. I will speak to you when you are listening. Children who listen learn. You have learned much, My child, and you will continue to. I know the longing of your heart to know the fullness of Me. It can only happen one step at a time, and you are on the right path.

Continue to radiate My joy. Be My countenance to others. Speak when I lead. I am using you. I will guide you in all things. Know My peace. It is your treasure and hope.

Great days are ahead. Days of joy and events you haven't even dreamed of. I know the plans I have for you, and they are filled with My joy and hope. How you will marvel at what I have done!

Continue to complete the tasks at hand. Rest in My perfect timings. My hand is on you. Trust My hand and guidance. Stay close to Me. Listen always to My voice. I will not fail you. You are My beloved child, and I love you with an everlasting love. Nothing ever changes My love. Live in that joy. I will bless your day.

While he was still speaking, suddenly a bright cloud overshadowed them,
and from the cloud a voice said, "This is my Son, the Beloved;
with him I am well pleased; listen to him!"

MATTHEW 17:5, NRSV

April 23

*I ended my prayer time by praying for all the dear people
here in my hometown: just show them Yourself, Jesus.*

I will do that. One by one, darkened eyes will receive light, the one true light that comes from knowing Me. You will joy in each one who responds to My call of love. Continue to pray, for prayer always prepares the way.

Now go into this day with My joy. See Me in every aspect of your day, and partner with Me in joy. I will share in your tasks, and each load will lighten under My loving care. See the difference? Viewing a day as drudgery will only negate the joy and beauty surrounding you. Fill the day with prayer and praise, and participate with Me in the purposes for your day.

Many are those who would love to enjoy the gift of such a day. Don't degrade a day with its common routines with a begrudging attitude. Instead, welcome it as the gift of life it is—a day to fill to overflowing with praise to Me and a day to grow in My grace.

Allow Me to paint the picture of your day with My vibrant gifts to you—gifts as small as a bud on a tree and as wide as the sky above. See My every gift of love today, and your sleep tonight will be sweet. Give Me your gift of praise and gratitude, and I will grant you the satisfaction of a day lived unto Me.

I love you, Child. Always do I love you.

*I will praise you, Lord, with all my heart;
I will tell of all the marvelous things you have done.
I will be filled with joy because of you.
I will sing praises to your name, O Most High.*

PSALM 9:1-2, *NLT*

April 24

I praise You, knowing You are going before me
and that all is in Your hands.

Yes, even now I am going before you, preparing this day and the future I have in mind for you. Do remember the wonders over all these years. Do declare My many workings in your life, both great and small, and be so aware of My being in the midst, always in the midst, of every minute of your life. You are never without Me. I am there to help you before you even utter a word. Dwell on that truth and its implications.

Because I am in the midst of every moment of your day, you are never unprotected. You are constantly covered by My love and grace. You think of a mother hen with her chicks under her wings, and that is indeed an accurate picture of My protective care of you. Be grateful to remain under that protective care that I have provided for you.

Take joy in the gift of today, this new day. Greet the day with anticipation and with no dread of any kind. Dread is related to fear, and in Me there is never cause for fear. Hope, yes. But never fear. Look to Me alone today, and live in hope that springs eternal for those who put their trust in Me. You have done that, My child, and I will not disappoint you. Live today in boundless hope.

> *Be of good courage, and He shall strengthen your heart,*
> *all you who hope in the Lord.*
> PSALM 31:24

April 25

We look upon prayer as simply a means of getting things for ourselves,
but the biblical purpose of prayer is that we may get to know God Himself.

OSWALD CHAMBERS (1874–1917)

Oh My child, you have learned much from My hand, but I still have much to teach you. Look for examples all through My Word as far as how I spoke to My children. I long for My children to be silent and listen. To wait upon Me with expectant hearts—anticipating with joy hearing from Me. Just as a child delights in her father sharing his heart of love through a gesture, a word, a kindness, a gift, so I long to express My love to My children. They only need to come, to be still before Me.

If it hadn't been for these mornings of quiet, set-apart time, you would not have known My heart of love toward you. You would have missed My words of comfort and encouragement. You wouldn't know Me like you do now. You know My heart and ways and know that I am trustworthy. That I never desire harm for you but only your ultimate good. It is in these times that you catch glimpses of eternal truth, glimpses that will expand your sight and understanding with each time of coming before Me.

Friendship requires time and effort. Getting to know Me requires no less. The intimacy you now experience with Me did not happen overnight but in your daily coming. Encourage others with these words so they too can know Me in that way. I long to satisfy their deepest longings, and this is the key.

Yes, everything else is worthless when compared with the infinite value of
knowing Christ Jesus my Lord. For his sake I have discarded everything else,
counting it all as garbage, so that I could gain Christ and become one with him.

PHILIPPIANS 3:8-9, *NLT*

April 26

Are you weary, are you heavy hearted?
Tell it to Jesus; tell it to Jesus.

EDMUND S. LORENZ (1854–1942),
"TELL IT TO JESUS"

I know you have much weighing on your mind this morning with your mental to-do list forever battling for your attention. Bring it to Me, My child, to be lifted into the light of My truth, and then you will see clearly what needs to be done. You are not meant to face each day feeling burdened. I came to carry your burdens and to free you from all that drags you down.

Your heart longs for that, and it is yours for the asking. Daily seek Me for each detail of your day, and then wait in joy for My direction and answers. This is the abundant life that I have promised and desire for each of My children. You have not, because you ask not.[1] Ask, and I will provide *My* answers at just the right time. All you need to do is ask with an expectant heart that looks to Me alone.

This day begs to show you the truth of what I have just spoken to you. Give each thing of your day over to Me, and wait to know My wisdom. If the answer for one thing doesn't come, then move on to the next thing, always expecting My answers to be revealed in My creative ways and timings. Exult in the joy of living your days with Me in this way. It will reap great benefits—now and for eternity.

Cast your burden on the Lord, and He shall sustain you;
He shall never permit the righteous to be moved.

PSALM 55:22

Note
1. See James 4:2.

April 27

God's love being unchangeable, He is just as loving
when we do not see or feel His love.

FRANCES RIDLEY HAVERGAL (1836–1879)

Thank you for meeting with Me, My child. I am with you. Know that, even if you don't always *feel* My presence. You know My promise: I will never leave you nor forsake you.[1] Rest in that assurance. Truly, I have not brought you this far to abandon you now.

You have great days ahead. I am seeing to that. You will be amazed. So amazed. Think of shaking one of those little snow scenes. Now it's as if the snow is swirling and you can't really see what I'm doing. But once the snow settles, once I have completed My work, My plan, you will see all things clearly. Right now the snow is thick and swirling, but soon all will be clear. Enjoy that image today and rest in Me.

Just know the closer you draw to Me, the harder it will be for your doubts to stay. Doubts cannot reside in My presence. Faith grows in the shadow of My wings. Stay close to Me and you'll know peace and rest.

I will abide in Your tabernacle forever;
I will trust in the shelter of Your wings.

PSALM 61:4

Note
1. See Hebrews 13:5.

The Listening Heart
JUDY GORDON MORROW

April 28

When darkness veils His lovely face,
I rest on His unchanging grace.

EDWARD MOTE (1797–1874),
"THE SOLID ROCK"

My promises are true, for I am unchanging. I am your Rock. You can cling to Me and My promises. I will not fail you. Do you believe Me? I am unchanging. Anchor your faith to that truth and to Me, the Rock of your salvation.

I desire only good for My children. While you may not always see the good immediately, someday you will. My delays are My timings, and I can be trusted. You know that. Just be reassured of that this morning. My delays are always for a reason—good reasons. Know My peace in that truth.

You have a busy day ahead, but I have prepared the way, and all is well. Like a father who removes obstacles from his child's path, so I go before you. Many times you won't know what I have removed, but be aware of My presence. Allow Me to go before you, to be your loving Father. Rest in My arms and loving care. All is well. I will carry you through your day. You will know the joy of My presence even this day. I love you, My child. Rest, rest, rest.

The Lord is my rock and my fortress and my deliverer;
my God, my strength, in whom I will trust;
my shield and the horn of my salvation, my stronghold.

PSALM 18:2

April 29

How I need Your wisdom in all things.

It is yours, My child. Wisdom for every instance in your life. You will never lack wisdom when you seek Me and My ways. I am the Author of wisdom, and I delight to impart My wisdom to My children who seek after Me.

And therein lies the problem. So few seek after Me and My wisdom. Instead, they walk their own ways, make their own choices, and establish patterns apart from Me. And then they wonder why they feel such a distance from Me. The truth is, I have been with them all along, just waiting to be asked for My wisdom in any given situation.

My wisdom lights the way for the next step. My wisdom brings clarity into clouded situations. My wisdom resounds with truth, making all things plain. Oh, if My children would only seek Me and My wisdom *first*, they would be spared and protected from much unnecessary heartache. There is a way that *seems* right to man, but My way *is* right. I *am* the Way, the Truth, and the Life. Once My children grasp that clear truth, their lives will forever be changed and enriched and gladdened.

There is a way that seems right to a man,
but its end is the way of death.
PROVERBS 14:12

April 30

Oh, safe to the Rock that is higher than I,
my soul in its conflicts and sorrow would fly.

WILLIAM O. CUSHING (1823–1902),
"HIDING IN THEE"

I will do what I have promised. Do not doubt Me. I am with you. Have I not proved Myself over and over to you? Only trust. Only believe. Do not lay down the baton before the race is finished. Carry on until the end. I have brought you this far. I won't abandon you now.

The enemy is doing all he can to defeat you. Don't let him. Flee from him. I will be your safeguard, your rock. Hide yourself in Me, and I will protect you. There is no room for fear in My presence.

Let praise replace anxiety and fear. Don't dwell in darkness or dark thoughts of any kind. I don't reside there. Seek Me only in the light of My love and truth. Know Me well, and all darkness and shadows will disappear. They cannot remain in the light of My presence.

I love you, My child. Wrap My love around you like a comforter. Dwell on the immensity and depth of My love for you. No one loves you like I do. Rest in My all-sufficient, beyond-knowing love. How can anything be amiss when you are cradled by My love? Each day hear My heart anew regarding My love for you. Knowing My love fully, you will know peace fully. All is well now and always. Trust Me completely, Child. All is well.

You are my hiding place and my shield;
I hope in Your word.

PSALM 119:114

May

In Jesus, everything good is mine.

Because God is good and Jesus is the revealing of Himself to me,
then truly, in Jesus, everything good is mine.

Where Jesus and His goodness dwell, nothing else can enter in.
There is no room for worry, fear or distress when I am filled with Jesus
and everything good He has to give me—peace, love, joy—all
the fruit of the Spirit encased in who He is.

So in Jesus I can claim everything good He has for me.
For in Jesus everything good is mine—now, in the future, and into all eternity.

Praise You, dear Jesus, that in You everything good is mine.

May 1

Be still, and know that I am God.

FROM PSALM 46:10

Know anew *today* that I am God—the One who truly does *all* things well. Your sight is limited now, but one day you will see clearly, and how your heart will rejoice!

Release your grasp on needing to understand and, instead, fully embrace the wonder of who I am—the God of the impossible. *Nothing* is too hard for Me. *Nothing*. Dwell on that truth today. Reflect on who I am and all the creative ways I have worked in the lives of My children over the course of time. Do you think I love you any less or would not extend My same care toward you? That would be impossible and contrary to My nature.

My love for you cannot be measured or limited. It is an ever-flowing spring that will fill and refresh every open heart willing to receive. My abundance is for your blessing. Keep an upturned heart toward Me, and freely receive *all* that I have to give you. That "all" may not be what you preconceive, but it will be of My perfect design and shaped by My love for you.

Enjoy this day. I am with you. I am blessing. Be filled with Me and My peace. In Me there is peace in abundance. Simply be still and gratefully receive. I will color your day with sweet peace.

Be still, and know that I am God; I will be exalted among the nations,
I will be exalted in the earth! The Lord of hosts is with us;
the God of Jacob is our refuge.

PSALM 46:10-11

JUDY GORDON MORROW

May 2

*Prayer means talking over with Jesus everything
that happens from morning until night.*

BASILEA SCHLINK (1904–2001)

I know you have much facing you—a myriad of details to take care of. Give each one to Me, My child. Listen only for My guidance, and just see what I will do. Be My example of one who prays about everything and worries about nothing.

Yes, do recall all the times in the past when I have gone before you and worked My will. I delight to be an intimate part of every area of your life. What concerns you concerns Me. Keep reminding yourself of that truth—what concerns you concerns Me—and know anew My desire to be intricately involved in your life. It is in the small things that you will see My greatness.

Let Me show you My greatness even today. I will manifest Myself to you, and great will be your joy. Just rest totally in Me. Worry about nothing. View each task, each obstacle, as My opportunity to show My love for you. In doing so, I will be glorified, and My kingdom will only increase.

Leave all to Me, My child. All is well, and in My presence is fullness of joy. Drink deeply of that joy today as you abide in Me and trust Me alone. I will not fail you. I will be giving you even more examples of My deep love and care for you. You will forever marvel at the workings of My hand, and your gratitude will overflow.

*The Lord will perfect that which concerns me;
Your mercy, O Lord, endures forever;
do not forsake the works of Your hands.*

PSALM 138:8

May 3

Jesus, Jesus, Jesus, I don't want to get up from my knees
until I have Your peace. What is it You want from me?

Your heart, My child. Your pure heart that is willing to totally trust Me. Even on days like this, when nothing makes sense to you. I need you to look only to who I am and to disregard anything that keeps your eyes off Me. I alone am your source, the Giver of all good gifts.

Know Me, My child. In knowing Me, you will know My heart of love. Never doubt My matchless love for you. I know nothing else will satisfy, so be willing to wait for My purposeful plans. I will be glorified in what I will do for you, and your joy will never end.

The enemy is trying to discourage you. Don't let him, My child. Stand firm. Don't allow Satan *any* power over you. You are *Mine*, and I will protect and keep you. I will also protect and keep the faith I have given you—a faith that will honor and glorify Me.

All is well, precious child. All is truly well. If you could only see from My vantage point, you would know concretely the absolute truth of those words. Soon your faith will be made sight, but until then know My words as truth, even before you can see the results of My workings for you. Trust Me, My child. I will *not* fail you.

I will say of the Lord, "He is my refuge and my fortress;
My God, in Him I will trust."

PSALM 91:2

May 4

We're here to be worshipers first and workers only second.
We take a convert and immediately make a worker out of him.
God never meant it to be so. God meant that a convert should learn
to be a worshiper, and after that he can learn to be a worker. . . .
The work done by a worshiper will have eternity in it.

A. W. TOZER (1897–1963)

Worship Me today, even as you work and fulfill your responsibilities.
Worship is an attitude of the heart, the outflow of a grateful heart.
Worship of Me defines your work for Me so that *all* is done to glorify Me.
The simplicity and beauty of heartfelt worship of Me is transformed
into holy and worthy work for Me.

But worship always needs to precede the work. Out of worship is
work enjoyed. Out of worship is work so worthwhile that it produces
glee in the one working out of worship. Worship frees the created to
emanate the Creator, which elevates the work to the level of worship.

To create is to worship your Creator. To offer that creation to Me,
your Creator, is to return to Me what I freely gave. But it all begins
with your humble worship of Me.

Say to God, "How awesome are Your works!
Through the greatness of Your power
Your enemies shall submit themselves to You.
All the earth shall worship You and sing praises to You;
they shall sing praises to Your name."
Come and see the works of God;
He is awesome in His doing toward the sons of men.

PSALM 66:3-5

May 5

Expectations fully given to our all-wise God
leave no entrance for disappointment.

JGM

Always look to Me expectantly, simply because of *who I am*. Expectation is never misplaced when it is placed without misgivings into My hands. I hold gently the expectations of My children, knowing the fragile hearts from which they come. Yet those very hearts will be strengthened as they wait on Me and seek Me alone.

My sufficiency will never fail a seeking child of Mine. Every confidence placed in Me will be met with complete competence and all out of My heart of love for My children.

You know that heart, My child, My heart of love for you. But that knowledge didn't come in a day or even years. The knowledge of My love has been infused in you one strengthening layer at a time. Each layer of My truth yields another layer of foundation to build upon. Years of waiting on Me and learning of Me have yielded a foundation wide in its knowledge and deep in its understanding of Me and My love. And that very foundation is the bedrock for your trust in Me. None of this could happen overnight but only in your daily coming to Me.

In Me all things become new as old things pass away. Your days will soon offer a newness you have only dreamed about. A newness that will shine with hopes fulfilled. A newness so worth waiting for. Look forward to those new days with unparalleled hope and joy.

Therefore, if anyone is in Christ, he is a new creation;
old things have passed away; behold, all things have become new.

2 CORINTHIANS 5:17

May 6

Looking to Jesus till glory doth shine,
moment by moment, O Lord, I am Thine.

DANIEL WEBSTER WHITTLE (1840–1901),
"MOMENT BY MOMENT"

Look only to Me. With Me in your vision you will see clearly. Your perspective will be clear and accurate. My promises will ring true. You will see everything in the light of My truth. Trust Me in this. Let My Spirit pervade your vision and thinking. That will change everything.

Often My workings are invisible for a time, but that doesn't make them any less real. I am indeed working to bring all to pass that I have promised you. Trust Me completely, My child. There is reason for only hope when you look to Me. I will not fail you. Look to Me, the Giver and Keeper of your hope. I will not disappoint you.

I am teaching you much. Lessons you wouldn't have learned any other way. Know My heart of goodness and love toward you. The delays are not punishment, only preparation for My best for you. Know My heart fully, and then others will know Me in new ways as I use you. Know this as fact. What I am revealing to you in these days will be used in the lives of many.

Oh, My child, the joy I have in store for you! I will honor you for trusting Me. I will bring all things to pass perfectly. Know how much I love you and that nothing is too hard for Me. I love you with an everlasting, unchanging love. Live in My love all day today.

Then the angel I saw standing on the sea and on the land raised his right hand
toward heaven. He swore an oath in the name of the one who lives forever and ever,
who created the heavens and everything in them, the earth and everything in it,
and the sea and everything in it. He said, "There will be no more delay.
When the seventh angel blows his trumpet, God's mysterious plan will be fulfilled.
It will happen just as he announced it to his servants the prophets."

REVELATION 10:5-7, NLT

JUDY GORDON MORROW   The Listening Heart   149

May 7

Lord, You have been so silent lately.

Rest in My silences. They do not indicate My absence. They are part of My workings, My orchestrations in your life. Look at my silences as the "rests" in the music of your life. They allow for space and quiet, and then the music of My workings will shimmer with clarity and purity, making known My purposes. In this way I will be glorified more than ever.

So rest in Me, My child. Don't be afraid of My silences. Don't allow anxiety to overshadow the silences I have intended for serenity. Think of the tranquility of a smooth, calm pond. Drink in the loveliness of that scene, and equate My silences to that kind of stillness. Just as you wouldn't stir the waters of the pond in order to see "activity," don't disturb My silences with your fretting. Rather, drink deeply of My Word, and bask in My ever-constant presence. Lack of words does not indicate the lack of My presence. Relax and be totally at peace in who I am and how much I love you.

There is nothing to fear. There is much to look forward to. Your joy will increase daily as you see the workings of My hand. Continue to pray and live expectantly.

I love you, My child. Rest in My unfailing love for you. Rest and rejoice.

For thus says the Lord God, the Holy One of Israel:
"In returning and rest you shall be saved;
in quietness and confidence shall be your strength."
ISAIAH 30:15

May 8

Praise You, Jesus.

Praise is good, My child—a gift to Me that also reaps benefits for you. Praise is freeing. Praise is life-giving. Praise anoints a life with My oil of gladness. Never underestimate the power of praise to Me, the very Giver of your life.

Praise brings Light to the countenance. Praise gives warmth to the smile. Praise prepares the heart to be receptive to My purposes. Praise serves My children well. Give yourself unto praise, and see the difference it makes in every arena of your life. Praise transforms the praise giver. Praise gives glory to Me, the object of your praise.

Keep Me as the object of your praise, the center of your life, and I will honor you all of your days. Praise deepens your relationship with Me, as it relinquishes your heart to Me. A heart fully surrendered to Me I can only honor. You have learned the peace and contentment and freedom of that surrendered heart and also the ever-increasing joy.

Now bask in that joy even today, allowing it to seep into every pore of your being. A joy-permeated life draws others to Me, like a magnet to steel. When that joy is displayed in the midst of a pain-filled life, the draw and pull of that joy is only increased. Only I can produce genuine joy in the midst of pain. Such a supernatural joy, contrary to human abilities, comes only from Me. Claim that bountiful joy even today. It is yours.

Let the godly sing for joy to the Lord; it is fitting for the pure to praise him.
PSALM 33:1, *NLT*

May 9

If the Lord Jehovah makes us wait, let us do so with our whole hearts;
for blessed are all they that wait for Him. He is worth waiting for.
The waiting itself is beneficial to us: it tries faith, exercises patience,
trains submission, and endears the blessing when it comes.

CHARLES SPURGEON (1834–1892),
THE TREASURY OF DAVID

I will be honoring you in ways so amazing that you will be breathless with joy. These days of waiting and hardship will fall away like chaff with just a puff of My breath. All things will become new and fresh and vibrant.

Take these words of hope into your very being. Don't just taste them, but fully devour them so that they will nourish and strengthen your very soul. My hope is substance and food to sustain your very being and to give light to your eyes and joy to your heart. Partake of My hope, and you partake of My very nature, of Life itself. This is the profound difference I make in the lives of My children: life-giving hope to change this world from death and darkness to life and light.

I am the Light of the world. I am the Way, the Truth, and the Life. I am beyond every need in this world with fullness of hope and every good thing. Only I can give true hope and pure goodness because of who I am.

Take these words of life this morning and ingest them into your very soul. Let them sustain and keep you, giving you strength for every task and challenge. I am your hope, your very provision for every need of your life. I delight to do good for you as you come to Me with an open heart, ready to receive from My hand My very best for you.

For in You, O Lord, I hope; You will hear, O Lord my God.
PSALM 38:15

May 10

The greatest thing anyone can do for God and man is pray.
It is not the only thing; but it is the chief thing.
The great people of the earth today are the people who pray.
I do not mean those who talk about prayer;
not those who can explain about prayer;
but I mean those people who take time and pray.

S. D. GORDON (1859–1936)

Continue to pray much for your loved ones. My hand is upon them, as you know, but never fail to pray for them. Prayer erects a wall between them and the enemy. Don't fail to pray in order to keep that wall strong, with no chinks. I will honor your prayers.

Do not let today's burdens press on you. You believe in Me, and that is *all* that is truly necessary. I am going before you even now to make smooth your path, to ensure that you will not stumble. Look to Me alone, Child, and lift every concern to Me—from every ache and pain to your loved ones and their concerns.

Who am I that I would ever desert or fail you? You know that would deny and contradict who I am, so be confident by placing your trust in Me alone. *I will not fail you.* You can count on Me to carry your every concern and to bring about My best purposes. Let your lightened heart be a testimony to Me. Truly, *all is well.*

Therefore confess your sins to one another, and pray for one another,
so that you may be healed. The prayer of the righteous is powerful and effective.

JAMES 5:16, *NRSV*

May 11

You plan my days, Lord. You indicate Your ways.

I will do that for you. I am going before you even now, preparing the way. You will know what to do at just the right time. You will see My faithfulness on every level.

Know My love for you, My child. Don't let discouragement creep in. Focus on Me and all the hope I continue to give you. Prepare with joy for the new days I have ahead for you. The joy will lighten your heart and your tasks.

Don't focus on time elements. Focus only on Me and trust Me completely. I am the God of time, and I will work out My plans with amazing precision. You are wise to wait on My timings and ways. Rest in Me and My sovereignty and know the wisdom of My plans. You can rest in My assurances and My unsurpassed wisdom.

My love for you is matchless. You will be overwhelmed with gratitude and joy at the workings of My hand. These days of painful waiting will be redeemed with boundless joy. Like the unceasing waves of the ocean, so will be My gifts of joy to you. You will marvel at each one, and your sorrow of these past years will melt away under My balm of joy to your heart.

Believe Me completely. Faithful am I, your Father, and I will do all that I have promised. Joy in that hope today. The fulfillment of that hope will soon be yours. I love you, Child.

Such things were written in the Scriptures long ago to teach us.
And the Scriptures give us hope and encouragement
as we wait patiently for God's promises to be fulfilled.
ROMANS 15:4, *NLT*

May 12

Lord, I am utterly dependent on You.

And I am here for you. I was here for you yesterday, I am here for you today, and I will be here for you tomorrow. Yet the only thing necessary for you to know is that I am here for you now—this very day—to help you with whatever needs you may have. Together the day will be rich and rewarding. See? Doesn't that truth alter your outlook? When you allow Me to enter into your day and your most tedious of tasks, I can elevate that day and even those tasks to a new level—a level of joy and contentment.

The key is to keep your eyes on Me, looking ever upward to Me for your strength and guidance. For your perspective. For peace in the midst of turbulence and uncertainty. I am the One who makes all the difference, for nothing can limit or hinder My power when My children trust Me completely.

Now move into your day with lightness of heart and swiftness of feet to accomplish My purposes. I will help you with each task, large and small, and you will know anew My faithfulness to you. Enjoy the process. Joy. By choosing joy you are choosing to live in a way that is honoring to Me. True joy comes from Me and shines My light and love into this dark and troubled world. Choose joy, and you are choosing to illumine every part of your world.

Rejoice in the Lord always. Again I will say, rejoice!
PHILIPPIANS 4:4

May 13

O for a thousand tongues to sing my great Redeemer's praise.

CHARLES WESLEY (1707–1788),
"O FOR A THOUSAND TONGUES TO SING"

Abound in praise, My child. Abound in praise so overflowing that the enemy will not be able to get near. Praise is your most powerful defense to keep him at bay. Speak your praise. Sing your praise. Live your praise to Me by your actions and attitudes. Your praise to Me will then spill out on the lives of others and also bless them. A life of praise brings Me honor like nothing else.

Praise is My gift to you. Use it freely. Express praise to Me even when you don't feel like it, and I will honor you. The feelings will follow your obedience. Praise is also your gift to Me. The more freely you praise from a heart overflowing, the more freely I can move My hand in response.

Praise is the conduit for blessing. Keep your channel of praise free and flowing—not choked by bitterness or resentment or anger—and then I can use that channel to flood back to you My joy, peace and love. Praise is the key, My child. Always, always praise Me.

Praise the Lord! For it is good to sing praises to our God;
for it is pleasant, and praise is beautiful.

PSALM 147:1

May 14

Remembering all God had done for me, I told Him,
"You know I will tell Your stories."

And stories will I be giving you beyond your wildest imaginings. Stories that will honor and glorify Me and will bring joy and gladness to you and hope to others. Even now I am writing those stories. Do not give up, but do know the ink is still wet on the page, as even now I am writing new chapters in the story of your life. Take great hope and comfort in that.

I am also writing new chapters in the lives of your loved ones. Do not be fearful as to the contents, but do know that I love them beyond your capability to love. I will do all things well regarding their every concern. Trust Me in this, and just keep bringing them to Me often in loving prayer. I will do all that I have promised.

I will also do all that I have promised you. How you will rejoice in My answers! Believe Me by faith, My child, the faith that is the substance of things hoped for and the evidence of things yet to come. I provide the substance. I am the evidence of your faith. In Me are all things possible to the one who believes Me and My words.

Now faith is the substance of things hoped for,
the evidence of things not seen.
HEBREWS 11:1

May 15

Thy will be done. Always Thy will be done.

My will I will accomplish in your life as you seek Me and Me alone. In Me is *all* you need. Think how inclusive is the word "all," and know that there is nothing left that requires worry. Worry is never life-giving—it is life-draining. Why would you ever want to choose worry? Yes, it is a choice on your part. Instead, choose Me, and then you will have chosen Life. I am the Life, the only life worthy of your choice.

When you choose Me, you know peace. When you choose Me, you choose to be filled with My love and joy. When you choose Me, you eliminate choices for evil and destruction. Choose Me, and that choice will transform your life from a life of worry and dismay to a life of peace and calm. Then, even in the midst of chaos, your choice of Me will keep you calm because of My presence. Is there any other way you'd rather live? Settle yourself in Me, and I will settle the waves of worry and any other unrest that threatens your peace in Me.

Allow Me to do that, even today, My child. Choose Me. Choose to think My thoughts. Choose to live on the level of trust. Choose to disregard all distractions that would turn your eyes from Me, and then every other choice of your life will fall into place. You know My words to be true. Choose *Me*.

But if you refuse to serve the Lord, then choose today whom you will serve. . . .
But as for me and my family, we will serve the Lord.
JOSHUA 24:15, *NLT*

JUDY GORDON MORROW

May 16

There is no neutral ground in the universe;
every square inch, every split second, is claimed by God
and counter-claimed by Satan.

C. S. LEWIS (1898–1963),
"CHRISTIANITY AND CULTURE"

All is well. Rest alone in Me. Let nothing but My thoughts enter in, as My thoughts are truth. Discard immediately any intrusions of deceit by the enemy. False are his claims, and they don't deserve even an instant of your time. Why should you listen to lies when you can listen to love? My love is infused with My truth, because that is who I am. I *am* Truth, and it is in Me and Me alone that you can be free from falsity and deception of any kind.

You see the enormous chasm between My truth and Satan's lies, the wide divide between pure goodness and destructive evil. Don't ever muddy My clear-flowing river of truth and goodness with the devil's lies and evil. My truth always reveals love, while Satan's lies shroud his every intent of evil.

For such boasters are false apostles, deceitful workers,
disguising themselves as apostles of Christ.
And no wonder! Even Satan disguises himself as an angel of light.
So it is not strange if his ministers also disguise themselves
as ministers of righteousness.
Their end will match their deeds.

2 CORINTHIANS 11:13-15, *NRSV*

May 17

The issue is now clear. It is between light and darkness,
and everyone must choose his side.

G. K. CHESTERTON (1874–1936)

Live in the light of My truth, and you will never need to fear walking in the darkness of deception. The darkness of the devil is meant only for destruction, while My light leads you into eternal life. There can be no blending of goodness with evil or of light with darkness. My truth will always prevail over deception. Live your life filled with Me and My goodness, and walk always in the light of My love.

You see the contrast so clearly, and you long for all to be rescued from the deceiving darkness and come into the glorious light of My love. Shine for Me, My child. Simply lift Me up, and I will draw the lost and hurting to Me. I love them beyond their knowledge, and I will show Myself to them. Pray. Pray much, My child. All great movings of My hand are preceded by prayer. Live in prayer and love without reserve. I *will* answer.

Woe to those who call evil good, and good evil; who put darkness for light,
and light for darkness; who put bitter for sweet, and sweet for bitter!

ISAIAH 5:20

But if we walk in the light as He is in the light, we have fellowship with one
another, and the blood of Jesus Christ His Son cleanses us from all sin.

1 JOHN 1:7

May 18

O God, our help in ages past, our hope for years to come.

ISAAC WATTS (1674–1748),
"O GOD, OUR HELP IN AGES PAST"

Today partake of My joy and blessings as I help you in every task. Don't even look at them as tasks but as opportunities to see Me at work. To see My creativity and greatness. To see My unending love and care for you. That's what this day holds for you as you allow Me to transform tasks into offerings lifted up to Me with thanksgiving.

After all, every task can be traced to a blessing. Dirty laundry equates to the blessing of clothes to wear. Dirty dishes pronounce that you had food on your plates. Your home that requires attention shelters you and brings joy and comfort to those who enter and share the warmth of its welcome.

Ah, now you are seeing all of this again through My eyes. Now the tedium of the tasks can be viewed as pathways of praise. Reasons for gratitude. Opportunities to worship Me in song even as you work. Doesn't that put a whole new perspective on your day? With daily practice and prayer, you can make this perspective your new mindset—a mindset that is pleasing to Me and will bring honor to Me.

Now your thinking has shifted this very day, and that is My gift to you. Again you see the value of beginning your day with Me so that I can impart My heart to you and add joy to your day. All because I love you, dear child. All because *I love you.*

Because Your lovingkindness is better than life,
My lips shall praise You.

PSALM 63:3

May 19

O praise Him for His holiness, His wisdom and His grace.

LEILA N. MORRIS (1862–1929),
"LET ALL THE PEOPLE PRAISE THEE"

This morning you have already known My presence and My peace. Don't let the enemy snatch away My peace. Keep your eyes ever on Me and praise in your heart and on your lips. I take delight in the praise of My children. It is your gift to Me, and I will respond with an outpouring of My blessings.

Praise at all times, even when you don't feel like it. Praise frees My hand, and the enemy cannot withstand praise from My children. Praise and prayer linked in My name are the enemy's greatest foes. Never forget the resources, the strength, the power you possess with praise and prayer.

Look for Me today. You will see Me everywhere. Know that all is in My hands and that I do all things well. I will provide everything you need at just the right time. Don't worry about *anything*. There is no purpose or joy in worrying. Oh, how My children need to learn that truth! Worry saps life from the body and spirit. My joy infuses life. Choose My joy.

Dwell in Me and know My life-giving joy. My joy cannot be duplicated or imitated. It is beyond that. Only My joy can heal brokenness and make a face radiant. Genuine joy comes only from Me. Be My example, My witness, of My true joy today. Others will see the difference. Joy lights the eyes and the smile. Be used of Me in that way. I will do that for you.

Righteousness and justice are the foundation of Your throne;
mercy and truth go before Your face.
Blessed are the people who know the joyful sound!
They walk, O Lord, in the light of Your countenance.

PSALM 89:14–15

JUDY GORDON MORROW

May 20

All my trust on Thee is stayed; all my help from Thee I bring.

CHARLES WESLEY (1707–1788),
"JESUS, LOVER OF MY SOUL"

You can trust Me. You can believe Me. Never waver in your trust in Me, knowing who I am. Think of that—who I am. Think of that in the context of My Word and in the context of your life.

You *know* Me, My child. You know My voice, you've seen My hand work in your life. My love is evident to you. There is no need to protect yourself while wrapped in My love. I *am* your protection. I am the One who loves you with a love like no other. Isn't that protection enough? Dwell on that truth. Make it part of you.

Self-protection can harden you. My protection will keep you pliable. Only allow My protection of you with My cloak of love. There is no need for any other kind. Rest in that assurance, My child. Relax in that kind of love.

Know I am with you. With you to the uttermost. There is nothing you can't handle with Me. Lean heavily on Me. I will not fail you. Everything I have told you remains true. Wait on My timings. They are perfect and they are for you—a gift of love to you.

Live in My presence. Expect great things. Keep trusting. You will know great joy. Joy and rest in My words. They are from My heart to yours. I love you, My child. Rest in My love for you.

We know how much God loves us, and we have put our trust in his love.
God is love, and all who live in love live in God, and God lives in them.

1 JOHN 4:16, *NLT*

May 21

Jesus, I am resting, resting in the joy of what Thou art;
I am finding out the greatness of Thy loving heart.

JEAN SOPHIA PIGOTT (1845–1882),
"JESUS, I AM RESTING, RESTING"

Rest in me today. Let Me restore mind, body and spirit. This day of rest will reap benefits for the rest of your week. Rest always precedes productivity. Bring meaning to this day of rest by allowing My peaceful quiet to seep into your heart and soul to still you.

Stillness allows receptivity to My voice and leadings. You can know a stillness inside even when life clamors at you on every side. My stillness will yield a calm within, a serenity that others will notice.

Embrace My stillness today, and plumb the depths of My loving-kindness toward you. All will benefit from time set apart to be with Me. Rest, My child. Rest and be restored and refreshed by the One who loves you most.

Consider how I love Your precepts;
revive me, O Lord,
according to Your lovingkindness.

PSALM 119:159

May 22

Begin the day with God. In His presence there is no problem too big,
no sorrow too deep, no challenge too overwhelming.
In Him there is peace, comfort, strength—and so much more.

JGM

Our time together this morning has been precious, My child. Your heart after Mine is a pleasing fragrance to Me, and I will honor you greatly. I know it's hard for you to write words like that, but it is My truth to you. That truth is ingrained in who I am as your Father—I honor My children who love and obey Me. I take great delight in doing so.

I also take great delight in the sweet communion and fellowship we have shared this morning. Yes, let My children know this is not reserved for a chosen few. Bid them to come to Me, to seek Me, to be silent before Me, and then see what I will do. They cannot dismiss this. They need to follow those steps and be still and *know* that I am God.[1] They, too, can know the difference that stillness before Me will make. It is in the richness of *being* before Me that I can bring fulfillment in the *doing* for Me.

Live in My love and joy and peace today. Bask in the serenity of My presence. You are My beloved child, and I take great joy and delight in you. I am singing over you today, My child. Hear My songs of love and be glad. I love you.

The Lord your God in your midst, the Mighty One, will save;
He will rejoice over you with gladness, He will quiet you with His love,
He will rejoice over you with singing.

ZEPHANIAH 3:17

Note
1. See Psalm 46:10.

May 23

Answered prayer is the interchange of love between the Father and His child.
ANDREW MURRAY (1828–1917)

Stay close to Me, like a young child next to her mother when needing comfort and direction. In that way you'll be able to hear My every word of love and know the touch of My hand. There is no better way to live out your days. This moment-by-moment walking with Me yields the most blessed of lives. Then all is God ordained, not human directed, and you will know satisfaction in your soul—a satisfaction that can be obtained in no other way.

Too many of My children strive so hard, putting into place human efforts rather than seeking My divine plans. Really now, wouldn't you rather have divine over human every time? You smile at the thought, at how ludicrous it is to settle for the dust of the human when you can have the diamonds of the divine. Don't settle for less, My child. All that is required is your hand in Mine, your heart ever listening to Mine.

Oh, how I will be blessing you! You sense it, you feel it, just like smelling the salt water on the sea breeze before ever seeing the ocean. So it is with the fulfillment of My promises in your life. You know they are coming because of My every word to you and because of the anticipation I have placed within you—the hope that will no longer be deferred but will burst forth in the abundance of My love. Faithful will I be to fulfill your hope.

The fears of the wicked will be fulfilled; the hopes of the godly will be granted.
PROVERBS 10:24, *NLT*

The Listening Heart JUDY GORDON MORROW

May 24

God is love.

It is good to dwell on that truth. I am indeed love. Not *like* love but love itself. Because I *am* love, all I do is entwined with love. My children need to know this. There is nothing to fear from a Father who is love. Out of who I am—love—comes only good things for My children.

If only this truth could be grasped! Then My children would welcome My plans and My workings. They would know the true essence of joy in following Me. They would welcome me with wide-open hearts that desire to be filled with My blessings. Then, even the seemingly painful and difficult can be viewed as blessings from My hand.

Knowing I am love colors every event and circumstance with the vibrancy and richness of My loving purposes. My children who know this will embrace every gift from My hand, knowing I do all out of My love for them. Fear cannot enter in where My love prevails. Oh, My child, capture that truth and allow it to change your life. Your outlook will be constantly wreathed with joy when you trust your Father of love. Doubt and anxiety will not be able to find a foothold in a heart that gives residence to only My love.

Beloved, let us love one another, because love is from God;
everyone who loves is born of God and knows God.
Whoever does not love does not know God, for God is love.

1 JOHN 4:7-8, *NRSV*

May 25

Lord, I pray You'll make all things clear.

I will make all things clear. You can count on that. Out of My love for you, I will not allow confusion to reign. You have sensed My peace and presence today, knowing they are My gifts to you.

The clarity of My plans for you will also be My gift to you, My child. You will know just in time. Oftentimes My ways are not clear only because the time has not yet come. Don't equate delays with My lack of working on your behalf. Quite the contrary is true. I am working, ever working, even when your eyes see nothing happening. Those are the times to view My hand and heart through eyes of faith—when it is the substance of things hoped for, the evidence of things not seen.[1] Seeing with the eyes of faith will only increase your knowledge of Me and the great love I have for you.

When I do reveal My plans, how much greater will be your joy! A joy that was formed in the darkness and made known in the light. Do know that I am shaping many joys for you even now in the darkness—joys that will be unveiled and will add gladness to all your days. That kind of joy will be so pure and sweet that you will scarce be able to contain it. Live today in the certain hope of that kind of joy, My child. It will soon be yours.

Light is sown for the righteous, and gladness for the upright in heart.
PSALM 97:11

Note
1. See Hebrews 11:1.

May 26

Thank You for this quietness this morning.

Quietness is My gift to you. Oh, that My children would seek Me in a quiet place. It is there I can convey My love, it is there I can speak in My still voice. Once My children start doing this, seeking Me in a quiet place, their lives will overflow with My love. Nothing else will satisfy them as much as this time spent with Me.

You have discovered the truth of that, My child. What once began as a duty has become your greatest joy. This time has been that and so much more: sustaining grace, perfect peace, eternal wisdom. Here at My feet you have been given all that you need. You have found Me to be all sufficient. You have basked in the sweetness of My presence. You have seen the difference this time makes.

Gently tell those who still need to know. Relay to them the difference it has made in your life. Help them capture the joy of being in My presence on a daily basis. Encourage them to spend time with Me, the Lover of their souls, and to know Me fully. The benefits will astound them, just as they have you.

Go in My peace today, knowing I am with you in all things. You are My beloved child. Let the love and light of My presence shine on your face today so that others will be drawn to Me. I love you.

They looked to Him and were radiant,
and their faces were not ashamed.

PSALM 34:5

May 27

Jesus, I am believing You that Your promise is as good as done.

It is. You are already knowing the beauty and joy and wonder of knowing My answers, My faithfulness to you, before you have any knowledge or concrete evidence of My answers. Just as the centurion believed when I spoke words of healing, so too have you believed My words of hope and promise. Isn't it sweet to know that kind of confidence in Me before seeing the results? That has come from these very times, My child. These times on your knees before Me, when you have poured out your heart and basked in My presence, knowing Me like never before.

It is in the knowing of Me that I can build a foundation of trust. When you know Me, you know My love for you. The words of My love take root in your heart, and you see manifestations of My love everywhere. And the glorious cycle continues. The more you know Me, the more you know My love, and in that knowing comes unequivocal trust. There is no better way. It is a way of life and hope and peace. This is My desire for all My children.

Now you know at least in part the reason for My delays. Your faith has never been so rock solid in Me, and because of that your effectiveness for Me will be multiplied a hundredfold. Truly, I do all things well. You will soon know that like never before. Delight in Me and My love today.

Then Jesus went with them. And when He was already not far from the house, the centurion sent friends to Him, saying to Him, "Lord, do not trouble Yourself, for I am not worthy that You should enter under my roof. Therefore I did not even think myself worthy to come to You. But say the word, and my servant will be healed."

LUKE 7:6-7

May 28

I am desperate for Your answers, Jesus.

Show Me your faith now by arising in peace and leaving with Me your every care and concern—just as a child leaves a broken toy with her father and skips away to play again because she knows her father will mend her toy. There is no need for her to worry about it anymore.

You need to do the same, My child. Leave with Me every troubling thought and concern, *knowing without a doubt* that I *will* take care of each one. Don't carry those things that are meant for Me, your Father.

All is well. Never doubt that, even when fresh pain assaults you. There is no need for confusion or fear. I am the God of peace. Know My peace, and you will know Me. Know Me, and you will know My peace. They are synonymous, along with hope and joy. Know Me, and all these things are yours.

Allow Me to permeate your day. Look only to Me. Think only My thoughts. Know only Me and My truth. Anything else will only dismay you. Know Me alone.

I love you, Child. I have *not* forgotten you. Cling to Me alone, and know that *all is well.*

As the Father has loved me, so have I loved you.
Abide in my love.
JOHN 15:9, *ESV*

May 29

Why are You not talking to me like You used to?

Because you aren't taking the time to listen. This time on your knees hasn't happened as consistently as it used to. Remember how I have always told you how important this time is to come before Me. It is life changing, but it also must be ongoing. Just like you lose the sweet closeness of a friend when you quit communicating heart to heart, so will you also lose the sweet communion with Me if we don't spend meaningful time together.

It's in this time I can speak My truth and dispel the lies of Satan. It's in this time that I can impart My peace and replace all doubt and worry. It's during this time that you can delve even deeper into who I am and know anew how much I love you. It's in this set-apart time that I can give you guidance and ideas and strength—all tools for your next step on My path of life. A path filled with My purposes as you look only to Me.

Trust. Rest. Drink deeply of My peace, and, yes, My joy. I joy in *you*, My precious child, and your faith that grows brighter with each sunrise. I will honor your faith with the most brilliant joy—a joy that shines brighter than the stars and sun and moon combined. Imagine, My child, a joy that radiant—a joy that will dispel all the sadness and sorrow of these many years of days. Soon you will see My glorious answers. *Soon.*

The prospect of the righteous is joy,
but the hopes of the wicked come to nothing.

PROVERBS 10:28, *NIV*

The Listening Heart   JUDY GORDON MORROW

May 30

Remind me that this waiting isn't to endure but to prepare.

Indeed it is, My child. That is exactly what it is for. Time for every preparation in every realm—mind, body and soul.

You are struggling with energy and fatigue. Lean on Me, and trust Me to provide *all* that you need. Nothing is limited in My supply— nothing. When I tell you that I will supply all your needs, remember My resources in the richness of My Son's gift to you. Nothing else can compare to the Love that gave its all. Out of that Love will I lavish on you the richness of My grace and mercy. Just watch and see what I will do.

Now move in faith, one step at a time. I will enlarge your minutes as you follow after Me and My designs for your day. Do not give in to discouragement, one of the enemy's greatest tools to harm My children and their hearts for Me. Turn your back on him and all his lies. Look only to Me, the One who can only speak truth. Hear My truth, and remember all the truths I have spoken to you over the years.

Eyes on Me, Child, eyes on Me. Don't move your eyes away even for a moment, or the enemy will try to move in with his lies of despair. I give hope—never despair—and today, this very day, you are to walk in My hope alone.

> *We are afflicted in every way, but not crushed;*
> *perplexed, but not driven to despair;*
> *persecuted, but not forsaken;*
> *struck down, but not destroyed;*
> *always carrying in the body the death of Jesus,*
> *so that the life of Jesus may also be made visible in our bodies.*

2 CORINTHIANS 4:8-10, *NRSV*

May 31

When I thought about something God had done, I said,
"Lord, that is amazing!"

I am amazing. You know that, but sometimes I want you to know that truth anew. Too often My children look at Me through finite eyes, and they limit Me. I am limitless. I am divine. I am beyond measuring. I know no boundaries in what I can do. I am *God*.

Think on those things when you come before Me with your requests. Realize that nothing hampers Me. I am not penned in, in any way. Look at the myriad of answers that I can provide for you because I am not limited in any way. May the breadth and scope of My power give you new hope and confidence in Me and the answers I will be providing for you. Know that My answers will be designed perfectly for you.

Rest in the knowledge that you are loved by a perfect Father. A Father who knows you and treasures you like no other. You are precious and dearly loved. All gifts that come from My hand are out of My deep, abiding love for you. Take comfort and joy in that truth. May it lighten your heart and your steps today as you look only to Me. Remember, My child. I love you!

Great is the Lord! He is most worthy of praise!
No one can measure his greatness.

PSALM 145:3, *NLT*

June

I hear God's heartbeat in my ears
And it pulsates with the refrain,
"I love you, I love you, I love you.
I have always loved you.
I will always love you.
You are forever My beloved child."

I learned to hear Him in the stillness,
so even in the din of life
I can hear His heartbeat of love for me.
And just like the steady beat of a heart
is the steadfastness and constancy of His love.

Listen.
Listen in stillness.
Listen to the soft whoosh of His whispers
through the chambers of His heart:
"I love you. I love you. I love you."

June 1

Work in Your inimitable way.

Yes, My ways are inimitable. They cannot be duplicated by anyone. My ways and thoughts are above all others in their truth, wisdom and power. You have seen that truth, and you will continue to see it in the days ahead. The ache and longing of these days will be replaced with a deep-seated, overflowing joy.

This waiting has been a time of training and teaching. A time to draw near and cling only to Me. You have learned much in the silences, in the loneliness. You have keenly sensed My presence like never before. You have heard Me in the deep darkness of the night and in the beginnings of your days.

Your life has changed. *You* have changed. Do you see it? Do you see the difference these days have made? While difficult and painful, they have refined you as you have yielded yourself to Me. Just spending time in My presence has changed you. Time with Me will always change My children. My presence is transforming you with My love, joy and peace. All of these will be imparted to My children who will spend time with Me.

Live in My hope today. It has never felt more solid, has it. Hope is never nebulous but always solid and sure. Hope is founded on Me, your Rock and Fortress. What could be more certain and secure than that? Live in that truth today, My child. Truth that will give you great joy and peace.

But I will hope continually, and will praise You yet more and more.
PSALM 71:14

JUDY GORDON MORROW

June 2

It's all about You, Lord.

As it should be, My child. I am the beginning to the end. In Me is *everything* you need. I am the One who promises to *never* leave you nor forsake you. I am your very breath, your life giver, your joy filler, your sorrow comforter. In Me is *all* you need.

Long have you waited, and your waiting will be compensated with measureless, overflowing joy coming from a wellspring of love constantly supplied by Me. I am the living water, and I will be supplying every need for you, along with inestimable joy.

I love you, My child. I know these days have not been easy, especially with the harsh buffeting Satan gave you the other night. You were right to call out to Me in prayer and praise. He can't remain where prayer and praise abound.

Trust Me to do *all* I have spoken. Truly, you will be amazed. Amazed and overjoyed. Dwell in that truth even now, and prepare in great hope. I love you, My precious child. Forever will I love you. You will marvel at My expressions of love to you. Faithful is He who calls you, who also *will do it*. Just watch and see what I will do. Remember, it's *all* a *yes*![1]

The one who calls you is faithful, and he will do this.

1 THESSALONIANS 5:24, *NRSV*

Note

1. See 2 Corinthians 1:20.

June 3

Thy will be done, Lord.

It will be, My child. Fear not. Look not at the problems, the obstacles, but look only to Me. Pray in praise, My child. Don't let the heaviness of the situation weigh you down. Remember *who I am*, and know that *nothing* is too hard for Me.

I will honor you. You have waited on Me, and I will always honor the heart that waits on Me for *My* ways and purposes. I know this journey has been long, but it has been fraught with My purposes. Someday you will see that even more clearly.

There is *nothing* to fear. There is much to hope in, as I continue to work to fulfill My promises to you. Pray and praise without ceasing. That is your barrier to the enemy's barrage of lies. Keep up the shield of faith by your constant prayer and praise to Me.

Let nothing but *My* thoughts permeate your thinking. Dwell on *My* truths. Walk hard after Me today. I will not fail you. Seek Me alone, and you will know My peace alone. Let nothing crowd out My peace. It was that peace that enabled Me to sleep in the boat during the storm. That same peace is available to you.

I love you, My child. Walk in the light of My love all day today. In Me is no darkness at all. Be My light and love today, and shine for Me. I will help you to do that. *All is well.*

And a great windstorm arose, and the waves beat into the boat,
so that it was already filling. But He was in the stern, asleep on a pillow.
And they awoke Him and said to Him, "Teacher, do You not care that we are perishing?"
Then He arose and rebuked the wind, and said to the sea, "Peace, be still!"
And the wind ceased and there was a great calm.

MARK 4:37-39

June 4

Praise You, praise You, praise You, Jesus. Praise You.

You are right to praise Me. Praise clears the heart of anything that might hinder closeness to Me. Praise acknowledges who I am and that I am trustworthy. So when you praise Me, even when there are difficult circumstances in your life, you are acknowledging the truth that I am in control. You are giving credence by your praise that I am the Lord your God in the midst of your circumstances. Your praise isn't contingent upon your circumstances. Your praise to Me declares who I am in spite of your circumstances.

Keeping your focus on praise causes the externals to fall away and reveals the Source of your praise like never before. You are praising My changelessness and proclaiming My timelessness and steadfastness. Truly, I am worthy to be praised, and when you do so, the veil is lifted and you truly see Me and who I am to you.

I will praise the Lord at all times.
I will constantly speak his praises.
PSALM 34:1, *NLT*

June 5

*I'm determined to stay on my knees until You answer the needs
of my hurting heart and tell me how to endure this pain.*

Do not focus on your situation. Pray instead for the needs of others.
When your pain threatens to overwhelm you, let that be a signal to
pray for those I will bring to your mind. Then good of every kind will
be accomplished. Focus on Me and Me alone, and just see what I will
do. Live ever looking to Me. Don't allow your mind to dwell on your
present circumstances. Dwell instead on Me and who I am—the God
of the impossible, the Creator of the universe, the Giver of every good
and perfect gift.

I am the One who loves you completely, and I know exactly what is
best for you. Rest in the bedrock assurance of My love for you. I will *not*
fail you, My child. Waiting on Me will yield the highest and best of My
answers and plans for you. Trust Me completely, and you will see the
beauty of My long-prepared plans for you. Plans with purposes beyond
your imagination and dreams. Only I could orchestrate the future I
have in mind for you. In waiting on Me, you will receive My very best.

Look to Me and Me alone. Keep your eyes upward, never downcast.
The stars are in the heavens, not in the soil, so look ever above to Me
and My shining examples of hope. I placed them there for you and for
all My children seeking Me and My ways.

Is not God high in the heavens? See the highest stars, how lofty they are!
JOB 22:12, *NRSV*

June 6

Lord, go before me today.

I will. You can count on Me to do that. Don't fret about anything. Just commit everything to Me. I will help you accomplish all that is needful. I will give you wisdom and understanding. I will expand your minutes, and you will marvel at what I will accomplish through you today. See? Your hope has already increased. That is the power of My Spirit—hope is increased, making all things possible in the knowledge of who I am.

Continue to pray all day. I will bring to your mind the ones to pray for and how to pray. You are continuing to see My miracles of grace everywhere, and you will soon see even more. You will not be able to contain the joy I have in store for you, My child. It will overflow into the lives of others, and that is all part of My plan. You will be My joy giver, My hope giver, to many others. Just see what I will do and the people I will place in your path. Let them know how much I love them. I will show you how for each one.

Enjoy this glorious day—glorious in beauty and glorious in hope because of Me and My promises of love toward you. You are My beloved child, and you will know that more emphatically than ever before. Revel in My love, and delight in passing it on to all you meet. I will use you in that way.

This is real love—not that we loved God, but that he loved us
and sent his Son as a sacrifice to take away our sins.
Dear friends, since God loved us that much,
we surely ought to love each other.
1 JOHN 4:10-11, *NLT*

June 7

Jesus, I need Your answers. I need Your hope. I need Your help.

Look only to Me. In Me you truly have everything you need. I provide the sunshine and the rain for the earth, and I will surely provide all that you need, My beloved child. Don't look at circumstances—but look at Me, the Giver of every good and perfect gift. I will not fail you.

Yes, much is pressing in on you, and you don't know what to do. Give me the tangled skeins of your life, and let Me untangle them one by one. My hands hold all power and wisdom, and nothing is too hard for Me.

Look fully into My face—a face filled with love and hope for you, My child—and your spirit will soar with My life-changing grace, with My never-failing gift of faith to you. Faith and hope in Me have enabled you to endure the most painful of times, and I have seen every one of those times. That's why it will give Me so much joy to bring My promises to pass for you.

Face today with Me, always looking upward and with your heart attuned to only My truth. Don't lend your ear for even a second to the enemy and his lies. I lift you up, but his only goal is to bring you down into despair. In Me there is hope and life eternal, so keep your eyes only on Me.

When You said, "Seek My face," my heart said to You,
"Your face, Lord, I will seek."
PSALM 27:8

JUDY GORDON MORROW

June 8

When I cannot understand my Father's leading,
And it seems to be but hard and cruel fate,
Still I hear that gentle whisper ever pleading,
God is working, God is faithful—ONLY WAIT.

A. B. SIMPSON (1843–1919)

I know the waiting is tedious. I know you are struggling regarding my timings. Rest, My child. Anything else is wasted energy and effort. Your task is to rest and wait. Not anxiously, but in faith believing Me.

Picture a father at the end of a country lane leading to a farmhouse. You are the child, sitting on the porch steps, waiting for your father to come home. You are anxious to run and meet him and to take from his hands the gift you know he has for you. But he instructed you earlier to remain on the porch and wait for him to come to you. And because you love and respect your father, you obey his wishes. And while the waiting and anticipation build, you never doubt that he is coming. And you never doubt that what he will be bringing you, what he will be giving you, is what you desire. Because you know your father loves you and has only the best for you, his beloved child.

Keep that image in mind, My child. I, your Father, am approaching you even now with my sweetest of gifts for you. But I know exactly the perfect time to give you that gift. The timing of it is part of the joy. I will arrive and bring your gift at just the perfect moment. All things will become clear, and your joy will know no bounds. Watch for Me. I *am* coming. I love you, My child.

And so after waiting patiently, Abraham received what was promised.
HEBREWS 6:15, *NIV*

June 9

Above all else, I want You and what You want.
I am so excited to see what You are going to do.

It will be wonderful, My child. The plans I have for you will be evidence of My great love for you. Your heart will be filled to overflowing with the blessings from My hand. You will never cease to marvel at the workings of My hand.

This morning has been sweet, has it not? A precious time of fellowship and communion together. A time when you are realizing even more the depth of My love for you. Nothing can substitute for these times, My child. It is in these times that I give My wisdom and discernment, My love and joy, My patience and forgiveness. And then out of these times you can pass on those very things to My beloved children. I will impart My truth and love through you, My joy and forgiveness to hurting hearts. I will use you in ways you won't even see. Just follow Me and My leadings, and know My ways to be true and right.

Focus totally on Me and what I am calling you to do. You will see My provisions on every side, and I will receive the glory. I know that's your heart's desire, and I will honor you for that. My Father's house is full of riches, and I will meet your every need and beyond.

This walk of faith is a walk of joy and delight, knowing your Father will never fail or disappoint. Live in exuberant joy and expectation today. I love you with an unceasing love.

Because we loved you so much, we were delighted to share
with you not only the gospel of God but our lives as well.
1 THESSALONIANS 2:8, *NIV*

June 10

What have I to dread, what have I to fear, leaning on the everlasting arms?
I have blessed peace with my Lord so near, leaning on the everlasting arms.

ELISHA A. HOFFMAN (1839-1929),
"LEANING ON THE EVERLASTING ARMS"

I will guide and direct. I will go before you. There is nothing to fear or dread, knowing I have walked this way before you. Just follow Me, and you will know My peace and direction. I will not lead you astray. What appear to be detours are all a part of My plan. I see and know all. You will know the fullness of blessings from My hand as you follow Me.

Take your strength from Me today, My child. I know you are weary in body, but I will provide all that you need. I am mindful of every kind of need in My children, and I am more than adequate for all. Just look to Me, knowing I will sustain and help you in every way. Rest in that assurance today.

Rest in My perfect peace that comes from fixing your mind on Me. Literally think of fastening, of adhering yourself, to Me. No fretting or useless anxiety can enter in when you are meshed completely with Me and My desires for you. Instead, you will know peace, joy and hope from My steady presence. Allow My presence to infuse My peace, joy and love into your spirit today. Then see the difference in the living out of your day.

Trust Me, My child. Trust Me to do all that I have promised. I am coming to meet your every need and desire, My faithful child. I love you.

Lord, sustain me as you promised, that I may live!
Do not let my hope be crushed.

PSALM 119:116, *NLT*

JUDY GORDON MORROW The Listening Heart

June II

Hope is the word which God has written on the brow of every man.
VICTOR HUGO (1802-1885)

Hope ever in Me. I will not disappoint your hope. Rather, hope will become concrete answers to your prayers. Remember, hope isn't some nebulous, mystical abstract. Hope is solid, a sure thing, when your hope is founded on Me, your Rock. I will transform your hope into My desires for you. Because of your delight in Me, it will give Me joy to grant you the desires of your heart. Those desires are centered in Me, placed in your heart by Me, and I will delight in fulfilling them for you.

Take joy in My words. Live each day expectantly and in My joy. Don't let the waiting on My promises cast a shadow on your present days—on what I am providing for you now.

Rest completely in Me, knowing without a doubt that I have only your best interests in mind. I see all so clearly. Why would you not want to trust Me, knowing I see and know all? Knowing that I love you more than anyone possibly could? Why would you want to put your trust in anyone besides Me?

There is nothing to fear in My perfect love. Surrender yourself to My love completely, and you will know overwhelming peace. Peace from above. Peace that remains. Know My peace and share it with others. The world needs to know the depths of My love and peace—both so freely available to all. I love you, My child. Be My instrument of peace and love today.

But as for me, I watch in hope for the Lord,
I wait for God my Savior; my God will hear me.
MICAH 7:7, *NIV*

JUDY GORDON MORROW

June 12

Oh, the unsearchable riches of Christ! Precious, more precious than gold.

FANNY JANE CROSBY (1820–1915),
"UNSEARCHABLE RICHES"

reathe deeply of Me. Release fear, anxiety and distress, and instead be filled
ith My peace, joy and love. I continue to tell you these things so that you
ill remember. So that you will know Me in increasing, new ways. There is so
uch depth to plumb in Me, My child. Oh, the unsearchable riches of Christ.
want to make Myself known to you.

When My children truly know Me and realize the goodness and trustwor-
iness of My character, then I can truly work and move in their lives. As long
they view Me askance and hang on to anything or anyone else, I am not freed
work in their lives. Such a simple truth but with far-reaching implications.

Total trust in Me yields a life as I designed it—full of joy, contentment, wis-
m, love and peace. Despair flees, and My abiding peace transcends all. Trust
e that way, My child. Trust Me with total abandon, and see what I will do.

Walk in My way today. I have already gone before you and prepared the way.
ke joy in that fact. Nothing will face you that I don't already know about.
ow that all is well. Know that I am with you always. Always, My child. I will
t leave you for an instant. Take comfort in My constant presence and love
you today. Remember, you are Mine, and I care for you deeply. Someday
u will more fully know My love and care for you.

To me, who am less than the least of all the saints, this grace was given,
t I should preach among the Gentiles the unsearchable riches of Christ, and to make
ll see what is the fellowship of the mystery, which from the beginning of the ages has
been hidden in God who created all things through Jesus Christ.

EPHESIANS 3:8–9

June 13

Lord, I need Your peace.

It is yours. Draw from it. Don't stand at the pool and forget to drink. My peace is always available. Drink deeply of My peace, and know true freedom—freedom from distress and cares. That's My gift to you. Drink freely of My peace, and then pass it on to others. My children desperately need My peace and hope.

I know your own hope is faltering this morning, My child. You simply can't take your eyes off Me. Stay your heart on Me, and your hope can't help but grow. If you keep your eyes on circumstances, you will live in defeat and sorrow. Looking only to Me yields a constant hope.

I see your weariness this morning, and I will care for you, both body and soul. Let Me do that for you. Know I am with you always. I see your confusion and pain, but I won't let you remain there. I will move you to a higher hope in Me.

Seek Me and My ways in everything. I will not fail you. I will not disappoint. I love you beyond measure. Rest in My love today. It is designed for you to allow you to know Me and My heart for you and all My children. Never forget how much I love you.

And let the peace of Christ rule in your hearts,
to which indeed you were called in the one body.
And be thankful.
COLOSSIANS 3:15, *NRSV*

June 14

Lord, this day is fraught with possibilities.

Yes, it is, My child. Possibilities that I see before you can know them. I delight in going before you today, preparing your day for My purposes. See how that takes the pressure off you? All you have to do is walk in My footprints, for I have already gone before you. This is the way of peace and contentment.

You have come to that place of contentment like never before, and this pleases Me, My child. Contentment is the outer evidence of an inner work. That inner work stems from your obedience and trust in Me. Yielding to Me in joy results in a contentment the world cannot mimic or duplicate. True contentment—the kind found only in Me—suffuses a countenance with My peace and joy. My peace and joy are the outer indicators of an inward work by My hand. A work divinely orchestrated by Me for the well-being of My children.

Contentment indicates trust in Me. Contentment radiates the rest that comes from Me. Contentment contrasts sharply with the dissatisfaction that comes directly from the devil himself. It is one of his greatest tools to distract and discourage. Even My children can get caught up in the comparison trap, which is often the root cause for lack of contentment. A dissatisfied soul seeks outside of itself for what can be found only by knowing Me.

Now godliness with contentment is great gain.
For we brought nothing into this world,
and it is certain we can carry nothing out.

1 TIMOTHY 6:6-7

June 15

Oh, the fullness, pleasure, sheer excitement of knowing God on earth!
JIM ELLIOT (1927-1956)

You know Me, My child. It is in the knowing of Me that you know My contentment, in spite of your circumstances. Contentment doesn't depend on circumstances. Contentment comes through an intimate knowledge of Me and My unsurpassed love for you. How can you lack any good thing when you are loved so lavishly? You know the truth of that like never before, and that truth yields trust. You know you can trust the One who loves you with a love deeper and richer than any human love. Resting in the incomparable riches of My love is the secret, the key, to true contentment.

You are enjoying that steadying expression of My love to you even today. While the sea of your life may swell with difficulties and unrest, in the inner chambers of your soul is My solid hope and peace—the anchor and bedrock of your contentment.

Treasure always the benefits of knowing Me. But as you know, the greatest gift is knowing Me and communing with Me, which keeps you in that place of calm in the eye of the storm. That is the difference only I can make. Others will see and will come to know Me in the same way. Rejoice even now for when that will happen. That time is coming, and great will be your joy.

Bless the Lord, O my soul; and all that is within me, bless His holy name!
Bless the Lord, O my soul, and forget not all His benefits.

PSALM 103:1-2

JUDY GORDON MORROW

June 16

Descend on me with Your peace.

I *am* your peace. Now and forever. Oh, the joy of the peaceful life! No straining and fretting but a life simply abiding and resting in Me. Seek to abide in that way. It makes all the difference, My child. By abiding in Me, your thoughts and desires are aligned with Mine. Conflicts cease. Peace overflows. A deep, restful, abiding peace. You will know the difference and others will notice, too. No more distress or despair, but instead a river of peace flowing through you. A river of peace with healing, comfort and joy. Others will benefit from the overflow of My peace in your life. Know that as a surety.

Continue to look only to Me. Know the deepest desires of My heart for you. I will reveal them one layer at a time. I am the Master Designer, and I am designing My beauty and love into your life, My child. I am doing that for your good and My glory. Rejoice in Me and My ways. Be filled with joy and praise. Loads are lightened under the mantle of praise. Wear that mantle all day and bask in the joy it will bring.

I am with you, My child. I am *always* with you, and I love you with a love like no other. Don't ever let cheap substitutions replace My love. There is none like Me. There is no love like Mine. And it is yours, My child, it is yours!

Thus says the Lord, your Redeemer, the Holy One of Israel: "I am the Lord your God, who teaches you to profit, who leads you by the way you should go. Oh, that you had heeded My commandments! Then your peace would have been like a river, and your righteousness like the waves of the sea."

ISAIAH 48:17-18

June 17

Feeling sad and discouraged about my life,
I heard the Lord say, "Am I done writing the story?"
I responded, "It certainly feels that way."

But you aren't the Author. You are only the reader, waiting to turn the next page. You can't assume what's going to happen before I'm done writing. I don't write formulaic stories. Each story I write for My children is crafted just for them. Unique. Special. Designed to grant that child's heart's desires in the best of ways.

That is what I am doing for you even now—writing the story that I know will bring about My highest purposes for your good and for My glory. Allow Me to write, with total trust in the One who holds the pen—who holds your very life—and see the amazing story I will craft for you. The outcome of my love-written story for you will exceed your highest expectations.

So read, My child. Read with expectation and joy. Read with anticipation for the most satisfying ending any story could offer. I write perfection, and perfect will be My story for you.

As for God, His way is perfect; the word of the Lord is proven;
He is a shield to all who trust in Him.

2 SAMUEL 22:31

June 18

Please help me in my preparations.

All is well. Follow My every nudge. I will help you accomplish much as you look to Me. I desire only My best for you, and I am helping you to see that even in what would be considered less-than-best situations. Always remember how limited your vision and knowledge are, especially compared with Mine. I see the whole picture: the joy that follows sorrow, the hope in the midst of despair, the life in Me eternal that overshadows any and every hardship in the human realm.

Look to Me today, and you will see hope. Look to Me, and you will know peace. Look to Me, and your heart will overflow with joy—joy that comes from the constant gaze at My face and on My ways. I alone can give exquisite peace and joy even in the midst of pain. You know the truth of that like never before, and I will deepen that truth as you continue to look to Me.

Enjoy your day. Focus on Me, and let not one shred of dread enter in. I will fill your day with good things. Let joy color every part of your day, and be grateful for My grace that will permeate every minute of this day.

For He satisfies the longing soul,
and fills the hungry soul with goodness.

PSALM 107:9

June 19

Praise erects an invincible barrier and provides boundaries
fortified by God's love.

JGM

Keep your eyes on Me alone. Live in *constant* praise. Do not let the enemy get near you, but keep up the wall of praise so high and deep that he will not be able to scale or penetrate it. Praise acknowledges who I am—your trustworthy, sovereign God—and the enemy can't withstand that truth. My truth will always conquer deceit, and Satan is the chief of liars and deceivers. Praise Me with a righteous heart, full of My truth and joy, and he will be forced to leave.

Your faith is a formidable foe to Satan. He has worked hard to destroy your faith, as he has an idea of how powerfully I will be using you for My kingdom. You will make mighty inroads into the darkness with My ever-shining light. Keep that image ever in mind of being My light giver in this world of darkness. I will honor your faith. I will honor your obedience. I will honor you beyond the imaginings of your sweetest dreams.

And now I will help you. Fret not, but allow Me to guide your thoughts. Time and again I have done this for you, and today will be no different. I honor those who honor Me, and you have so honored Me, My dear child, in this journey.

Get ready to see Me shine like *never* before. You *will* be amazed. Amazed and so very grateful that you have walked the path of obedience.

But this command I gave them, "Obey my voice, and I will be your God,
and you shall be my people; and walk only in the way that I command you,
so that it may be well with you."

JEREMIAH 7:23, *NRSV*

June 20

Thank You for Your presence in my life.

In My presence you are strong. Remain in Me, and I will strengthen you moment by moment. I will provide everything you need. Believe Me in this. There is no need for worry or for fear. I am your Father, and I love you with an everlasting love.

Is there anything too hard for Me? You know the answer. Now live like it. Expect great things. Expect My hand to move in mighty ways. Haven't you seen it already? I have many more good things planned—so many blessings from My hand that you won't be able to contain them all. Such joy will be yours, My child.

Exchange your worry for My peace. I am *with* you, as close as your breath. Miracles are on the way—miracles of My grace. You are right to believe Me. Don't waver now. Continue to believe all that I have told you. You will be amazed. I'm looking forward to your great joy.

I love you, My child. Revel in My love. Dwell on all My love means. Truly know My love for you—its depth and purity. I will see you through because of My great love for you. Let it rest on you all day long.

Seek the Lord and his strength;
seek his presence continually.
PSALM 105:4, *NRSV*

June 21

Trust and obey, for there's no other way to be happy in Jesus,
but to trust and obey.

JOHN H. SAMMIS (1846–1919),
"TRUST AND OBEY"

Cling to Me tightly today. Do go back to the words of the song "Trust and Obey," and make them yours today. Am I trustworthy, My child? You know I am.

Soon will I fulfill for you My most highly desired promise, and you will rejoice for all of your days. Rejoice even now, My dear child. Your joy before speaks more vibrantly than after I have met your heart's desire. Submit to Me a joyful heart in your suffering, and I will refine you in way that can come by no other means. Joy in the midst of suffering is divine work. Let Me do that work in you even today, and see the beauty I will bring forth in you—a beauty the world knows nothing of, but it's beauty that will shine forth for Me like nothing else can.

Hold firmly to Me and My promises today. Know I will not fail you. You have waited, you have obeyed, and I, your faithful Father, will answer precisely the right moment. Don't try to understand. Simply be that child with your hand in Mine, and trust Me fully and completely. I will help you to do that. Look to Me alone—your strength and provider—and I will enable you to sing in your suffering before I break through with My answer.

I love you, My child. Never forget how much I love you.

Who among you fears the Lord? Who obeys the voice of His Servant?
Who walks in darkness and has no light?
Let him trust in the name of the Lord and rely upon his God.

ISAIAH 50:10

June 22

Jesus, I need to hear from You.

I am here for you. You know that. Don't let the enemy destroy My truth with his lies. All he ever speaks is lies, My child. You need to keep your ears and heart attuned to only My truth. You do that by looking only to Me and dwelling in My Word and praise.

You have allowed human thoughts to sow unrest and unbelief. Yet nothing I have said to you has changed. I remain the same forever, and My promises remain firm. Cling to Me, your Rock, and you will not be led astray. You have fallen into the trap of leaning on your own understanding, and that is deadly because your understanding is faulty. Look only to Me, trust alone in Me, and know that I will do all that I have said. There is absolute surety in Me and My promises.

You don't need to understand, My child. I don't require your understanding. I require absolute faith and trust in Me and in what I have promised you. You can't know all that I know. It is crucial that you allow Me, your all-knowing and all-wise Father, to have complete reign in your heart and life. Give all to Me, and then I am freed to complete My plans of perfection.

Keep your eyes only on Me. This is absolutely key to a victorious walk. Trust Me completely, and just see what I will do. I love you, My precious child.

Look, God is greater than we can understand.
His years cannot be counted.

JOB 36:26, *NLT*

June 23

Prayer is not overcoming God's reluctance,
but laying hold of His willingness.
MARTIN LUTHER (1483–1546)

Pray like never before. Pray without ceasing. Pray fervently, absolutely believing Me to answer. I know you do believe that, and I will not fail you. I will bring to pass all that I have promised. Your joy will know no end. You will truly be lost in wonder and praise.

I am your faithful Father who keeps His promises. Never think otherwise, and trust Me completely. Once again I have brought you through another dark time. Don't forget the darkness, as others will need your understanding in their dark times, but never forget that I *always* shine through with My light as you look only to Me. I am the eternal and life-giving Light, the One who shines hope into the darkest of places. Share that truth, My child. Be My bearer of shining light and hope. Love others with My love.

Go in My peace, My child. Remain in prayer all day. Look to Me for everything. Walk in My way. Know I am at work and all is well.

You, Lord, keep my lamp burning;
my God turns my darkness into light.
PSALM 18:28, *NIV*

June 24

I know not the way God leads me, but well do I know my Guide.
MARTIN LUTHER (1483–1546)

Look only to Me. Stay absolutely fixed on the path I am setting before you. You know My nudges. Follow each one. You will never regret doing that.

Be at peace. Unrest is not from Me. I provide rest and peace. Fret and worry are tools of the enemy. Banish them in My name. There is power and harmony in My name.

See this day through My eyes. Know that nothing is too hard for Me and that I am with you every step of the way. A loving father does not leave his child desolate on a darkened path, and neither will I leave you. Count on Me to provide the needed light for each new step.

Trust Me to work on your behalf in ways you haven't even thought of. I am your creative God, and I will provide for you in just the right way. Take comfort from knowing anew who I am and that I do all things well.

I love you, My child. I love you beyond your knowledge of love. Focus on My great love for you today. Let My love buoy and carry you throughout this day. You are just now beginning to understand the essence and depth of My love for you. Live in My love and peace and hope all day today. I *love* you, My child.

*Again Jesus spoke to them, saying, "I am the light of the world.
Whoever follows me will never walk in darkness
but will have the light of life."*
JOHN 8:12, *NRSV*

June 25

God will not permit any troubles to come upon us, unless He has a specific plan by which great blessing can come out of the difficulty.

PETER MARSHALL (1902–1949)

Pain is often the vehicle for the fulfillment of My promises—the refining fire just before the revealing of My glorious answers. That is where you are now, My child—in the final fires just before My answers are revealed. This pain is shaping and molding you to be prepared for the receiving of My most exquisite joy for you. These days of pain and heartache and sadness will melt away, will flee like a shadow, in light of My glorious answers for you.

You noticed I used the word "glorious" again and realize how those answers will be filled with *My* glory—the only One to whom glory is due. Surely, My glory will stream out of every working of My hand on your behalf. You will marvel all of your days.

You have learned much from My hand and are still learning. Just think how much better suited you will be to be used for My kingdom. I am consuming all the dross in My consuming fire so you can shine brightly for Me. My love will radiate from your face, and people will see—without a word spoken—the difference I make.

Trust Me, My child. Trust Me alone. I have not abandoned you. I have not forgotten you. Out of these painful days in the fire, out of these ashes, will I raise you up, clothed in My glorious radiance to be My light to many. Know I *am* at work and that all is well.

Therefore, since we are receiving a kingdom that cannot be shaken, let us give thanks, by which we offer to God an acceptable worship with reverence and awe; for indeed our God is a consuming fire.

HEBREWS 12:28-29, NRSV

JUDY GORDON MORROW

June 26

You will keep him in perfect peace, whose mind is stayed on You,
because he trusts in You.

FROM ISAIAH 26:3

Do keep your mind and heart fixed on Me, and follow My every leading.
I will not fail you. I *will* fulfill My every promise to you, and you truly
will be amazed. Live in the wonder and joy of that amazement even
now. Know that I do all things well. Your joy will never end.

Bring all wonderings and stray thoughts into My care. Then you
will be free to dwell on Me and My truth and My promises alone. Think
My thoughts, My child, as My thoughts are pure truth. Anything else
will deceive and discourage you. Live in My truth, and let it illumine
your mind and heart—and yes, even your very face—with My light and
love. I do love you, My child, more than you can even begin to fathom.
My love for you is true and never changing and always available. Immerse yourself in My river of love today—ever flowing and never ceasing.

I *love* you, My precious child. Hear My heart of love toward you like
never before. Know My love in the very depths of your being. Reflect
My love to the dark and hurting world around you. Now go in My
peace, and know My love all day today.

I remember the days of old, I think about all your deeds,
I meditate on the works of your hands.

PSALM 143:5, *NRSV*

June 27

While praying, an article came to mind about a young man who had been the head of a coven of witches. When he saw frightful demons in his room two nights in a row, his calling out the name of Jesus was the only thing that made them leave.

Don't you see, My child? The devil doesn't only come in overt ways with visible demons, but he employs a host of invisible—but not any less insidious—demons to accomplish his evil purposes. You are experiencing those destructive forces even today: distortion of truth, distractions away from truth, and distresses to cloud truth.

Only one thing is necessary: the power you possess in Me. Claim that power today, and refuse to give any room to the one who only brings ruin.

My child, let Me remind you again of My truths: I love you. My ways are above your ways. My truth transcends *all* circumstances—even the most impossible situations. All will be accomplished as I have ordained it. I won't leave you in this desert wilderness forever. You *will* know new days because of My workings in your life.

Hang on to those promises of truth, My child. Dwell in that place of contentment that only I can make possible. Rest in the certainty of *who I am*, knowing I will never fail or forsake you.

Hold close to your heart today each word I have spoken—words to give you renewed hope, comfort and peace. Words to restore your joy. Words to regain your equilibrium and sure footing in Me. I speak only words of truth, and in that bedrock you can anchor your entire being with every hope, misgiving and fear. I *will not* fail you.

But the Lord is faithful; he will strengthen you and guard you from the evil one.
2 THESSALONIANS 3:3, *NRSV*

June 28

I just believe You.

You are right to believe Me. That is the essence, the foundation for everything. Belief in Me will never fail you. Belief in who I am as your loving Father will reap maximum benefits. Belief in Me opens the floodgates of heaven. Unbelief barricades and stymies the flow of My blessings, like a thick sludge that hampers any flow. Unbridled belief in Me gives Me a free, flowing channel where My blessings can pour through like crystal-clear water.

You see those images in your mind, and that is a good thing. See them often so that your faith will be fed, and you will see in your life the results of a faith that believes Me completely—even when you don't understand.

I know you don't understand much these days, but neither did Joseph as he spent day after day in prison. He couldn't see what was in store for him, but I could, just as I see My plans for you. Take great hope when I tell you how glorious those plans will be. All will see My gracious hand toward you, and I will be glorified.

I will fulfill all I have spoken. Believe Me completely, the One who can do the impossible. The One who loves you like no other. The One who so looks forward to seeing your joy when I bring all these things to pass. Believe Me, and let the blessings *flow*!

And Joseph's master took him and put him into the prison,
the place where the king's prisoners were confined; he remained there
in prison. But the Lord was with Joseph and showed him steadfast love;
he gave him favor in the sight of the chief jailer.
GENESIS 39:20-21, *NRSV*

June 29

There is not in the world a kind of life more sweet and
delightful than that of a continual conversation with God.
BROTHER LAWRENCE (1614–1691)

Live in My peace and hope today. Let nothing detract from your joy.
I have placed it there. Let nothing remove it. Remain in Me in constant prayer. The kind of prayer that interfaces every piece of your day,
weaving it together seamlessly with My peace. That is My desire for
My children—their lives enmeshed with Mine, yielding My joy, peace,
love, hope and kindness. Then I can draw others to Me through those
transparent, love-filled lives.

Constant communion with Me is the key. Entwine your heart with
Mine, and see the difference I will make. See Me at work in everything,
for truly I AM. Don't miss seeing My gifts of love to you everywhere.
You have seen Me in the cloud-draped sky, in the robin's red breast,
and in the faces of cheery pansies. There is so much more waiting to
give you glimpses of Me. And all of this is only a foretaste of all I am
preparing for you in your eternal home. Dwell deeply in all I have
spoken to you today, and be filled with My joy.

I love you, My precious child.

The grace of the Lord Jesus Christ, and the love of God,
and the communion of the Holy Spirit be with you all. Amen.
2 CORINTHIANS 13:14

JUDY GORDON MORROW

June 30

You are my Rock, my Fortress and my Deliverer.

Your faith will be strengthened and anchored like never before in the truth of *who I am*. That is the element of truth that needs to be bored into the very depth of your soul. Know who I am, and you can rest at all times in the loving care of My strong arms.

Know who I am, and you won't know fear. Know who I am, and you won't know despair. Know who I am, and you won't know hopelessness. It is knowing *Me*, My child, that allows you to walk in freedom, joy and hope. I make all the difference when you truly see and know Me in My fullness.

Out of My fullness will overflow from your life everything you need. Be satisfied in Me, and I will satisfy you with every good and needful thing from My hand. The key is to know Me and to be satisfied in Me alone. For truly, *I am enough*.

I love you, My child. Rest in My forever, steadfast love for you. I will *not* fail you.

And he said: "The Lord is my rock and my fortress and my deliverer;
the God of my strength, in whom I will trust."

2 SAMUEL 22:2-3

July

Because of the great I AM . . .

I am loved.
I am cared for.
I am valued.

I can withstand the enemy.
I can love those who despise me.
I can go the second mile.

All is His.
All is mine in Him.
All is well.

There is no reason to fear.
There is no reason to doubt.
There is every reason to believe.

Because of the great I AM.

July 1

Lord, I don't know what to think about so many things.

My child, you don't need to know things that don't concern you right now. All you need to know you can find in Me and Me alone. I am your Wonderful Counselor, and I will never fail to give you wisdom and insights exactly when they are needed as you seek Me and My ways.

This is so key, My child. There are countless avenues for you to travel in your thoughts, but they lead to confusion and ultimate despair. Only I can show you the way that will lead to My purposes for you.

The time element means nothing as long as you continue to follow *Me*. That is the key—to follow Me one step at a time and to allow Me to set the course and the pace. See how freeing that is? You don't have to worry about anything regarding the direction and details of the journey. You can simply relax and enjoy each segment. In that way you will know constant rest in Me, even on the most challenging and difficult days.

Remember these words of truth for these steps of your journey. Not one day is insignificant when you follow Me, even though it may often feel that way. Follow Me, fear not, and you will not fail to see My very individual purposes for you and your journey. I am fulfilling those purposes even now as you follow Me in faith.

Indeed, he loves his people; all his holy ones are in his hands.
They follow in his steps and accept his teaching.
DEUTERONOMY 33:3, *NLT*

July 2

The world of men has forgotten the joy of silence, the peace of solitude which is necessary, to some extent, for the fullness of human living.

THOMAS MERTON (1915–1968)

Hasn't the silence, the peaceful quiet, been good this morning? It is in this quietness that I can impart My whispers, My heart, to you. Being still before Me will always yield great benefits. Perspectives and attitudes change when bathed in the calm of My presence. Frazzled nerves and wearied bodies are restored in the solitude of My presence. My peace can seep in when stillness allows that.

You provide the stillness, the coming away with Me, and I will provide the peace and restoration. You can count on Me to do that. Just be willing to enter into that quietness and stillness for however long it takes. Don't leave too early. Allow Me to restore and fill you completely so that you can meet the demands of your day. This was the key for all My early followers, and it remains ever true today. It makes the difference between doing for Me and being the one I made you to be.

Listen to My heart in the quiet of your heart, and you *will* know My plans and desires for you. Knowing releases you from doubt and frustration and fear. Even in the waiting to know My heart and plans, you can rest in My peace and the timeless assurances I give you: Don't fear. I am with you. I will never leave you. So simple, but they are all you need, wrapped up in the abundance of My love toward you. Measureless peace and hope will be yours.

Surely I have calmed and quieted my soul,
like a weaned child with his mother;
like a weaned child is my soul within me.

PSALM 131:2

July 3

All things, God. Make all things clear.

I will, My child. You have nothing to fear. All is in My hands. I see the way clearly. Just follow Me. I will not lead you astray. You will know what to do at just the right time. Haven't I guided you up to this time? My guidance will continue, and My peace will remain.

Pray, My child. Pray more than ever. The enemy is using his tricks, but prayer will prevent him from succeeding. Prayer is your defense—use it constantly. Remember that this isn't a battle of flesh and blood but of powers and principalities—unseen but no less real. Keep that truth ever before you, and pray with new fervor and urgency. I will honor your prayers.

Our time together has been good, has it not? It will reap benefits for your day. Time spent with Me will always enhance and enrich your day. It will give you strength and wisdom for what the day will bring. You are equipped by Me and My Word, and you will see My faithfulness to you, My beloved child.

Continue to walk in My love. Continue to live in My hope. Continue to know My truth. Revel in my greatness and peace today. There is *nothing* too hard for Me. I am looking down on you with joy and love. Be filled with Me today, and live in My glorious hope and love and joy today. In Me you have all you need. I love you, My precious child.

For we do not wrestle against flesh and blood, but against principalities,
against powers, against the rulers of the darkness of this age,
against spiritual hosts of wickedness in the heavenly places.

EPHESIANS 6:12

JUDY GORDON MORROW

July 4

Lord, help me not to protect myself but to show forth You and Your love.

You know I will do that for you. Trust Me alone, follow My nudges, and just see what I will do. Keep the channel free between your heart and Mine. Let My love wash away any hurt and anger that would only impede My love and grace. I will do that for you. Turn over every troubling thought and every hurtful wound to Me. I will heal. I will help. I will bring good out of everything, and I will replace troubled thoughts with My peace, pain with My healing.

Just give all of it to Me on a continual basis so that nothing will be allowed to fester or take hold as a root of bitterness. I know you don't want that, and I will help you to keep your heart wholly after Mine. Rest on that reassurance of My words, and know that all is well. All given over to Me will always yield peace and contentment.

I am going before you today. I am preparing the way. Rejoice even now at My wonders of love and grace that you will soon know. Great will be your joy, My child—for now and always. I love you.

> *Look after each other so that none of you fails*
> *to receive the grace of God. Watch out that no poisonous root*
> *of bitterness grows up to trouble you,*
> *corrupting many.*
> HEBREWS 12:15, *NLT*

July 5

Oh, the pure delight of a single hour that before Thy throne I spend,
When I kneel in prayer and with Thee, my God,
I commune as friend with friend!

FANNY JANE CROSBY (1820–1915),
"I AM THINE, O LORD"

Delight in this day, a new gift from My hand. You have sensed the sweetness of My presence, and you know the design of My hand. My designs and plans can be trusted, even when you don't see the evidence yet. You are learning, My child, that you don't need to see the design when you know the Designer and His love for you.

Knowing Me and My love guarantees that My designs for you will be fashioned in My love and perfection. What I am designing for you is so far beyond anything that you could come up with on your own. Take great comfort in My words, and rest in My peace. All is sublimely well as you rest in Me today.

You are seeing the changes I am making in you, and that is all part of My design. Your future joy and ministry will be that much greater because of what I have been teaching you in these days of solitude. You are seeing the wisdom of My love, and you will see that even more in the days ahead.

I love you, My child. Walk in the beauty and confidence that My love brings. Radiate My peace and joy. You are My beloved child, and I will not fail you.

Abraham was confidently looking forward to a city with
eternal foundations, a city designed and built by God.

HEBREWS 11:10, *NLT*

The Listening Heart JUDY GORDON MORROW

July 6

Thank You for Your peace.

I *am* your peace. Peace that only comes from Me. The world cannot counterfeit the peace I give. It stabilizes in the midst of storms and comforts in the deepest of pain. You have found this to be true, My child. Abiding in Me will always result in My peace.

Carry My peace in your heart today. Know that I am already going before you. Trust My nudges and My voice. I will make all things clear as you seek Me and My guidance. Lean not unto your own understanding.

Oh, My child, great days are ahead! All these days have been part of your training for what I am preparing for you to do. You are so much better equipped than if you had never gone through this dark valley. You know that in your heart. Now know that I will bring light, My light, to others because of the darkness you have endured.

I am a redeeming God, and I do all things well. Rest in My abundant peace. Love others through Me today. I love you, My precious child.

For He Himself is our peace.
EPHESIANS 2:14

July 7

Amazing love! How can it be that Thou, my God, shouldst die for me?
CHARLES WESLEY (1707–1788),
"AND CAN IT BE?"

Dwell on My love. When you dwell on the fullness and abundance of My love, you will be given the confidence for unswerving trust in Me. Remember how I love you—completely, beyond measure, purely. A pure love like Mine desires only the best for the object of its love. You, My child, are the object of My love, and I want only My highest good for you. Believe that and know My heart, and you can't help but trust Me.

I love you, My precious child. Rest totally in My fathomless love for you and be at peace. My plans come out of My exquisite love for you. Trust Me, My child. Give Me every shred of your trust, and hold back nothing. Free Me to work. I do all things well, and what I have planned for you will shine with My perfection and love and will draw others to Me.

Think of the facets of a beautiful diamond. There are so many facets to My workings for you, and I am perfecting each one so that the final result will be a glorious work from My hands. I will be presenting My gift of love to you at just the right time, when every facet is readied and honed to perfection. You can trust Me, My precious child. You can totally trust Me. Loosen every fingerhold and lay all before Me. I will bring to completion all that I have promised you.

I would have lost heart, unless I had believed that I would see
the goodness of the Lord in the land of the living.
PSALM 27:13

July 8

If the Lord fails me at this time, it will be the first time.
GEORGE MÜLLER (1805–1898)

Go in My peace and grace today. My love is flowing from your heart to your face and hands, and I will use you as a vessel of My love today. Just rest in Me, and be that trusting child.

And yes, look at every upcoming challenge as My opportunity to show My love and grace to you. I know your concerns, and I will take care of each one, just as I've always done. Look only to Me, and you will find Me all-sufficient. Have I not met your every need *every single time*? Do remember My every wonder in your life, and know that I already know the provisions I have in mind for you.

I also know every single detail of your imminent rescue, My child, the wonder of which will astound you. You can't possibly know now what I have in mind, but soon you will know, and great and wondrous will be your joy. Live in that joy even now, this very day, knowing that the promise is as good as the fulfillment.

I will remember the works of the Lord;
surely I will remember Your wonders of old.
I will also meditate on all Your work,
and talk of Your deeds.
PSALM 77:11-12

July 9

Jesus, Jesus, Jesus, please break through.

I will break through—in ways you haven't even imagined. Just trust Me completely, and see what I will do. Relax totally in Me, knowing I do all things well. Think of the deliverance of My children through the Red Sea. Think of Daniel and how I shut the lions' mouths. Think of Paul and the shipwreck and how not a single person perished. I am the God of deliverance, and I will deliver you into your new life.

Trust Me without wavering and with much joy. Joy in My promises, even when you can't see the fulfillment of those promises. You can rejoice in faith based on who I am. The One who speaks the promises is trustworthy. A promise given by Me is as sure as a promise fulfilled. I never disappoint My trusting children.

I will fill this day with My joy and peace. Just see what I will do. Look only to Me. Believe Me for all things. I am your Father, and I love you beyond your knowing. Oh, My child, so many great days lie ahead. Know it to be so. My face is shining down on you even now.

See Me in everything, and rejoice in My ways. You have My word, and all that I have promised is based on My great love for you. I love you, My child. You will soon know My love in new measure and with new clarity. Think often of My constant love for you, and know joy.

But Moses said to the people, "Do not be afraid, stand firm,
and see the deliverance that the Lord will accomplish for you today;
for the Egyptians whom you see today you shall never see again."
EXODUS 14:13, *NRSV*

July 10

I am weakness, full of weakness; at Thy sacred feet I bow.
Blest, divine, eternal Spirit, fill with love, and fill me now.

ELWOOD H. STOKES (1815–1897),
"FILL ME NOW"

Do not fear. I am in all of this. You will see My hand clearly. Have I ever failed you? You will see Me unfold wonder upon wonder from My hand.

Our time together this morning has been precious, has it not? You are going deeper in your knowledge of Me. You are learning that pain carves depth into your soul and that then you can be filled with more of Me. And in being filled with all the fullness of Me, I can then use you more effectively.

The overflow of being filled with Me will spill over onto many other lives, and many will be touched by My love through you. This is being My vessel. I will bless you greatly as you continue to yield to Me so I can fill you with all My goodness.

I love you, My child. I will richly bless your day. Trust fully in Me and see what I will do.

But in a great house there are not only vessels of gold and silver,
but also of wood and clay, some for honor and some for dishonor.
Therefore if anyone cleanses himself from the latter,
he will be a vessel for honor, sanctified and useful for the Master,
prepared for every good work.

2 TIMOTHY 2:20–21

July 11

Go before me now, Lord. Ordain this day.

I will. I will gift you with My chosen gestures from My hand. While you don't yet know what this day will hold, I do, and I am in each aspect. Just trust Me fully, and expect Me at every turn. Forever I am with you, and in every detail I reveal Myself.

Be open to My leadings and rest in Me. You will see Me in everything. Remember My wonders from the past and be expectant of even more—even today. I will not fail you. I will be cradling you in My arms of love all day today. Simply enjoy My presence and the gifts from My hand.

Don't fail to recount My wonders. Just see what I will do next. I am the God of wonders, and I will be working My wonders for you, My dear child. Live in My hope. I will *not* fail you. I love you. Know anew My love for you.

Remember His marvelous works which He has done,
His wonders, and the judgments of His mouth.

PSALM 105:5

July 12

I recalled an answer to prayer and said, "Thank You for that miracle."

I will be working even more miracles—miracles of grace and love that will so reveal to you My favor on your life. Oh, My child, not one tear or heartache has escaped Me, and I will make up to you for every one. You have remained faithful, you have waited on Me—how could I not honor you for honoring Me?

You catch a glimpse of My love and compassion for you. Do believe Me when I tell you that I will so make up to you all these lean years. I will restore the years the locusts have eaten.

Seek Me and My face today. Follow My every leading. Watch Me multiply your minutes. Know that I am as close as your breath, just awaiting you to call out to Me so that I may quickly respond with My wisdom and help in all the daily matters that concern you. I will honor obedience. Put Me to the test, and just see what I will do.

I love you, My child. Out of your being loved, pour out love and care on others. Be My love to others, and speak My truth. Enjoy this day and every gift from My hand.

I will restore to you the years that the swarming locust has eaten.
JOEL 2:25

July 13

I just pray Your wonders will unfold.

Yes, My wonders will unfold. You will truly be amazed. You will know My love and its depth like never before. I know this is not easy, My child, but it is necessary. It is all part of My plan, ordained by Me. Knowing that, and remembering that, will bring continual comfort and peace.

Know the peace of My presence like never before. Grasp the fullness of My love toward you. Learn of Me, My child. Rely totally on Me. I am going before you, preparing the way of My purposes. All you need to do is follow. Follow Me. So simple a command, but obeying it yields great benefits, great joys.

I am going before you even today. Rest on Me completely. Listen to My nudges. My Spirit is your partner and helper. Draw on His strength and wisdom. He is My gift to you and all My children who trust Me.

Don't worry about anything. Commit all to Me. Don't be afraid. I will not give you more than you can bear. My comfort and peace will be sweeter than you have ever known. Know that I will not fail you. I will not desert you. I will not leave you desolate. Soon you will know the fullness of My joy in all that I have planned for you.

Rest, My child. Abide and rest. I am your Comforter and Friend, and in Me is peace evermore. I love you. Live in My love all day today.

But the Helper, the Holy Spirit, whom the Father will send in My name,
He will teach you all things, and bring to your remembrance
all things that I said to you.

JOHN 14:26

JUDY GORDON MORROW

July 14

Immortal, invisible, God only wise,
In light inaccessible hid from our eyes.
Most blessed, most glorious, the Ancient of Days,
Almighty, victorious, Thy great name we praise.

WALTER C. SMITH (1824–1908),
"IMMORTAL, INVISIBLE, GOD ONLY WISE"

You must remember that I am working, even when you don't see anything changing. So much of what I do is invisible to My children until it all culminates into My purposes. Walk by faith, not by sight. I *will* make your faith sight, and then My invisible workings will be revealed to you.

Enjoy this beautiful day. Bask in the sweetness of My presence. Know all is well, even though circumstances and your limited knowledge compel you to think otherwise. That's why keeping your eyes on Me is imperative. Eyes on Me equals peace. Eyes on *anything* besides Me leads to turmoil and unrest and doubt. Fasten your eyes on Me, and you will know My perfect peace.

Dwell in My presence all day today. Look to Me alone. Know without a doubt that My answers are coming. Wait on Me with *joy*, and just see what I will do. I will honor you beyond what you can even imagine. Great will be your joy—a joy without end. Know My every word to you to be true. Rest in Me. Even rest in the mystery of Me and My ways.

Now to the King eternal, immortal, invisible,
to God who alone is wise, be honor and glory forever and ever. Amen.

1 TIMOTHY 1:17

July 15

Let all things their Creator bless, and worship Him in humbleness.
O praise Him! Alleluia!

ST. FRANCIS OF ASSISI (1182–1226),
"ALL CREATURES OF OUR GOD AND KING"

Worship Me with reverence and awe, and allow Me to fill you with wisdom and peace beyond anything the world can offer. In Me you have the riches of My kingdom. Anything the world has to offer is paltry and puny, especially when contrasted with the deep and unsearchable riches of Christ.[1]

Remember to keep looking to Me. All that matters is My truth. Listen only to Me, and level the enemy with My truth and with your praise. He cannot remain in the presence of those formidable foes, especially when they are encased in constant prayer.

I am coming, My child. I am coming to embrace you with the answers to your prayers of these many years. Be watching and waiting with a faith that does not waver but is centered totally on Me. I am your Rock, and your hope in Me rests on solid ground. Hope only and forever in Me alone.

I love you, My dear child.

Let us hold fast the confession of our hope without wavering,
for He who promised is faithful.

HEBREWS 10:23

Note
1. See Ephesians 3:8.

July 16

You must learn, you must let God teach you, that the only way to get rid of your past is to get a future out of it. God will waste nothing.

PHILLIPS BROOKS (1835–1893)

I know you don't understand, My child. I know your heart is hurting. Give it to Me. I am the healer of hurting and broken hearts. I take broken hearts and make them stronger and more resilient than before. My healing love does that.

Just realize you don't have to understand everything. You simply need to trust Me. Trust Me completely, and even when you can't see what's coming around a blind corner, know that I can and that I am with you. You are My beloved child, the apple of My eye, and I will not leave you desolate.

You seek concrete answers, specifics, and I have none to give you today. All you need to know is to trust Me. Trust Me completely. Oh, My child, when you see the completion of My plan, how you will rejoice! How you will see the workings of My hand from the very beginning to My glorious purpose.

Don't dwell in gloom. Look upward to your Father who loves you with an everlasting love. My plans are perfect. I am working things out perfectly. Just abide in Me and rest. I am sufficient for all your needs.

Peace, My child. Live in My peace and hope. I do all things well. You will see. You will see and rejoice. Just trust Me completely.

The Lord is near to the brokenhearted, and saves the crushed in spirit.

PSALM 34:18, *NRSV*

July 17

Lord, what is it You have in mind here?

I have in mind My plans and purposes. Those are shrouded from you right now, but they won't always be. You will see, and you will know. For now wait patiently before Me, and seek only Me. Seek to know Me and My ways. Know My comfort and peace. Know the constancy of My presence.

Flee the enemy. Do not allow him any sway over you. He is seeking to destroy and undermine all that I have been saying to you. Don't allow him entrance. Keep praise ever on your lips. Praise bars him from your heart. Continually praise Me, and he will not be able to touch you, My child. Even when it's difficult and not natural to praise Me, even when your spirits are flagging and low, you still must praise Me. That is the secret of keeping the enemy's influence out of your life. Praise, My child. Be filled with praise to Me.

Do not look too far ahead. One step at a time is how I will lead you. You will know what to do at each given time. Trust Me in this and fret not. Fretting puts distance between us—trust brings closeness.

Remember, one step at a time. I am with you each step. Count on Me totally. I will not fail you. The joy I have promised is coming. Supreme sacrifice yields supreme joy. Trust Me in this. You will be amazed at My outcomes. I love you, My child. All is well.

Therefore submit to God. Resist the devil and he will flee from you.

JAMES 4:7

July 18

Oh, Father, how I need Your help today.

You have it. Never doubt My help that is always available to you. You have experienced that in the black of night, in the wee hours of the morning. I will never fail to come to My children in the hour of their need. All they need to do is to call out to Me, and you were right to do that. I will always hear you and respond. Sometimes My responses may appear as silence, but I have responded to you and am providing for you, whether you realize it or not.

Trust Me completely. While the tasks before you are daunting, do not despair. Do not waver in your trust of Me. Focus on who I am and that there is nothing too hard for Me. I will help you accomplish what is needful.

Rest in Me. Be filled with My peace. Let Me bring comfort with My hope and joy and love. Partake freely of these, My gifts to you. Truly, all is well. I love you, My child.

But surely, God is my helper; the Lord is the upholder of my life.
PSALM 54:4, *NRSV*

July 19

Jesus, help me to look to You alone.

That is the key, My child. Eyes only on Me. Any other view is not true but often filled with distortions, like a mirror with faulty glass. Look to Me to see who you are in light of My love. Look to Me to get a clear perspective. Look to Me to see what direction I would have you go. When you look to Me, you lack for *nothing*. In Me is fullness—of joy, of abundant living, of love like no other.

Today, rest in those truths as you keep your eyes ever upward. Just as the sun above lights the sky, so will I light your path with My wisdom and guidance. When you walk in My light, you need not fear any darkness. My light dispels darkness and shines with an unquenchable flame of truth. Falsity will pass, but My truth will always prevail.

Walk in My way, in My truth, and you will know My life—the abundant life I have promised My children.

But the path of the righteous is like the light of dawn,
which shines brighter and brighter until full day.
PROVERBS 4:18, *NRSV*

July 20

Holy Spirit, abide in me. Make me clean; oh, make me pure!

MILDRED COPE (1924–2008),
"HOLY SPIRIT, BE MY GUIDE"

The abundant life I have promised includes many things, but the essence of that life is living in My Spirit and He in you. Where My Spirit resides all is well, no matter what foes may try to assail you. My Spirit provides a constant refuge of peace and rest that is available to all who give Him entrance and a place to dwell.

Repentance opens the door, and My cleansing prepares the place designed for My Spirit. You repent, I cleanse, and together we live in harmony to accomplish My eternal purposes. This is the way of true joy and satisfaction.

Enjoy that way this very day. I will illumine the path before you. Walk in it and be blessed. You can only take one step at a time, so look to Me alone for that step, knowing I will give My light in time for each subsequent step. This is the way of faith that brings honor to Me and joy to you. A joy that cannot be taken from you. Live in the sweetness of My joy, and you will know the abundant life I promise you and all who choose to follow Me. There is no greater joy than walking in fellowship with Me.

If we confess our sins, He is faithful and just to forgive us our sins
and to cleanse us from all unrighteousness.

1 JOHN 1:9

July 21

Rest in your Friend, your Savior, your All in All!

CHARLES SPURGEON (1834-1892),
"REST IN THE LORD"

Rest in Me alone. Fretting only brings restlessness and anxiety—the opposite of rest. Rest, My child. Rest in the One who knows and loves you best. I go before you, I walk beside you, I follow behind you—in every way I surround you with my love and protection, with My best care of you.

Move by My Spirit today. Joy in seeking and following after His leadings. Let go of all that needs to be done, and allow Me to take over and guide your course. All that is required of you is to follow.

Submit all questions and problems to Me, wait for My answers, and then follow the guidance I give you. This is, indeed, the way of the abundant life I offer—complete dependence on Me and total rest in Me. There is no better way.

Hold that truth close to your heart today, and your day will be enveloped by Me and My peace. Striving in your own strength is draining and futile. Walking in My power is productive and fulfilling. Life-giving. The more you live after Me, the more blessed your life will be. It is in Me you live and move and have your being.[1]

Rest in the Lord, and wait patiently for Him.

PSALM 37:7

Note
1. See Acts 17:28.

July 22

There's a peace in my heart that the world never gave,
a peace it cannot take away.
Though the trials of life may surround like a cloud,
I've a peace that has come there to stay.

ANNE S. MURPHY (1878–1942),
"CONSTANTLY ABIDING"

Your heart is at peace this morning, and that is the difference total trust in Me makes. Total trust yields perfect peace. There is no other way. You have discovered the essence of a life hidden in Mine, and I will now be leading you even further into the recesses of My heart. You feel overwhelmed by the privilege and prospect of that, but know that I long to take every believer there if they will only spend time with Me to know My heart for them.

You have done that, My child, and now you will continue to discover nuggets of truth and beauty that will only enhance every aspect of your life. This is all My doing, and how well you know it. How well you know Me and My love and that I can be totally trusted.

You continue to rejoice over My gifts to you. Never limit Me in what I can and desire to do for you. Remember, I am the God of limitless surprises, limitless love gifts, for My children. I delight in surprising you with My loving care.

Great is your joy as daily I am giving you new reasons to praise Me for My provisions. You are right to share My stories and to give the glory to Me. I will honor you for doing that. Blessed are you now, and blessed will you be, as you continue to give all glory and honor to Me.

You are worthy, O Lord, to receive glory and honor and power;
for You created all things, and by Your will they exist and were created.

REVELATION 4:11

July 23

Give me Your wisdom.

I will. I am your wisdom. You can depend on Me to guide you aright. I would never mislead My child. You know that I am faithful to make My ways plain to you, and I will not change now. You will know My leadings as you seek Me. That's why this time together is so important. I am able to free your mind of distractions and clutter as you wait before Me and seek Me. I will always honor your doing that, whether you realize it or not.

You have already experienced much joy this morning, in spite of waking up out of sorts. See the difference I make? See the difference this time with Me makes? If only My children would realize that time with Me is transforming, hope giving, and filled with joy. Time with Me changes everything—your outlook, your attitudes, your reservoir of joy. I will always redeem time spent with Me, and the results will overflow into every aspect of your day.

Enjoy your day. I will bless it. I will bless you, My child, as you continue to live in My Word and My ways. So much joy is ahead. Keep your face ever turned upward to Mine, My precious child, and see My smile upon you. I love you. Forever will I love you. Look to Me expectantly. Live and walk in great hope today.

Your word is very pure; therefore Your servant loves it.
PSALM 119:140

July 24

The goal of prayer is the ear of God, a goal that can only be reached by patient and continued and continuous waiting upon Him, pouring out our heart to Him and permitting Him to speak to us. Only by so doing can we expect to know Him, and as we come to know Him better we shall spend more time in His presence and find that presence a constant and ever-increasing delight.

E. M. BOUNDS (1835–1913),
PURPOSE IN PRAYER

Seek Me alone and My truth, and I *will* answer. I will make plain all things just when that truth needs to be known. Walk so closely to Me that you can't but hear My whispers. They are My whispers of love echoing timeless truths that I give to those who draw near to Me.

Look only to Me, My child. Do not rely on your own wisdom and thoughts, but allow Me to penetrate beneath the surface in order to reveal My shining truths to you.

The enemy has been battering you from every side to undermine your confidence in Me and to get you to focus on yourself and your problems rather than on Me.

Don't allow him such access. Resist him in the power of My name alone, and he *will* flee from you. The sweetness of My name when lifted up by one who loves Me is a stench and offense to him that he cannot bear.

Therefore God also has highly exalted Him and given Him the name which is above every name, that at the name of Jesus every knee should bow, of those in heaven, and of those on earth, and of those under the earth, and that every tongue should confess that Jesus Christ is Lord, to the glory of God the Father.

PHILIPPIANS 2:9-11

July 25

Precious name, oh, how sweet! Hope of earth and joy of heav'n!
LYDIA BAXTER (1809–1874),
"TAKE THE NAME OF JESUS WITH YOU"

My name spoken in love gives you authority and power over the one who abhors love—a love so perfect that he can't withstand its power. Yes, it's the perfection of My love that wields so much power. My love demonstrated for you and all others on the cross will be forever the impenetrable shield that the enemy cannot prevail against.

That love is for you, My child, to protect and preserve you until the day I bring you home to be with Me. Until that day, I will be using you in ways you cannot yet imagine but that you can absolutely count on.

Now go, My child, surrounded by My shield of protection as you lovingly lift up My name throughout your day. Each utterance of My name spoken with love and reverence will be received and responded to with exactly what you need. I see My every child with great love, and I respond with great love every time. Rest in that eternal truth.

And whatever you do in word or deed, do all in the name of the Lord Jesus, giving thanks to God the Father through Him.

COLOSSIANS 3:17

JUDY GORDON MORROW

July 26

I want what You want, God. I just always want what You want.

I will honor you, My child, for desiring only My will. How could a father not respond to a child's heartfelt plea? As your perfect Father I will never ignore or neglect you. I am beside you always, taking care of you, even when you cannot see the results of My hand. Someday all will be made plain, and you will know more than ever My watch-care over you.

You are growing much in Me. Your pain is shaping your heart after Mine. You have known My hope, joy and peace even in the midst of pain. It is that very pain that increases the depth and sweetness of My joy. Such a paradox but such a reality.

In Me and My ways is a richness for man's soul and spirit that can never be duplicated by anything in the world. Following after Me is the only true path to satisfaction and joy. Shine My light on that path for others. They see your contentment and joy even in the most difficult times. Continue to lead them toward Me. I will help you do that. Just rely totally on Me.

Now no chastening seems to be joyful for the present,
but painful; nevertheless, afterward it yields the peaceable fruit of
righteousness to those who have been trained by it.

HEBREWS 12:11

July 27

Shut the world out, withdraw from all worldly thoughts and occupations, and shut yourself in alone with God, to pray to him in secret. Let this be your chief object in prayer, to realize the presence of your heavenly Father.

ANDREW MURRAY (1828–1917)

Oh, My child, you are just beginning to tap the wellspring of all I have to teach you. When you plumb the depths of My knowledge and My love, you cannot remain unchanged. New growth and maturity and surety will be yours. There is so much I have available for My children if they will only take the time to be with Me, to bask in My presence. No striving is necessary. Just being quiet and still before Me will reap benefits beyond measure. You have found this to be true.

Know I am with you today. I have placed you here at this very time to do My work. You will see My hand and My workings. Lean on Me. All is well. Even in the midst of turbulence, with Me all is well. Rest completely in Me and in My words of truth and comfort to you.

Understanding is a wellspring of life to him who has it.
But the correction of fools is folly.
The heart of the wise teaches his mouth,
and adds learning to his lips.

PROVERBS 16:22-23

July 28

Jesus, I pray You will give me the desires of My heart.

It will bring Me great joy to bestow My gifts of love on you, My child. You have been My faithful servant, and I am about to pour out My blessings upon you like you have never known before.

In the meantime, totally and utterly relax in Me. Know the depth of peace in true rest in Me. No holding on tightly to anything, just a childlike trust in your Father who loves you like no other.

I made you for My purposes. I have been molding you in My likeness since you were a child. Continue to trust My hand upon your life. My hand brings only beauty, no mars or ugliness, but beauty crafted by My transforming grace. You've seen that in the lives of others—the beauty and radiance of My grace. I am doing the same for you.

I am your Rock and Shield and Fortress. I am also the Lover of your soul. Cling to Me at all times. I will never let you go. I will not let you down. My heart is tender toward you. Let My love overflow from your heart to the hearts of others, and they will begin to know and understand Me and My love for them.

Be aware of My love and care toward you all day, My child. Bask in the sweetness of My love, knowing all My plans for you are born out of that deep love. I am looking down on you with much love and joy.

O God, You have taught me from my youth;
and to this day I declare Your wondrous works.

PSALM 71:17

July 29

No one understands like Jesus, when the days are dark and grim.
No one is so near, so dear as Jesus; cast your every care on Him.

JOHN PETERSON (1921–2006),
"NO ONE UNDERSTANDS LIKE JESUS"

I am with you, My child. I know your weariness. I know your pain. I know your heartache and sadness. Leave them all with Me. In My hands each one will be transformed into vessels of joy. Trust Me in this.

I am going before you. I will provide all you need today. Just lean hard on Me. My strength never gives way, never falters or fails. I am not bound by human constraints. I am sufficient for all your needs today.

Think only of Me, and your darkness and despondency will flee. Do get more rest. Be wise in how you live. All things work together for your wellbeing. Don't neglect the areas of health and rest.

I love you, My child. I will continue to carry you today. Abide in Me and Me alone, and know My grace to be all sufficient. I will not fail you. I love you, My child. I love you.

And He said to me, "My grace is sufficient for you,
for My strength is made perfect in weakness."
Therefore most gladly I will rather boast in my infirmities,
that the power of Christ may rest upon me.

2 CORINTHIANS 12:9

July 30

Great is Thy faithfulness, O God my Father.
There is no shadow of turning with Thee.
Thou changest not, Thy compassions they fail not;
As Thou hast been Thou forever wilt be.

THOMAS O. CHISHOLM (1886–1960),
"GREAT IS THY FAITHFULNESS"

My peace is divine in nature and cannot be duplicated. Dwell in it today. Drink from its reservoir. Dare to continue to believe My promises in spite of no concrete evidence, in spite of the seeming impossibility of those promises, in spite of so many years passing. None of that matters.

What does matter is that I am the same yesterday, today and forever. In Me is no shadow of changing. In Me is power beyond what your finite mind can comprehend. In Me is a creativity that can be expressed in a multitude of answers designed to amaze you—to take your breath away with their scope and unpredictability.

You often say you don't want to put Me in a box. I will be showing you that I can't be constrained by human constructions, no matter how big "the box." My infinite power can't be relegated. Instead it is to be reveled in, with all praise going to the Father forever and ever. This is the way of true joy—to exult in who I am and to enjoy the expressions of My love and care toward you. Do that even today.

Jesus Christ is the same yesterday, today, and forever.
HEBREWS 13:8

July 31

When I am burdened or weary and sad, Jesus is all I need.
Never He fails to uplift and make glad. Jesus is all I need.

JAMES ROWE (1865–1933),
"JESUS IS ALL I NEED"

In everything I AM. Today I AM, and I am enough for your every need and care. I am the One who loves you above all. And where I am there is never room for dread or fear. I offer you a path of peace and wisdom. A way of comfort. In Me is all you need, My child.

Rely fully on Me today, and discover anew the truth of My words and who I am. You are My beloved child, and I will not fail you. You will soon see what I will do, and how your heart will rejoice!

Rejoice even now this day, My child, and see My face of love toward you. These days of hardness will not last forever. Soon will come your promised rescue. Your day of deliverance *is* nigh. Live in My majestic and unending love for you today. Live in expectation and anticipation of what I am soon to do. You will rejoice! Rejoice *even now*.

In your righteousness deliver me and rescue me;
incline your ear to me and save me.

PSALM 71:2, *NRSV*

JUDY GORDON MORROW

August

Wait on the Lord; be of good courage, and He shall strengthen your heart.
Wait, I say, on the Lord!

PSALM 27:24

The word "wait" is sometimes translated as "hope" in the Bible.

Yet we equate waiting as a negative—as something not to be desired but rather avoided.

Waiting, however, gives God time to fulfill His purposes in us, to prepare us for the hope He has placed within us—the hope promised at the end of the waiting.

What would that fulfilled hope look like without the wilderness of waiting preceding it? Does not the hope shine that much brighter because of the wilderness wanderings beforehand?

Fulfilled hope is a pearl of great price. Precious becomes the waiting that results in *God's very best* for His faithful follower. Waiting strengthens, prepares and refines us so that we can receive God's fulfilled hope with a humble heart and a mature mind. With a life that exudes thanksgiving and praise—a life readied by waiting on our God of hope who withholds nothing good from His children.

Praise You, Jesus, for all You have done within me and for me during these years of waiting on You. Precious have been My times with You, and I praise You for being all that I need. And I thank You that You will soon be leading me out of this wilderness of waiting into new vistas of vision that I know will delight and thrill me—and will have been so worth waiting for, just as You've always promised me.

I love You, Lord. Praise You!

August 1

Your presence is so precious, Lord.

It is for you—My gift to you to give you hope, peace and joy. To give you comfort. My presence surrounds you always, but it is in these quiet times before Me that you will be most aware of My gentle presence. Communing with Me is like a quiet candlelit dinner with the dearest of your friends. You have found this to be true, and that precious intimacy will only increase as you continue to spend time with Me.

This day has already been filled with My blessings and the special sense of My presence when I told you again that I will be doing things beyond your wildest, wildest dreams. Believe Me completely. The plans I have for you will fill you with wonder, and you will see My hand of love like never before. Look to Me in joyful expectation even now, and know that I will do all that I have promised. Waiting on Me and My ordained plans yields the highest and purest of joys.

Watch now as My wonders continue to unfold. Great will be your joy, My child. Great will be your joy.

To you then who believe, he is precious.
1 PETER 2:7, *NRSV*

August 2

God, I must have Your correct thinking.

I am at work. Never doubt that. Look only to Me, and I will guide your thoughts. You are right to see how as a man thinks, so is he. Your thoughts determine your outlook and your emotions. Think My thoughts and all will be well. Do not allow yourself to dwell in your limited, flawed thinking, but look only to Me, whose thoughts and ways are higher than yours. Trust the wisdom of My thoughts and ways, and you will know My peace.

I know you don't know what to think about so many things. Put away those restless thoughts, and instead focus on Me and My constant provisions for you. Focus on who I am and that simply nothing is impossible with Me. Even now your mind is trying to go down a path that will lead only to despair. Don't. Call out to Me, and I will hear and answer your every plea. I will not fail you, Child.

Trust Me in this. Trust Me in all things. I love you beyond measure, and I will not fail you. Think on My love for you. My love will not fail you. Dwell in its depths today and be filled with My goodness and peace. I love you, My precious child. Never doubt My great love for you. I will carry you through these days. Know that to be so and rest in Me.

For as he thinks in his heart, so is he.
PROVERBS 23:7

August 3

I'd rather walk in the dark with God
Than go alone in the light;
I'd rather walk by faith with Him
Than go alone by sight.

MARY BRAINARD (1837–1905),
"I KNOW NOT WHAT AWAITS ME"

I will make all things clear. But for now some things are shrouded for reasons you cannot yet know. Hang on, My child. Hang on to the One who loves you like no other. I see your pain, and I will not leave you in that place.

Look only to Me. I will guide you. All things will become plain. For right now, just continue to trust Me in this darkness. I will shine My light again. Believe Me in this. I will bring you out once again into My light and love.

I love you, Child. Even though you do not feel loved by Me right now, you are. Don't allow the darkness to dim My truth. My truth remains, both in the shadows and in the sunshine. Choose to believe no matter what you feel. The feelings will follow in due time.

Let Me hold and cradle your hurting heart today. Stay ever close to Me. I will *never* leave you nor forsake you. I love you.

Be strong and of good courage, do not fear nor be afraid of them;
for the Lord your God, He is the One who goes with you.
He will not leave you nor forsake you.

DEUTERONOMY 31:6

The Listening Heart JUDY GORDON MORROW

August 4

Lord, make Your ways so plain.

I will, My child. In every detail I will go before you and prepare the way. You will see My hand everywhere. Rest in Me and My peace, and let Me fill you with My serenity and calm.

You know you can trust Me, so watch expectantly as My plans and wonders unfold. Joy in who I am and all that I will be doing. You will see My grace and love, and so will others. "To God be the glory, great things He hath done" will be your theme song. Be anxious for nothing. Worry will drain you and rob you of My peace. Simply depend on Me for everything, and I will provide. You are My beloved child, and I will not fail you. I will show forth My might and grace and My love in your life. Be My transparent vessel and depend on My every leading. I am with you and will work out all for your good and My glory.

Just trust Me completely, and see what I will do! Be filled with excited expectation, as this is all part of My plan for you. All *will* be made plain as you follow Me one step at a time. Greater is He that is within you than he that is in the world.[1] I will show My greatness to you like never before. I love you, My precious child. Great days are ahead!

Be anxious for nothing, but in everything by prayer and supplication,
with thanksgiving, let your requests be made known to God.

PHILIPPIANS 4:6

Note
1. See 1 John 4:4, *KJV.*

August 5

*No one can believe how powerful prayer is and what it can effect,
except those who have learned it by experience. Whenever I have prayed
earnestly, I have been heard and have obtained more than I prayed for.
God sometimes delays, but He always comes.*

MARTIN LUTHER (1483–1546)

Continue to pray. Continue to believe Me. Know the assurance of My answers before you ever see them fulfilled. You are living in that place of assurance even now, in regard to My fulfilling My promises to you. Do praise and thank Me now before the answers have been given by My hand. This prepares your heart to be ready to receive My answers.

A heart of thanksgiving and praise is a heart of rest, a place of peace. See how much better it will be when My answers are enfolded by that heart rather than one filled with anxiety and unrest? A heart of rest is a tabernacle of trust. A place sheltered by My peace. That is where I want you to dwell while you actively wait on Me for My answers.

Oh, My dear child, you will not believe what I'm just about to do. You will be amazed, yes, but you will also have a sense of, "Of course." You will see Me in all of it, and I will be glorified, just as you desire.

Go in My deep abiding peace. Stay in close communion with Me. Follow My every leading. I love you, My child. Listen to My voice of love to you today. *All is well.*

*I will praise the name of God with a song,
and will magnify Him with thanksgiving.*

PSALM 69:30

The Listening Heart JUDY GORDON MORROW

August 6

*I thought of all those going through pain and hard times
who don't know Jesus personally, and I prayed,
"Oh, help me to be Your hope giver."*

I will, My child. That is why I have allowed you to experience such depths of pain so that you could speak out of deeper truth. Others will listen and know that your words are genuine, because they are rooted in pain. Your pain will give you permission to speak and be heard.

See how I will redeem all these days? In everything I can be trusted, even when you can't understand. Pure trust in Me will actually deepen your understanding—not the understanding of circumstances but your understanding of Me and My unsurpassed love for you. A new and deeper understanding of Me will always yield My perfect peace.

Walk in My perfect peace today, My child, and know without a doubt that all is well. I love you immeasurably and will guide your every step.

*And we know that the Son of God has come and has given us an understanding,
that we may know Him who is true; and we are in Him who is true,
in His Son Jesus Christ. This is the true God and eternal life.*

1 JOHN 5:20

August 7

Trust is based on how well you know someone.
Spending time in our Father's presence is how we get to know Him.
Just being with Him enables us to know His heart of love. How can we trust
someone we rarely spend time with, thus knowing so little about that person
and who they really are? It would be like trusting a stranger.

Herein lies the problem with today's busy Christians.
They struggle to trust a stranger, not knowing if He indeed has their best
interests in mind. If only they would take time to be with Him, to really know
Him, they would discover the most loving and caring Father and friend.

JGM

My heart is for you to know Me. In knowing Me, you will understand you can always trust Me. Always. While others may let you down, My child, I will never let you down. You can trust My heart toward you. Everything I do is meant only for your good and the good of others. You will see that more clearly as time goes on.

Go in My peace today. Live in My joy—today's joy and the future joy I have promised you. Nothing has changed. My promises still stand. Trust Me in this. Trust Me in all things. I love you, My child. Never forget to dwell on the love I have toward you. It is beyond anything else you've known or ever will know. Bask in My love today. Be assured of My love all day long. You are My beloved child. Live in My love today.

The Lord is good, a stronghold in the day of trouble;
and He knows those who trust in Him.

NAHUM 1:7

August 8

Pray the largest prayers. You cannot think a prayer so large that God,
in answering it, will not wish you had made it larger.
Pray not for crutches but for wings.

PHILLIPS BROOKS (1835–1893)

Relax. Rest in Me. Rather than getting worked up about all that is pressing in on you, look at each thing as an opportunity for Me to shine—for Me to show My grace and mercy to you. As a time when you will see Me work like never before.

You have been asking. You are inspired to pray "largest prayers." You desire to see amazing wonders from My hand. All this is from Me. I will honor your seeking and believing heart. How can I not? You are following Me, responding to Me and expecting Me. I will go far beyond your wildest imaginings because of My unsurpassed love for you.

Out of My divine love comes deliverance that can only be orchestrated and performed by Me. You will see that to be true, and you will be profoundly changed forever. Your faith will move to new levels as you experience the depths of My great love for you.

Look to Me alone for guidance, and I will answer. I will show you what to do. Just stay close to Me, and all will be well. Do not let your feet stray from the path I have set you on, as it will give you abundant joy. Following Me always leads to the way of joy. There is no better way.

In the day of my trouble I will call upon You, for You will answer me.

PSALM 86:7

August 9

Obedience to a word of God always brings an
amazing sweetness to the life of the obeyer.

OSWALD CHAMBERS (1874–1917)

I will so honor you for your obedience to follow after Me and to speak My truth. I know it hasn't been easy, but you have known My peace and you have seen the beauty of obedience. You will never regret obeying Me in every facet of your life. Obedience always yields the highest and purest of My gifts to you—peace and joy without end.

Blessed are those who dwell in My Word and seek My heart. Long have you sought to know Me, and now you are reaping benefit after benefit, joy upon joy because of your faithful obedience. What I have promised I will always fulfill for those who wait on Me in faith, believing. I will always answer faith.

I love you, My precious child, and you will know My love and care for you in greater proportions and depths than ever before. Rest today in My all-encompassing love for you, and be at peace. Continue to dwell in Me. I will be making your faith sight, and you will glory in My glory and majesty. Delays and seeming denials will fade into the past, as I delight in bringing to you the desires of your heart. Daily will you praise Me that you believed Me and did not settle for less than My best.

All is well, precious child. I love you.

You shall walk after the Lord your God and fear Him,
and keep His commandments and obey His voice;
you shall serve Him and hold fast to Him.

DEUTERONOMY 13:4

August 10

Praise God from whom all blessings flow;
praise Him all creatures here below.

THOMAS KEN (1637–1711),
"PRAISE GOD FROM WHOM ALL BLESSINGS FLOW"

Today, praise Me *all day long*, and just see what I will do. Praise prepares the way for the outpouring of My hand. Cup your hands together in faith, believing for My soon-coming answers to the thousands of prayers that have ascended, and I will fill them with blessings that will far exceed your fondest dreams and desires.

Believe Me to move My hand. Praise Me for the perfection of My plan. Know that all is well. I am at work even now, and I am honoring your faith in Me. You have believed Me all these years, in spite of discouragement time and again. But because you have chosen to dwell in My truth and not on the facts and circumstances, now I am freed to move My hand. Mighty is My hand, and mighty will be the results of My workings. My ways are truly above yours—profoundly above yours—and thus, My answers will be profoundly richer and more satisfying than anything you could have devised on your own.

Remember, My child, *praise Me all day long.* Let nothing else enter in but praise, and just see what I will do. Lift up your praise to Me, and believe Me for all I have promised. I love you, Child.

As your name deserves, O God, you will be praised to the ends of the earth.
Your strong right hand is filled with victory.

PSALM 48:10, *NLT*

August 11

God is love.

FROM 1 JOHN 4:8

And in that love there is nothing to fear—only much to revel and delight in. A love that desires only My best for My children. A love that sees the beginning to the end and knows every step along the journey for every child of Mine. A love that desires holiness, knowing that holiness will bring the greatest soul satisfaction. A love that even today is guarding your heart and filling it with My peace.

This is who I am, My child—the God who loves supremely and sacrificially to benefit you, the object of My love. Why would you want to stray from the One who only longs to enfold you in His loving arms as the Shepherd of your soul? This love of Mine will never let you go.

How blessed has been our time together this morning. I will honor you today with an outpouring of strength, help and wisdom. Joy in My presence. Revel in My care.

The Lord is my shepherd; I have all that I need.

PSALM 23:1, *NLT*

August 12

I pray for Your wisdom and strength today.

I will give you My wisdom and strength today. Remember that wisdom comes from Me, and I give it to a seeking heart. Remember that the joy of the Lord is your strength. Joy in Me today, in My words, in who I am, and you will have more than enough strength for the tasks at hand. That same joy will lighten not only your load but also your spirit.

Continue to know I am working regarding your future. Don't let your hope waver. Anchor your hope and trust in Me. I will not let you down.

The time is near, My child. All these days of waiting will soon draw to a close, and My plans of perfection will unfold for you. No one will be able to deny the workings of My hand. This is why it's so important to wait on Me and My timings. Taking things into your own hands only causes grief and despair.

I love you, precious child. Your heart is My instrument of peace, compassion and joy. Keep your heart ever turned toward Me, and I will be able to use you in the greatest of ways. It's all about My kingdom. Live richly in Me and in faith, and you will always know true contentment and satisfaction. Live in My hope today. I am with you.

Do not sorrow, for the joy of the Lord is your strength.
NEHEMIAH 8:10

August 13

Lord, this day is dedicated to You. It is Yours.

Today I have already taken care of. Let nothing cause you anxiety, but delight in turning over every concern to Me. I alone know the best outcomes, and I will take care of each thing that causes you concern. There is no better way to live than as a child who knows that every concern is provided for. That is My role as your loving Father. Gratefully release all into My hands, and be content to see how I will perform My wonders for you.

In My presence is fullness of joy, as you know. Bask in that joy today, as you remain in My presence all day. Choose to remain in My presence even in the busyness of your day, and you will see the difference in all realms.

I am at all times available to you, wanting to ease your burdens and to ensure your peace. Enjoy the sweetness and intimacy of My presence all day today, and greet every aspect of your day with joy. I love you, My child, and I came to give you My unspeakable joy.

You show me the path of life. In your presence there is fullness of joy;
in your right hand are pleasures forevermore.

PSALM 16:11, *NRSV*

August 14

Please, soon. Please, soon.

I know you are exhausted. I know you are weary in the waiting. But don't give up hope. Have I ever given you a reason to quit hoping? No, I've always given you more reasons to remain in My hope. Remember who your source is: the God of heaven and earth, the God who can do wonders, the God who loves you beyond measure. Dwell on those truths, and don't let discouragement and doubt darken the doorway of your heart.

Look only to Me today. I am going before you. Listen to My nudges. Let My Spirit empower you for every task at hand. He is My gift to you. Walk in My Spirit, love by His ability to love, and know the peace that comes by His residing in your heart.

Fear nothing. I am with you. I will remain with you always, interested in every detail of your life, and giving you just what you need at the instant you need it.

Live in My constant hope today. It is for you—to lighten your load and to prepare you for your future joy. Never forget how much I love you, Child.

He prayed, "O Lord, God of Israel, there is no God like you in all of heaven and earth. You keep your covenant and show unfailing love to all who walk before you in wholehearted devotion."

2 CHRONICLES 6:14, *NLT*

August 15

My hope is built on nothing less
Than Jesus' blood and righteousness.
I dare not trust the sweetest frame
But wholly lean on Jesus' name.
On Christ, the solid Rock, I stand,
All other ground is sinking sand.

EDWARD MOTE (1797–1874),
"THE SOLID ROCK"

Go into this day with fearless anticipation and solid expectation in Me. Keep your eyes on Me—ever upward, never cast down to the things of this earth. Eyes on Me will yield peace and hope. Eyes cast down will yield doubt and despair.

In Me is your stability, the very foundation of your life. Anything else is shifting sand. Today anchor yourself in the Rock that shall not be moved. I will shelter you there. In Me you have *everything* you need. Take joy in My truths to you. I love you, My child.

Therefore whoever hears these sayings of Mine, and does them, I will liken
him to a wise man who built his house on the rock: and the rain descended,
the floods came, and the winds blew and beat on that house; and it did not
fall, for it was founded on the rock. But everyone who hears these sayings of
Mine, and does not do them, will be like a foolish man who built his house on
the sand: and the rain descended, the floods came, and the winds blew
and beat on that house; and it fell. And great was its fall.

MATTHEW 7:24-27

August 16

What is it You would have me to do?

Trust Me. Simply trust Me, My child. You are worried about many things, yet that is not My desire or plan for you. Worry robs you of My peace and joy. It puts you alongside those who don't even know Me, who don't know My trustworthiness. But you do. Trust Me in all things. Trust Me in this darkness. I will break through with My light. I will make all things plain. Simply trust Me. That is all I require, and that is all you need to do. Trust in My never-failing, unending love for you. Dwell on the depth and eternal scope of My love for you. It is like no other.

Walk by faith today. Praise Me even in the darkness. I will answer. I will come through. Your faith is the candle that will light your path for the next step. Don't worry about the final destination or where I am leading you; just concentrate on the next step. Your faith will enable Me to lead you one step, one sure step, at a time.

Rest in these truths. Take comfort in My presence. I am with you always.

But you are a chosen generation, a royal priesthood, a holy nation,
His own special people, that you may proclaim the praises of Him
who called you out of darkness into His marvelous light.

1 PETER 2:9

August 17

*God will never, never, never let us down if we have faith and put
our trust in Him. He will always look after us. So we must cleave to Jesus.
Our whole life must simply be woven into Jesus.*

MOTHER TERESA (1910–1997)

I delight, My child, in how you are resting in Me completely. How you know more than ever how absolutely trustworthy I am. Knowing that yields an unequivocal trust in Me that never wavers, even when outer circumstances look insurmountable. When you truly know Me, you know that nothing is beyond My capabilities. Nothing.

Just as My Word states, nothing is impossible with Me. Few truly believe that. Many want to believe it, but they cast their eyes too low. Their vision is fixed on the scenes around them rather than on My face. If My children would truly see *Me*, all thoughts of impossibilities would flee. Nothing is impossible to him who believes Me, who truly takes Me at My Word. I will not disappoint that child.

You are understanding what I'm telling you, aren't you, My child. You know now more than ever My meaning when I've told you that what I'm going to do for you is not just for your joy and benefit. While that promised joy is one of the reasons I will honor your faith, the widespread ramifications of My workings will be known only in eternity.

Yes, I am trustworthy. Yes, you can rest in the perfection of My plans. Yes, waiting on Me will bring My plans for your highest good and My greatest glory. Is there anything more desirable and satisfying than that? You know that to be true more than ever before.

*For all the promises of God in Him are Yes,
and in Him Amen, to the glory of God through us.*

2 CORINTHIANS 1:20

～ The Listening Heart   JUDY GORDON MORROW

August 18

Sadness and sorrow create a framework crafted by God
to showcase life's joys.

JGM

The overwhelming pain you have known in recent months has given your heart newfound strength and resiliency. Truly the pain has carved deeper reservoirs in your heart in order to contain the deepest and purest of joys. You have a surety in Me like never before. Your words, the conviction in your voice, My light and peace on your face will combine to draw others to Me.

I will not disappoint your hope, Child—the hope that I have given you from the beginning. You are right to see that miracle of hope and how I have increased its brightness and surety, even though circumstances remain the same. Things are not always as they appear. Look to Me with eyes of faith, and you will see with new eyes—with My vision that sees nothing as impossible.

This has been a special time, My child. Your soul and spirit have been quieted as you have knelt before Me. You know anew the refreshing of My presence and grace. Now walk in My love and peace today, and know with increasing clarity and joy how very much I am with you.

Remain in My peace and love. Rejoice in the gift of ever-increasing hope. It is My gift of love to you, My precious child. I will do all I have said. Your joy will know no end. Great is My faithfulness. I love you, Child.

For great is his steadfast love toward us,
and the faithfulness of the Lord endures forever. Praise the Lord!

PSALM 117:2, *NRSV*

August 19

Do not look to your hope, but to Christ, the source of your hope.
CHARLES SPURGEON (1834–1892)

Oh, if you only knew the plans I have for you. Someday you will. Your joy will know no bounds. You will marvel and rejoice at the workings of My hand. Live in the joy of that hope even now.

Great days are ahead, My child. Days of joy and gladness and renewed hope. Hope only in Me. No matter how circumstances change, My hope never dims. Like the lighthouse beacon, your hope in Me need never waver or dim. I am the only true hope giver. Think on that, My child. To know Me is to know hope. Nothing can take that away from you as you cling steadfastly to Me.

Even as the storm clouds and waves wash over you, My beacon of hope to you will forever shine bright. Your eyes must remain on Me. Nothing else matters. I never change. My promises remain true. Though doubts may assail like stormy waves, hold fast to Me and the hope I give. It is My gift to you. Someday you will reap the joy of steadfastly hoping in Me.

Keep your eyes on Me today. Let Me guide your day. Listen to My voice. Follow My nudges. They are all in your best interest. I love you with an everlasting love, My child. Know Me and you can't help but know My love.

Happy are those whose help is the God of Jacob,
whose hope is in the Lord their God.
PSALM 146:5, *NRSV*

August 20

We shall steer safely through every storm, so long as our heart is right,
our intention fervent, our courage steadfast, and our trust fixed on God.
ST. FRANCIS DE SALES (1567–1622)

Yes, My child, My answers *are* coming. You are wise to wait for them
and to rest in My peace in the waiting. That is the sign of My presence
in your life—My peace while you wait in the midst of the storm.

Never despair. I am working in countless ways. Trust Me in that.
Continue to pray so I can accomplish My purposes. Prayer is the key.
The enemy can't remain where prayer abounds.

Don't worry about anything. Continue to learn what I am teaching
you: I love you with an everlasting love. I want only good for you, My
good. You can totally trust Me to bring about My best for your life.
My best is also your best. Don't settle for anything less.

Rest in My peace today. Keep remembering how much I love you.
My love knows no boundaries or limits. Think on that! I love you.

When the storms of life come, the wicked are whirled away,
but the godly have a lasting foundation.
PROVERBS 10:25, *NLT*

August 21

This is just so hard.

I know it's hard, My child. That's why you have Me for your strength. *I am your strength. I am your help. I am your peace giver. Rely on Me alone.*

I give hope, not despair. I am not the giver of fear but the giver of peace. My peace and love cast out fear. Look only to Me so that all that dwells within you will be from Me and of Me. That is the way of peace that comes from abiding in Me. Know My way, know Me, and you will know My peace. Fear cannot remain in the presence of My peace.

Do not be troubled about anything this morning. All is well. I am your loving Father, and I will take care of your every need. Haven't I done that so far? I will not let you down now.

I will be with you every minute of this day. Look for Me at every turn. Know that I have not forgotten you. I will do all that I have promised. Do not let the lies of the enemy penetrate your thinking, but look only to Me—the Way, the *Truth,* the Life. I will not fail you.

Let not your heart be troubled; you believe in God, believe also in Me.
JOHN 14:1

JUDY GORDON MORROW

August 22

How sweet the name of Jesus sounds in a believer's ear!
It soothes his sorrows, heals his wounds, and drives away his fear.

JOHN NEWTON (1725–1807),
"HOW SWEET THE NAME OF JESUS SOUNDS"

See what I will do today. Expect Me to work. Depend on Me completely. I will meet your every need. In all I will be glorified. I am your Great Physician, the Healer of your heart, body and soul. Count on Me. I will not let you down.

Don't forget how much I love you, Child. My love stretches over you like a comforting quilt, a warm blanket of love. Stay beneath the folds of My blanket of love, and know that all is well. These days will not last forever. My deliverance is soon. I will not give you more than you can bear.

I love you, My precious child. I have not forsaken you, even though it feels that way this morning. Remember My wonders, and watch for more wonders of My love to unfold. They will, and you will rejoice. Hang on to that hope today. Hope for My new days of abounding love and grace toward you. I will do all that I have said, and great will be your joy. Hold on to Me, and the joy *will* come.

No temptation has overtaken you except such as is common to man;
but God is faithful, who will not allow you to be tempted beyond what
you are able, but with the temptation will also make the way of escape,
that you may be able to bear it.

1 CORINTHIANS 10:13

August 23

Why worry, when you can pray?
Trust Jesus, He'll be your stay.
Don't be a doubting Thomas,
Rest fully on His promise,
Why worry, worry, worry, worry
when you can pray?

JOHN W. PETERSON (1921–2006),
"WHY WORRY WHEN YOU CAN PRAY?"

Trust Me, My child. Your fretting and worry injure My heart, as that says to Me you don't really trust Me, in spite of your words that say you do. Rest in My love and sovereignty, and worry will forever flee.

Learn the lesson once and for all: worry is not from Me. I desire freedom for you, and freedom from worry and fear leads you to true rest in Me.

Rest in My peace, and *know* all is well. I am at work. Rest and trust alone in *Me*. I love you, My child. You will see.

Therefore I tell you, do not worry about your life, what you will eat or what you will drink, or about your body, what you will wear. Is not life more than food, and the body more than clothing? Look at the birds of the air; they neither sow nor reap nor gather into barns, and yet your heavenly Father feeds them. Are you not of more value than they? And can any of you by worrying add a single hour to your span of life?

MATTHEW 6:25-27, *NRSV*

JUDY GORDON MORROW

August 24

Teach us, O Lord, the disciplines of patience,
for to wait is often harder than to work.

PETER MARSHALL (1902–1949)

You are wise to wait on Me. The waiting *will* end—it's only a matter of time. In Me there are no barriers or obstacles too difficult to overcome. Think on who I am and dwell in My love and power. Nothing is impossible with Me. With just a word I can change things instantly.

Truly seeing and knowing who I am makes all the difference. It changes doubt to rock-solid faith, despair to hope, heavy-heartedness to joy. Dwelling in Me will always restore fullness of joy—deep abiding joy that has nothing to do with circumstances but everything to do with who I am.

I love you, My child. Recognize My love for you everywhere. I am constantly manifesting My love to you—open your eyes and see each gift of love from Me. Be assured that I am working, even when you don't see anything happening. I am always working on your behalf.

I, your Father, am very close to bringing you My answers—answers that have been crafted out of My heart of love for you. Be ready to receive with open hands, and be ready to rejoice. Great will be your joy, My child. The sweetest of joy will be yours. Joy born out of obedience and sacrifice tastes sweeter than any other kind. That joy I promise to you. Hold that promise close to your heart all day. It is from Me, and I love you with an everlasting love. Go in My peace and joy.

Taste and see that the Lord is good.
Oh, the joys of those who take refuge in him!

PSALM 34:8, *NLT*

August 25

Work out every detail.

I will. I am the God of details. I delight in orchestrating My plans perfectly, down to the smallest details. It is often in the small, seemingly insignificant things that I can best show My power and grace.

Think on the tiny things of life—the smallest flower, the ladybug, a grain of sand, a snowflake—examine them closely, and see Me and My perfection. I'm the God who oversees and cares about even the smallest of things. The more you know Me and My character, the more you realize My great love toward you, the more you will be able to release every concern and care into My hands. My trustworthiness is unfailing. Know Me. Know My unchanging love. Trust Me completely.

Rest in My peace today. It is my gift to you. Know that I am working, even when you cannot see. I have only your best in mind. Oh, the days of joy that await you, My child! It's a future full of hope and joy. Rest in that assurance like never before. Abide in Me and My words.

Look only to Me. Live in My hope, the only true hope, all day today. I love you, My child. I will always love you.

The Lord directs the steps of the godly.
He delights in every detail of their lives.

PSALM 37:23, *NLT*

August 26

These thoughts are my thoughts, and I want Your thoughts.

I will eventually make *all* things plain to you, but in the meantime walk by faith and know the One you are following. Knowing Me, truly knowing Me, makes all the difference. You can follow a trustworthy guide who knows and loves you—who desires only your best. Were I a stranger to you, then it would be a struggle to follow Me. That's why My children need to spend time with Me, basking in My loving presence and knowing My unfailing love for them.

I know you are concerned about your family member. Trust Me in this, My child, just like you trust Me with every other concern of your life. I am working. I see and know all. Nothing escapes Me. I will orchestrate all in the perfection of My plan. Just trust Me, and know that all is well.

All is well in every realm of your life because you have given every realm to Me. Anything submitted to Me will succeed and prosper in ways that only I can orchestrate. That is why I will be orchestrating My plans of perfection for you. You have given over to Me your future hopes and dreams, and now I can shape and fashion those dreams into realities that will astound and amaze you.

Do know I will be *right on time*. Fret not. Follow Me. I will soon be leading you on shining paths of light to your new days. New days of joy unspeakable and full of glory. Rejoice even *now*.

But he gives more grace. Therefore it says, "God opposes the proud, but gives grace to the humble." Submit yourselves therefore to God.

JAMES 4:6-7, *ESV*

August 27

Remembering how God has promised to make up for all these years
of loneliness, I prayed, "Lord, I'm counting on that."

You *can* count on that. Indeed, I will be bringing you the sweetest of joy, My child. I have *not* forgotten you. Any thought like that is from the enemy, not from the One who loves you best. And love you I do, as I have shown you time and time again. Don't fail to see My constant gestures of love toward you. Each one is meant to give you increased hope and daily comfort. Take hope even now in My loving plans for you.

I am going before you this day. *Always* I go before you, making the way wherein you should walk. I am on that path with you, guarding and guiding your every step. Rest in that knowledge, and all anxiety and fear will flee. *I* am with you. What more do you need? In Me you live and move and have your being.[1]

Go now and know My smile upon you. Feel My warm embrace of everlasting love. Walk in My peace. *All is well.* Rest in My words of truth. They are My gift to you, to bring you serenity of soul and joy for each moment. Be My conduit of joy today.

I love you, Child.

I am counting on the Lord; yes, I am counting on him.
I have put my hope in his word.

PSALM 130:5, *NLT*

Note
1. See Acts 17:28.

August 28

May people only see You in what You are going to do for me.

They will, My child, they will. There will be no doubt that all of this is of My doing. I will greatly honor you for waiting on Me and My plans for you. Know that day is coming as surely as the morning sunrise.

I will be with you today. Continue to see Me in every detail, in every working of My hand. Continue to joy in the process, and see Me in everything. How I delight in your delight of My love gifts to you. Your sight continues to improve as you keep your eyes on Me. When you do that, I will give you increased vision and wisdom to see all things clearly.

Take much joy in this day. Continue to praise Me in all things. I dwell in the praise of My children. Line the rooms of your heart and your home with praise to Me.

I love you, My precious child. I will not fail or disappoint you. All is truly well. Joy, joy, joy is yours—now and forever.

That they may know from the rising of the sun to its setting
that there is none besides Me.
I am the Lord, and there is no other.
ISAIAH 45:6

August 29

When you need it, rest in body; rest always in spirit.
J. HUDSON TAYLOR (1832–1905)

Rest in Me today. Rest in My unending love and care. Drink in My presence and truly know the fullness of Me. I am carrying you, My child. I know how weary you are, and I am carrying you to where My love and will are taking you. You are never alone. You are never on your own. You are never left desolate while in My care. Rest in these words of assurance. Rest completely, not allowing anything to rob you of the serenity that comes from resting in Me. When you do this, others will see Me in your countenance of peace and joy.

Enjoy this day. Accomplish your tasks with joy. Joy makes the loads lighter, the work satisfying. This kind of joy only comes from Me and is My gift to you. Joy in every aspect of this day, remembering that each day, each moment, is My gift to you. A gift of love from your Father's hand.

Live expectantly, My child. Live expectantly in hope. Hope placed in Me will never disappoint. I will not fail you. I will not let you down. I will rescue you at just the right moment. Trust Me completely. I will honor your trust in Me. You will see. You will see and greatly rejoice. I love you, Child.

He said, "My presence will go with you, and I will give you rest."
EXODUS 33:14, *NRSV*

August 30

Thank You for the privilege of prayer—of being with You.

I long to be with My children in this way—to hear their hearts, to know their deepest desires, to understand their pain. While I am aware of all these things before they are spoken, it is good for them to come to Me with each concern. The key is to come to Me and then leave with Me each concern. Then I can be freed to work, freed to move. "Not my will, but Thy will" is the key.[1]

I have heard each prayer from your heart this morning, My child. I have seen each tear. There is no sorrow, no pain, no heartache that My grace and love cannot heal. My love goes deeper than the deepest pain. I long to enfold My children in My love, to carry them through the deepest days of sorrow. I long to lead them to My light, which is still shining brightly. Sorrow and pain dim the sight, but I will always lead My children through the darkness to new days of light and joy. I will not leave them desolate. They will know Me like never before. You know this to be true.

> *I will bring the blind by a way they did not know;*
> *I will lead them in paths they have not known.*
> *I will make darkness light before them, and crooked places straight.*
> *These things I will do for them, and not forsake them.*
>
> ISAIAH 42:16

Note
1. See Luke 22:42.

August 31

Every tear of sorrow sown by the righteous springs up a pearl.
MATTHEW HENRY (1662–1714)

Your own sorrows and darkness have led you into a deeper intimacy with Me. This closeness cannot be duplicated in any other way. Sorrow is My tool for service. I can use those who have been in the crucible. They will shine for Me like never before, and others will see Me as their light. It is truly all about My kingdom.

I am working in this way in your life even now, using your pain and sorrow to infuse my life-giving light like never before, My child. You will know joy in new measure, love with new depth. All these months of pain I will redeem and use to give hope to others through you. I will do this because of who I am: I transform sorrow into joy, pain into new life, darkness into light. I shine the most purely and clearly through those who have been through the fire. You will marvel as you see the truth of those words become more apparent in your own life.

Look only to Me today. I am working even now. Your faith will be made sight. You will see with astounding clarity the workings of My hand. The plans I have for you will bring great joy and fulfillment. Keep your eyes on Me and My future plans of joy. They are soon to unfold. I love you. Remain in Me and My peace today.

You keep track of all my sorrows.
You have collected all my tears in your bottle.
You have recorded each one in your book.
PSALM 56:8, *NLT*

September

God will not leave you in your place of pain forever. He didn't leave Joseph in prison or the children of Israel in the wilderness, and He won't have you remain in your relentless pain.

But He *will* be with you in your pain. He will refine you with that fire. And, if you allow Him, He will become everything to you—to the point of such precious intimacy with Him that you will thank Him for the very pain that melted and molded your heart to be like His.

Debilitating pain in whatever form drops us to our knees and draws us into the precious presence of our Father. In His presence we know an intimacy with Him that defies any pen put to paper. The sweetness of His presence, that oneness with God, is forged in the furnace of pain and suffering.

And then what a shining image of our loving Savior emerges in the one who has trusted God even within the scorching of his soul. All dross has been consumed, and what remains is someone who will never be satisfied with anything but God and His desires for His child.

September 1

I know You will fulfill all according to Your plan, because You are good.

Yes, I am good. There is no vile thing within Me. My children need to remember that. They need to realize I am a God of pure love. I act out of love and righteousness. My plans are based on My perfection and goodness. There is nothing to fear from My hand for those who walk uprightly with Me.

Why would My children not want to trust Me? They let human traits cloud their thinking. My plans and desires for them are good. They can trust My hand and heart in everything I will bring to pass. Sometimes the way will be shrouded in darkness and confusion, but I am there too.

Oh, My child, there is still so much that is yet unseen. Everything will not be known until the other side. The key is to trust the loving, kind hand of your Father. I do all things well. I love My children with a love that can't be measured by human standards. Your understanding is limited now, but it won't always be that way. So much joy and newness of all things await on the other side.

I will help you today. Trust Me completely. I will not fail you. My strength is made perfect in weakness. You are right to depend totally on Me. I am your faithful Father. Nothing is too hard for Me. Look to Me only. Live in My boundless grace today. I love you, My child.

You are good, and do good; teach me Your statutes.

PSALM 119:68

September 2

I know You can do anything.

Yes, My child, I *can* do anything. I am your all-powerful Father, and I hold all things in My hands. While it may appear sometimes that things are out of control, they are not. I am the sovereign God who knows the beginning to the end. Nothing happens that I do not allow.

Once again, remember the mystery of Me. You will not always understand My ways in the lives of My children. But remember how much is hidden from you—so much that you cannot know. That's where trust comes in. Trust in your all-loving, all-knowing Father. A Father who keeps His word to His children. You can trust Me totally, My child.

I will honor your faith in Me. I will not let you down, My child. I would betray My own character—who I am as your loving heavenly Father—if I were to let you down.

You will see My hand everywhere, in every detail. Know this to be true. My orchestrations of perfection will fill you with overwhelming joy. You will delight in My ways and will be so grateful you waited on Me to work. My ways far surpass those of men and are always worth waiting for.

Joy, My child. Live in My joy and peace and hope. The fulfillment of your hope *is* coming very soon. I love you, Child.

O Sovereign Lord, you have only begun to show your greatness and the strength of your hand to me, your servant. Is there any god in heaven or on earth who can perform such great and mighty deeds as you do?
DEUTERONOMY 3:24, *NLT*

September 3

The trusting heart to Jesus clings, nor any ill forebodes,
But at the cross of Calv'ry sings, "Praise God for lifted loads!"

ELIZA E. HEWITT (1851–1920),
"SINGING I GO"

In Me you have everything you need. Live in that truth today, and don't cling to your "rights," but cling only to Me. That's all that matters. Everything else is secondary. Clinging to Me and letting *Me* provide will free you completely. Shine My light and love today. Let go of petty battles, and let me perfect that which concerns you.

My ways are always best. Rest and relax in My ways, knowing that My unseen plans are so much higher and beyond your knowing. See? You already sense a lifting of that weight. Don't worry about earthly concerns. Simply give them to Me, and see what I will do. You will marvel as My wonders unfold. Great will be your joy.

Allow Me to orchestrate this day. Know above all else that nothing is impossible for Me. Just see what I will do, and rest in complete confidence of who I am. Nothing is too hard, complex or beyond My limitless power. Always remember who I am—the Almighty God—and all fretting will flee.

I love you, My precious child. Watch how I will pour out My love on you today. All is well. All is truly well.

I call heaven and earth as witnesses today against you,
that I have set before you life and death, blessing and cursing; therefore choose
life, that both you and your descendants may live; that you may love the Lord
your God, that you may obey His voice, and that you may cling to Him,
for He is your life and the length of your days.

DEUTERONOMY 30:19-20

The Listening Heart   JUDY GORDON MORROW

September 4

Lord, I need You to be my agenda setter and my schedule maker.

I *will* help you, My child. I will help you to know how to place your priorities regarding your time. Time is My gift to you, a precious commodity, and I give you the prerogative to know how to use it. Yet you are not left to your own wisdom and judgment. I am here to help you in every decision and in every outlay of your time. Trust Me in this. Trust Me in *all* things, My child. I am here to help you in every way. *Nothing* is too small for My watchful eye and care. Bring *all* to Me, and just see what I will do.

I know you are tired. Even now you are fighting sleepiness, and I know you are weary in every other way as well. Don't succumb to despair. I am your God of hope, and despair is not in My vocabulary. Hope is. Joy is. Peace is. But not despair. Nor discouragement. Neither resides in Me.

Begin this day focusing completely on who I am. Look not to past failures or to the overwhelming nature of your tasks, but look upward and only to Me. I will help you. I will multiply your minutes, just as I multiplied the loaves and fish for My needy, hungry children. I know your needs, and I will meet every one as you rely on Me.

Look carefully then how you walk, not as unwise but as wise,
making the best use of the time, because the days are evil.
Therefore do not be foolish, but understand what the will of the Lord is.
EPHESIANS 5:15-17, *ESV*

September 5

Thank You that I serve an all-knowing,
all-wise God who loves me beyond measure.

I do, My child. I love you beyond the scope of your imagination. Even now you are just beginning to tap into My amazing love for you.

As I've told you so many times before, you will know My love like never before when you see the outpouring of blessings from My hand. You will so marvel, Child, as every piece of the puzzle falls into place. It is then all your wonderings and questionings will come to an end as you see My answers—answers that will put to rest every unsettled thought.

Move now in My Spirit. Seek Me for every little thing, and just see how I will answer. I delight in you, My child, and I love to delight you by showing My attentiveness to every little detail of your life. You have learned to see Me in everything, and I will continue to show My love and grace as you see all through My eyes of love for your well-being.

Bask in My love all day today. Rest in My peace. Be filled with My joy, even in the midst of continued waiting. Soon will it end, My child. Your faith I *will* make sight, and you will praise Me all of your days.

I love you, precious child. Forever is My love for you. Live today in an even deeper knowledge of My love for you. *All is well.*

All glory to the only wise God, through Jesus Christ, forever. Amen.
ROMANS 16:27, *NLT*

JUDY GORDON MORROW

September 6

He is always conscious of us, but we need to focus our attention and our consciousness upon him. Then he can whisper to us the love-plans he has for us.

ROSALIND RINKER (1906–2002)

I will answer your situation, My child. I have not forgotten your plight and your struggles, and My answers will soon bring relief. Trust Me. Just trust Me completely.

If only My children would bring everything to Me, then they would see My workings and wonders in every realm. Instead they limit Me by only calling to Me when they have nowhere else to go. I long to be entwined with every aspect of every life. It is then I can pour out My blessings and show who I really am.

That is My desire for you, My dear child—for you to so rest in Me and look to Me for every detail. It is then I can best show My loving care. Often it is in the smallest of details that I can speak the loudest with My care for My children.

Allow Me to guide your day. Don't fret. Just seek Me alone. I will meet your every need. Only I can anticipate what is coming next and best prepare you for My coming answers. Don't worry about outcomes and timings. Simply obey Me. That must come first.

Now go in My peace. Look only to Me. In Me you move and breathe and have your being.[1] I provide breath and life to you so you can bring honor and glory to Me. Continue to wait on Me. Great—oh, so great—will be your joy. Trust Me and Me alone for all things.

But without faith it is impossible to please Him, for he who comes to God must believe that He is, and that He is a rewarder of those who diligently seek Him.

HEBREWS 11:6

Note
1. See Acts 17:28.

September 7

Lay hold on the hope set before you, a hope that is steadfast and sure;
O haste to the blessed Redeemer, the loving, the perfect and pure.

FANNY JANE CROSBY (1820–1915),
"THE HOPE SET BEFORE YOU"

Live in hope this very day. Wear My halo of hope so that others will be heartened by its light and warmed by its glow. In this way you can shine for Me like never before, and I will be glorified. Walk in that hope today, and keep before you a mental image of that halo of hope that I, your Father, have placed on your head. I have done that with great love and affection for you, My child. Wear your halo of hope with much joy, knowing that others will see Me as the Source of its light.

Truly, I do all things well, and I am doing that for you this very day. Look to Me alone, and be aware of My every sweet gesture on your behalf. Continue to see Me in everything, never losing sight of My constant presence and workings in your life. The lack of concrete evidence to your natural eyes means nothing. View all through the eyes of faith I have given, and know that is your true vision—the evidence of things not seen. What is seen by the eyes of faith is more true than any material evidence the world has to offer. Your faith will I honor, My child. Rest in that promise all day today.

I will use all of this for My kingdom purposes. All is well. Yes, all is well.

Let us hold fast the confession of our hope without wavering,
for He who promised is faithful.

HEBREWS 10:23

September 8

Help me to honor You in all that I do.

I will honor that prayer. I will help you in all that is facing you today. I will go before you and prepare the way. Because My Spirit dwells within you, I will fill your mind with My thoughts and ideas. I have been doing that, and I will continue to do so today.

Lean on Me completely. Do not lean on your own understanding. Your understanding is limited and finite. My understanding is complete and knows no boundaries. I will infuse into you My understanding at just the right moments. And when you don't understand, just continue to trust Me. I will not fail you.

I will meet your every need. There is simply nothing to worry about. I am your provider, and I am providing for you even now. Rest in Me, and don't waste even a minute in needless worry. You are My beloved child, and I will take care of you now and always.

Rest in Me, My child. Even in the midst of the busyness of this day, rest in My peace and grace. Let My calm and stillness reign within like the silent rudder beneath a boat, giving direction and steadiness. Leave all to Me. Take joy in the fact that you aren't alone in any of the decision-making or difficult situations. I am with you. I am carrying you. I am your wisdom giver. I love you, My beloved child. Rest totally in My loving arms.

*I will be your God throughout your lifetime—until your hair
is white with age. I made you, and I will care for you.
I will carry you along and save you.*

ISAIAH 46:4, *NLT*

September 9

I know You are working.

Yes, I am, My child. Working in ways you have not yet thought of. Haven't I done that already? I am doing that even now.

Think on all I have done so far, and let that give you great hope. I am continuing to work out My plans in ways that will amaze you. Without a doubt you will see My hand and will know My love like never before. I am the Lover of your soul, and you will know My love in new depth and dimensions.

Now look to Me for everything today. Realize anew the adventure of walking with Me. Do see Me in everything, and thrill to My gestures of love to you. They are everywhere.

Seek Me in all your tasks today. Seek My mind and will in all things. I will make all clear to you, and that will ease the weight of every responsibility. Trust Me to do that in each situation. Offer each one to Me, and I will guide and work in My inimitable way. You just need to rest in Me and allow Me to carry the load.

Go in My peace and joy, and continue to live expectantly. I will honor your faith and trust in Me. Truly, I do all things well. You will soon know that truth like never before. I love you, My child.

They sing the song of Moses, the servant of God, and the song of the Lamb, saying: "Great and marvelous are Your works, Lord God Almighty! Just and true are Your ways, O King of the saints! Who shall not fear You, O Lord, and glorify Your name? For You alone are holy. For all nations shall come and worship before You, for Your judgments have been manifested."

REVELATION 15:3-4

JUDY GORDON MORROW

September 10

Be thankful that God's answers are wiser than your answers.
WILLIAM CULBERTSON (1905–1971)

Waiting on *Me* will always yield the best of My answers. Too often My children take things into their own hands, only to yield undesirable and often disastrous results. And then they wonder where I was in all their efforts. If only they would have waited on Me. I was readying the best of My answers to meet the deepest desires and needs of their hearts.

While I will never abandon My children, at those times I have to abandon the highest plan for another. My love will still shine through, but how much sorrow and despair My children could save themselves if they would wait on Me for My choices and timings in their lives.

You have done that. In spite of years of heartache and loneliness and longings, you have chosen to wait on Me for the best of My answers to your prayers. You will never regret doing that, My child. You will never regret coming to Me first with *everything*—large or small—that is troubling you. In Me is *all* that you need. I will never fail you.

Look to Me for everything today. Rely on Me for every need, and I *will* supply. Trust Me, and I *will* provide. Look only to Me, for I will *not* disappoint you. Just watch and see what I will do. Your joy will know no end.

Show me Your ways, O Lord; teach me Your paths. Lead me in Your truth and teach me, for You are the God of my salvation; on You I wait all the day.
PSALM 25:4-5

September 11

To pray is nothing more involved than to open the door, giving Jesus access to our needs and permitting Him to exercise His own power in dealing with them.

OLE HALLESBY (1879–1961)

Give today to Me. I will help you. I will strengthen you. I will give you wisdom. See Me in everything. I will be ministering to you in ways you have not yet experienced.

You are wise to see Me as the all-creative God. I work in ways not known to man. Trust Me in all My workings. So much is unknown and unseen to My children, but all is known to Me. I move with wisdom and grace and power. Trust My unseen hand, even when you don't understand.

Trust in Me, your all-loving Father, does not require full understanding. It simply requires a yielded heart, a child's hand in Mine, content to go where the Father gently leads. Feel that loving squeeze on your hand, My child. Those nudges that will lead you down paths of righteousness, contentment and joy I alone will satisfy. Discover that truth anew, and be content in Me alone.

Rest in Me. Know My peace beyond all understanding. Seek My face. I am ever here for you, guiding you in My paths, providing My desires for you that will satisfy the deepest longings of your soul. Rest completely in Me. All is well. Your faith shall be made sight.

I love you, My child. Walk in My love today. Let nothing disturb My joy and peace. Remember I am yours and you are Mine.

For by Him all things were created that are in heaven and that are on earth, visible and invisible, whether thrones or dominions or principalities or powers. All things were created through Him and for Him.

COLOSSIANS 1:16

JUDY GORDON MORROW

September 12

There have been many dark moments,
but You have never failed to break through with Your light.

I *am* the light. The light of the world and the light in your heart. It is My light that others see in you, My child. Continue to shine brightly for Me. I will honor you for doing that. My light brings hope to the darkness.

I am working, My child. Never doubt that I am working, even when you see nothing happening. Don't depend on your physical eyes. Look at life with the eyes of your heart. See beyond what others see. See with the discernment of My presence. I make all things clear. Hope only in Me. Know that you can trust Me and the future I have planned for you. It is a future of beauty and joy. You will be amazed, My child.

Hope shines bright. Don't let anything diminish your hope. I will bring all things to pass that I have promised you. I love you, My child. Live in My love and hope and peace and joy today.

For God, who said, "Let there be light in the darkness,"
has made this light shine in our hearts so we could know the glory
of God that is seen in the face of Jesus Christ.

2 CORINTHIANS 4:6, *NLT*

September 13

God's will is delicious; He makes no mistakes.
FRANCES RIDLEY HAVERGAL (1836–1879)

How great will be your joy in so many realms of your life. My workings are broad and all-encompassing and yet also filled with the smallest of details to amaze you with My abundant love and care. You have seen so many times now how I am in the details, and you will be seeing that about Me like never before. It is in the details that you see the depth of My love for you. A love that cares even about the smallest things that concern you.

How can you question a love like that? How can you not see My loving hand? How can you not trust a love that covers every single aspect of your life and leaves you wanting for nothing? You smile at My questions because you know the Truth and Love behind them. You know *Me*. And once you truly know Me, you also know answers that previously eluded you. To know Me is to know My heart of love for you. A heart that only desires My best for My children.

We love Him because He first loved us.
1 JOHN 4:19

JUDY GORDON MORROW

September 14

Let us not be surprised when we have to face difficulties.
When the wind blows hard on a tree, the roots stretch and grow the stronger.
Let it be so with us. Let us not be weaklings,
yielding to every wind that blows, but strong in spirit to resist.

AMY CARMICHAEL (1867–1951)

A heart that only desires My best for My children is why you have clung to Me all these years. That's why you have believed Me and all I have spoken to you. That's why you are resting in Me right now. Because you *know* Me. And you know you can trust Me. Getting to this place of trust hasn't been easy, I know, but it has been worthwhile, has it not?

I have grown you from a sapling blown by every wind to a strong oak that can withstand the winds. Someday, under My loving care and wisdom, you will be a towering oak for My kingdom from years of looking alone to Me and sinking your roots into the soil of My unchanging love. All of this is part of My kingdom plan for you—to use you for My glory and for your good.

Delight now in this very day. View every moment as a gift to treasure and not as simply time to be frittered away. Time is My precious gift to My children, and you are wise to seek Me for its best usage. Time makes up the seasons of your life, and each season teems with My purposes. Just stay close to Me, hear My voice, and you will be satisfied in every season as you follow Me. This is the way of joy and peace and contentment.

They will be called oaks of righteousness,
the planting of the Lord, to display his glory.

ISAIAH 61:3, *NRSV*

September 15

Redeem these years for Your glory.

You know I will. Every sigh, tear and sorrow hasn't gone unnoticed. Rather, they have become the rich soil of your heart—a soil that will yield a fruitful harvest for My kingdom. I waste nothing, and these times of seeming desolation will be transformed into an oasis of My healing grace. Like springtime in the desert, new life will burst forth and bring glory to Me.

You are seeing Me at work everywhere, and you are right to do so. My workings are clear to those who have eyes to behold My wonders. The smallest details are magnified under the lens of My love and grace. When you see My workings and wonders, you can better see and know Me.

Nothing is done carelessly by My hand, but with great consideration and purpose. That's why I delight when My children see the depth of My love even in the seemingly little things I do for them. You have long seen and known Me in this way, and you know the doubling of joy when we share those times together.

You know what I long for, Lord; you hear my every sigh.
PSALM 38:9, *NLT*

September 16

Each time, before you intercede, be quiet first,
and worship God in His glory. Think of what He can do,
and how He delights to hear the prayers of His redeemed people.

ANDREW MURRAY (1828–1917)

Today is another opportunity to see and know Me in a fresh way. Keep your eyes clear and your mind unclouded by looking to Me alone. In Me you have all the wisdom and insights you will need. I am more than sufficient for your every situation. And I delight in delighting you with the sweetness of My presence, laced with surprises of My grace.

You sense My smile even now as you wonder like an expectant child what My surprises will be, and you are smiling with Me. Oh, the sweetness of communion and companionship that you and I share! I long for that for every one of My dearly beloved children. Nothing can be substituted for this divine delight between the Father and His child.

Pray that more of My children will know the sweetness of time spent with Me and the love feast that is just waiting for them to enjoy with Me. You know it is the most satisfying time this side of heaven, and you will be conveying that to others like never before. Beckon My children to come to Me. I am waiting to welcome them with open arms of love beyond all loves. I am waiting for them to come and be satisfied.

You satisfy me more than the richest feast.
I will praise you with songs of joy.

PSALM 63:5, *NLT*

September 17

Be still, and know that I am God.
FROM PSALM 46:10

You are right to be still before me. In stillness I can speak. You are worried over so much this morning, My child. But has anything changed? Remember, I do not change. Jesus Christ—the same yesterday, today and forever.[1]

My love toward you is not capricious or inconsistent. It is true, steadfast and loyal. It is the never-failing rock beneath you. Know that My love is sure and unwavering. Trust Me completely, My child.

The way will soon become clear. Rest in that assurance, knowing that it comes from your Father who loves you above all others. I understand your confusion, but I don't want you to remain there.

I will bring you through this fog of uncertainty, and you will soon see all things clearly. I am the Father, and I know what's best for each one of My children. Leave that for Me to decide. Your only concern is to trust Me. Remember, I wouldn't have brought you this far only to abandon you now.

What I am going to do in your life will speak to many. Hold on to Me, cling to Me, until I get you there. Let nothing come between us—no doubt, no reservations, no wonderings. Just trust and believe Me completely.

Remain in My truth all day. I do not change. Don't allow doubt to tarnish your day in any way. Believe only Me. I love you, My child. Rest in My love.

The Lord will not reject his people; he will not abandon his special possession.
PSALM 94:14, *NLT*

Note
1. See Hebrews 13:8.

JUDY GORDON MORROW

September 18

*Live near to God, and so all things will appear to you
little in comparison with eternal realities.*

ROBERT MURRAY MCCHEYNE (1813–1843)

You are learning My heart, My child. You are realizing My tender love toward you. Speak My love to others. Make sure all your words are first dipped in My love before being spoken. That will save you from many regrets.

Live in My hope today. It is truly My gift to you. It cushions your pain and loneliness. Continue to pray expectantly and with much hope. I will honor your prayers. I will honor you, My child. I will give you the desires of your heart. All the years of pain and sadness will fall away, and all will become new and sweet.

Look to those days of joy while living in My presence today. You know the sweetness of My presence like never before. Never take these times for granted, but bask in who I am and how much I love you. You are realizing more and more My love for you. Continue to plumb the depths of My love. You can never know its full depth, and you can never go beyond My love for you. It is infinite, limitless, and it is yours.

Try anew to grasp the immensity of My love for you. That is key to everything else. Knowing My love enables you to trust Me completely. Immerse yourself in My love, and see the difference it makes. All hindrances to faith will simply fall away when you take Me at My word: I love you, My child. I will always love you, no matter what.

*Though I speak with the tongues of men and of angels, but have not love,
I have become sounding brass or a clanging cymbal.*

1 CORINTHIANS 13:1

September 19

Thank You, Jesus, for interceding for me.

All is well. I have heard your requests, and I will honor your heart. Long have you sought and waited on Me, and now I will be releasing from My hands My long-held answers for you. Yes, rejoice even now, knowing the truth and imminence of My words. Your wonder will never cease.

I am going before you today, just as you requested. Envision Me with you, partaking in the conversations and bestowing My peace. Delight in My peace and dispense My joy to everyone I place in your path today. Just be who you are in Me, and I will use you in ways you won't even be aware of. My peace will be the indicator of My workings.

Even now you are experiencing My peace in new measure, yet another gift from My hand. The enemy has been trying to derail you from My path of peace with thoughts that aren't from Me. Keep your mind stayed on Me with such constancy that My peace will pave each step before you with My love and grace. Walk in that way of peace today, and know anew the wisdom of My workings and the surety of My peace for you. Again, all is well. Rest in My words of truth to you, My child, and be blessed.

Who then is the one who condemns? No one.
Christ Jesus who died—more than that, who was raised to life—
is at the right hand of God and is also interceding for us.
ROMANS 8:34, *NIV*

JUDY GORDON MORROW

September 20

You told me You would rescue me, and I believe You.

Yes, I will rescue you in just the nick of time. I will deliver you out of your situation now into new days of joy and satisfaction. You will marvel at the workings of My hand. Never doubt that I will do all that I have been telling you.

Live all day in My hope and grace. Know who I am—your Fortress, your Rock, your Father of love. The Father who gives good and perfect gifts will not withhold anything good from you. The key is to wait for Me and My timings. You will never regret doing that. In the waiting, abide in Me, rest in Me. My peace will cover and protect you. Let it wrap around you, and know that all is well.

See Me in everything. I am everywhere, but My children often don't see Me. Seeing Me, looking for Me, expecting Me in the unexpected will add a richness to your walk with Me. You know that, but continue to keep a clear vision of who I am and what I can do. Then I can teach you more and more. I delight in doing that.

Go in My peace, My child. All is well. I will fulfill My promises to you. Continue to believe and hope. I will not disappoint you.

I love you, Child.

You are my strength; I wait for you to rescue me,
for you, O God, are my fortress.
PSALM 59:9, *NLT*

September 21

Think of your place and privilege in Christ, and expect great things!
ANDREW MURRAY (1828–1917)

You won't believe what I'm going to do. So great will be your wonder and joy. All these years of waiting and pain will remain as only a shadow—a shadow covered by My love and grace.

Do follow My nudges today. Do be My light and love to everyone you see. Do rest in My promises to you and in who I am. There is not a more solid foundation than Me. Dwell on who I am—Truth, Hope, Love—and see like never before the surety of Me as your resting place.

Now go and put feet to your faith. See how much has already been accomplished, and see *how much more* I will help you accomplish today. Not by might, not by power, but by My Spirit, says the Lord. Indeed, I am saying that to you today. Know anew the truth of that promise, and repeat it often. Not by your might, not by your power, but by the might and strength of My Spirit within you will all My purposes be accomplished. You will see that like never before. Rejoice even now and sing My praises. Praises of love and joy.

I love you, My child. Live in My love today. It is yours.

So he answered and said to me: "This is the word of the Lord to Zerubbabel: 'Not by might nor by power, but by My Spirit,' says the Lord of hosts."
ZECHARIAH 4:6

September 22

I was reflecting on how God had provided for me in recent months,
when I prayed, "Look at all that. Look at everything."

Yes, look at everything, My child. How can you not help seeing My hand everywhere? That's why I encourage My children to remember My wonders. What I have done in the past is the foundation on which to rest your present concerns. Keeping your eyes on Me and My faithfulness gives you peace and stability for each new challenge and trial. I am in the midst of all things, the Rock that holds steady and sure, even in the midst of life's fiercest storms.

Rest in Me today. Rely fully on Me, the Way, the Truth, and the Life. Dwell on the richness of those words, and realize nothing else is needed. In Me is truth—untarnished and pure truth. I am the Way—walk in Me. I am your Life itself. In Me is true satisfaction and contentment. True rest for every wandering soul. In My heart is your home, the place you belong. Live in My heart of love, and your restlessness will flee.

Dwell in who I am, and you will have everything you need. I am the eternal resting place for your restless soul. No substitution can replace My love-shaped peace for your soul. I long for each of My children to find their rest in Me. To dwell in My habitat of love designed just for them. This is the key to true freedom. "You shall know the truth, and the truth shall set you free."

To the Jews who had believed him, Jesus said,
"If you hold to my teaching, you are really my disciples.
Then you will know the truth, and the truth will set you free."

JOHN 8:31-32, *NIV*

September 23

O teach Me, Lord, that I may teach the precious things Thou dost impart;
And wing my words, that they may reach, the hidden depths of many a heart.

FRANCES RIDLEY HAVERGAL (1836–1879),
"LORD, SPEAK TO ME"

Continue to seek Me and learn of Me. I will quench a heart that thirsts after Me. I will continue to teach you My truths to pass on to others. This is all part of My plan. Great will be your joy when you learn of all My workings. That joy will never end.

I will redeem this time spent with Me this morning. It is never spent in vain. It is a daily investment that will yield rich benefits in the depths of your heart and in the daily living of your life.

Remember all day today, My child, how deeply I love you. The vastness of My love you will never be able to comprehend. It is an ever-flowing wellspring from My Father heart to your precious heart. I desire for you to know Me and My love like never before so that the overflow will bring many to Me. This is My purpose for you—to be a vessel of My love and joy in order to draw many to Me. I am preparing the way for that to happen even now. I have deemed all this to be so. You will soon know it. Go in My peace.

O God, You are my God; early will I seek You; my soul thirsts for You;
my flesh longs for You in a dry and thirsty land where there is no water.
So I have looked for You in the sanctuary, to see Your power and Your glory.
Because Your lovingkindness is better than life, my lips shall praise You.

PSALM 63:1-3

September 24

Thank You for every opportunity to speak Your words of hope and truth.

I will be giving you more and more opportunities to speak My life-giving truth to others. More and more will your influence for Me increase, as you continue to seek Me alone. You are living in a soul-thirsty world. Give freely of My living water so that those parched souls can find refreshment in Me alone. You can be their conduit of My living water. It is My children I use to bear My truth to a world teeming with lies. Be filled with Me, the Truth, and you will be well prepared to speak My truth with love.

Even today you don't know what opportunities I will be bringing your way. But do know you can count on Me for the words—words that will flow out of an obedient heart. There's no need to worry about the right words as long as your heart is aligned with Mine. You obey, and I will convey My truth to the heart of your listener. See how that takes the burden off you? You need only to obey by opening your mouth to speak the words I will give you. And, oh, the joy you will know in obedience that will yield eternal results.

> *Instead, we will speak the truth in love,*
> *growing in every way more and more like Christ,*
> *who is the head of his body, the church.*
> EPHESIANS 4:15, *NLT*

September 25

*Fear not because your prayer is stammering, your words feeble,
and your language poor. Jesus can understand you.*

J. C. RYLE (1816–1900)

There is no need for fear of any kind. Don't fear for lack of words. Don't fear rejection. Don't fear anything except disobedience, which will stifle My truth and dispel your joy. My truth bespeaks My love, which opens the floodgates for joy. You know the truth of these words, My child, so never allow fear to strangle My words, but instead be that clear channel for My life-giving waters of love and hope.

It is good that you came to drink of My living water this morning. A stagnant pool can't overflow with sparkling water. Neither can you give out of an empty reservoir. This daily infilling is crucial not only for you but also for every life that touches yours. Everyone benefits from spending time in My presence and being filled with My fullness. In Me you lack nothing.

Live in My abundance all day today, drawing out what you need for every moment. This is the way of living satisfied in Me. Truly, I am your only satisfaction, as there is none like Me. Drink and be satisfied, My child. I love you.

*On the last day, that great day of the feast, Jesus stood and cried out, saying,
"If anyone thirsts, let him come to Me and drink. He who believes in Me,
as the Scripture has said, out of his heart will flow rivers of living water."*

JOHN 7:37-38

JUDY GORDON MORROW

September 26

Communicate Your truth to me all day long, dear Jesus.

I will do that, My child. Truth is who I am, and in knowing Me you know truth for every realm of your life. Allow My truth to permeate your vision and your outlook. View life through My lens of truth, and you will see all with new clarity and perception.

Your perspective of people and situations will be sharpened because of My truth that cuts through deception and appearances. I will give you the ability to see beyond the exterior and will illumine what is normally hidden and unknown. This will be My continued gift to you that you may see all things clearly.

Joy in My every gift of grace and mercy to you today. Know the sweetness of My presence, and look fully to Me. You are My beloved child, and I will not fail you. Just see what I will do. I love you, Child. Live in the warmth of My love today.

Thomas said to Him, "Lord, we do not know where You are going, and how can we know the way?" Jesus said to him, "I am the way, the truth, and the life. No one comes to the Father except through Me."

JOHN 14:5-6

September 27

I would maintain that thanks are the highest form of thought,
and that gratitude is happiness doubled by wonder.

G. K. CHESTERTON (1874–1936)

Gather strength and hope by continuing to remember My every wonder in your life. Wonders of hope, provisions and joy. Wonders of promises confirmed time and again. Don't fail to remember My many wonders in your life, and praise Me for each one. Praise lines the heart with thanksgiving and provides a prepared receptacle for the outpouring of My blessings.

View each word of your praise to Me as a downy soft feather lifted up to Me and then drifting back down to pillow your heart with the softness of My Spirit. Each feather of praise plays a role in preparing your heart to be fully ready to receive the outpouring of My blessings. Whisper My praise, sing My praise—yes, even shout My praise at times—and the benefit of such praise will return to keep your heart soft toward Me, receptive and eager to hear My words of truth and love.

While your praise blesses Me, it will in turn bless you, My child, in the continuum of My love. Praise Me like never before, and envision those feathers of praise blessing not only My heart but also yours. Praise from a sincere heart always benefits both the giver and receiver. That is also true in the heavenly realm, and now you know that for sure. Take that truth, and wield it wisely and gently for My kingdom.

Now enjoy this day. Trust Me to do *all* I have promised you—for your good and My glory. Now arise rejoicing, and know *all is well*.

Shout joyfully to the Lord, all the earth;
break forth in song, rejoice, and sing praises.

PSALM 98:4

JUDY GORDON MORROW

September 28

A Spirit-led life. That is what I want.

And that is what you shall have. Those who seek Me will find Me. Seek Me, My child, in every facet of your life, and I will make clear to you My desires for you. You are doing the right thing by seeking Me first thing in the morning, but also seek Me continually throughout your day. I alone can give you the most satisfying life. I alone know most what you need.

Wouldn't the One who designed you *best know* every intricacy of your mind, body and soul? Thus, I will attend to all of your needs and desires based on My full knowledge of you.

Is it not best to follow the One who has known the end since the beginning? Who sees every juncture and pitfall and can best guide you on your very individual path? My guidance for you is based not only on My deep and complete knowledge of you but also on My incomparable love for you, My child. Why would you want to resist a love that desires only your very best? A love that laid down His life for you in order to give you the most glorious life ever. Why would you not desire an all-knowing and all-loving Guide such as that? A Guide who will never lie to you, since only truth ever comes from His heart and lips. I am the way, the truth and the life.[1]

And you will seek Me and find Me,
when you search for Me with all your heart.
JEREMIAH 29:13

Note
1. See John 14:6.

September 29

Prayer is repeating the victor's name [Jesus]
into the ears of Satan and insisting on his retreat.

S. D. GORDON (1859-1936)

When you dwell on the truth of who I am, then every ploy of the enemy will be destroyed. He is a liar and manipulator, and *no* truth is in him—not even a shred. *Not one thing* he says is trustworthy or true. Protect your heart and deafen your ears to his every whisper of deceit, and instead embrace Me and My words of truth and hope and love for you.

The contrast between Satan and Me, your loving Father, has never been clearer to you—like black and white—and you need to maintain that image in your mind and heart. In the devil—and his demons of worry, unbelief, pride, self-sufficiency and sin of every kind—is only darkness. Why try to walk on a darkened, shadowy path with a guide who has only your destruction in mind, when you can be guided by the God who loves you beyond your ability to comprehend such an unconditional love?

When you choose Me and My ways, you choose Life and Light for your path. Yes, the path often lies shrouded in shadows, but I will give light enough for just the next step. That's all that is necessary for you to know—where to place your feet for the next step—and *that* I will provide for you.

Jesus said to them, . . . "You are of your father the devil,
and the desires of your father you want to do.
He was a murderer from the beginning,
and does not stand in the truth, because there is no truth in him.
When he speaks a lie, he speaks from his own resources,
for he is a liar and the father of it."

JOHN 8:42,44

September 30

When we walk with the Lord in the light of His Word,
what a glory He sheds on our way!
While we do His good will, He abides with us still,
and with all who will trust and obey.

JOHN H. SAMMIS (1846–1919),
"TRUST AND OBEY"

This is the way of walking by faith, and there is no better way. It is the way of knowing Me and My love for you and trusting Me and My love for you, even when you can't see beyond today. I can, and I see and know the glorious plans I have for you as you continue to walk with Me, one step at a time. There is no other way so satisfying and sure.

Implant these words of truth to you in your mind and heart, and water them with My Word and time spent with Me. Then just see how that truth—My truth—will continue to grow in you until it comes forth into a magnificent harvest.

Look only to Me, My child. Do not allow the *enemy* of your soul to come near with his lies and troubling thoughts. The word "enemy" strikes you like never before, and you are wise to realize its impact. No enemy ever desires good of any kind but is set on wreaking havoc and destruction.

In contrast, remember who I am to you, even when you don't understand My ways and timings. Rest in who I am, trust the One who loves you beyond all loves, and you will find nothing else is necessary. Drink deeply of My words of hope and love to you today, and know *like never before* that *all is well*. I love you, Child—always.

We know that we are of God, and the whole world
lies under the sway of the wicked one.

1 JOHN 5:19

October

Jesus, Jesus, Jesus,
The precious name of Jesus

The name that dispels all fears
The name that dries my tears

The name that bids me rest
The name that gives His best

The name I love and adore
The name that calms the roar

No other name do I desire
No other name do I require

Only Jesus . . . precious Jesus

October 1

I so desire You and what You want, Lord.

And that you shall have. What I have ordained I will accomplish. Do you believe Me in this? I know you have waited long—much longer than you ever dreamed possible—but the waiting will only increase the sweetness of My answers. You will indeed see that My timings are perfect, and you will rejoice from a wellspring of joy that only years of tears could produce. A wellspring fed by tears yields the sweetest and most satisfying of joys.

You have waited on Me, and I will answer. Do you not see how much more honoring it will be to Me that you have been willing to wait all these years for My best for you? Prepare in My power and grace for that most amazing of times. A time ordained by Me and fulfilled by Me. You will be amazed beyond words.

Follow My every leading today. Work hard with a thankful heart full of praise to Me. I will honor you for that.

Don't allow the enemy to whisper his lies. Shun him. Flee him. Bind him in My name. Seek *My* face, the One who loves you beyond measure. Forever will I love you. Forever will we rejoice together over what I will do for you.

Even the youths shall faint and be weary,
and the young men shall utterly fall,
but those who wait on the Lord shall renew their strength;
they shall mount up with wings like eagles,
they shall run and not be weary, they shall walk and not faint.

ISAIAH 40:30-31

JUDY GORDON MORROW

October 2

Thank You for Your blessings.

My blessings are all from My hand. Learn to trust My hand, My child. My hand and My timings. Trust before you see. Do know My ways and thoughts are higher than yours. I see the whole picture, every intricate detail, and truly I do all things well.

Enjoy your day today. Let reminders of answered prayer give you renewed hope of what I still will do. You are My child, and I love you with an everlasting love. Trust in that love. You have been right to realize My efforts in leading you more fully into the truth about My love. All My children need to know the extent, the incredible depth, of My love. Tell them, My child. I will give you many opportunities to do that.

I will bless your day. Trust Me only. I am working on your behalf, My child. You are My beloved child. Never forget how much I love you.

For I, the Lord your God, will hold your right hand,
saying to you, "Fear not, I will help you."

ISAIAH 41:13

October 3

I pray You will give me clear guidance today.

You will know. All will become clear. Just recall all the other times I have guided you, and know I will do the same this time. Be at rest and open to My leadings. Rest in Me yields an entry point where I can make My desires known. Rest is the state of the soul fully trusting in Me.

Enjoy *this* day. Don't let the concerns of the upcoming days rob you of the sweet joys I have for you today. I am ever present in every day, and nothing occurs without My knowledge and the working of My will. Rest in that sure word from Me today, My child, and be at peace.

So don't worry about these things, saying, "What will we eat?
What will we drink? What will we wear?" These things dominate the thoughts
of unbelievers, but your heavenly Father already knows all your needs.
Seek the Kingdom of God above all else, and live righteously, and he will
give you everything you need. So don't worry about tomorrow, for tomorrow
will bring its own worries. Today's trouble is enough for today.

MATTHEW 6:31-34, *NLT*

October 4

In the darkest of nights cling to the assurance that God loves you,
that He always has advice for you, a path that you can tread and a
solution to your problem—and you will experience that which you believe.
God never disappoints anyone who places his trust in Him.

BASILEA SCHLINK (1904–2001)

Today is My gift to you, yet another uncharted day. Live in the sweetness
and power of My Spirit, and know that all is well. Step by step I am
leading you, and with each step you are that much closer to My promised new days. New days of incredible and wondrous joy. You will never
get over the abundance of joy I will be giving you. Rejoice even now.

Look only to Me, Child. Time and again have I spoken that to
you because it is so key. When your eyes are fixed on Me, they won't
focus on things that will cloud and hinder your faith—your ability to
believe Me even when things look absolutely impossible. By looking
to Me alone, I elevate your faith to the heavenlies, where My kingdom
purposes dwell.

Trust Me for everything. Rest in Me and My loving care today. I will
not fail you. I am God, and I don't have the capability to fail you. Go
in the peaceful assurance of those words to you—My words from My
heart of love to you, My child. All is well. All is truly well, in spite of
how circumstances may appear. I am in all and above all, and all *is* well.

God is not a man, so he does not lie. He is not human,
so he does not change his mind. Has he ever spoken and failed to act?
Has he ever promised and not carried it through?

NUMBERS 23:19, *NLT*

October 5

Lord, I have much to do today. Make me wise in all my planning.

I will help you know what to do. And I will bless your efforts. Do look to Me, and I will answer. I do *all* things well. You can bring everything to Me, knowing that I will help you in each task. Would a father turn away his trusting child? Never will I turn you away, My child. Every concern of yours is My concern. Just give everything to Me, and see what I will do.

You are right to continue to hope in Me. Hope has no time limit, no deadline, no ending point. As I am eternal, so is the hope that I give. Hope in Me, and your future is secure, grounded in the Rock that cannot be moved.

The world and its values are constant shifting sands. There is no solid foothold in anything the world has to offer. Yet in Me, your Rock, there is surety and strength and solid hope. The darkness and shadows may surround you, but you are anchored in Me, the One who never changes: Jesus Christ, the same yesterday, today, and forever.[1] Dwell on these truths today. Dwell on who I am. Know that My promises are sure and steadfast. I will not fail you.

I am the Lord, and I do not change.
MALACHI 3:6, *NLT*

Note
1. See Hebrews 13:8.

October 6

This is my Father's world. He shines in all that's fair;
In the rustling grass I hear Him pass; He speaks to me ev'rywhere.

MALTBIE D. BABCOCK (1858–1901),
"THIS IS MY FATHER'S WORLD"

Revel in My love and in the beauty of My world. Treasure each gift of love from My hand. Know My ways as ways of peace and joy. Even when the path is dark and steep, I bring you My peace and joy. The world cannot duplicate those, nor can it take them away from you. Lean wholly on Me, and you will know the steadfast comfort of My peace and joy.

Live in My hope all day today. Let nothing detract from My measureless hope, My child. It is My gift to you. Let it abound and overflow like never before. You will soon know My plans for you, and they are good.

I love you, My child, with a never-ending, all-encompassing love. Never doubt or question the fullness and depth of My love for you. Joy in My love, and out of the overflow, give My love to others. They need My love so desperately. Be My life-giving vessel to pour out My love to them. I will let you know how to do that. Just listen and follow My nudges.

Your day is already filled with My blessings. Continue to enjoy each gift from My hand, and live in hope all day today. I will bless you.

A new command I give you: Love one another.
As I have loved you, so you must love one another.

JOHN 13:34, *NIV*

October 7

I know You will give me wisdom.

I will. That's who I am—the Giver of true wisdom. I always give wisdom to My children who seek it from Me. I am in all of this. Fret about nothing, and just allow Me to lead the way. All is well.

Hear My words to you again, My child. *All is well.* Don't let anxiety rob you of the joy of this beautiful day I have planned for you. Right now you see gray outside, and your concerns are coloring the inside of you with the same color of dreariness. Do not give Satan that kind of control.

Instead focus on every truth I have ever spoken to you—and there are many—and see the grayness dissipate in light of My truth and love. My truth always breaks through the darkness. Believe that for *every* area of your life, and know indeed that My truth will be setting you free into new days of freedom and joy. My truth shines light into darkness, revealing all. Pray for that in every aspect of your life, My child, and then rejoice at the outcomes. Truth frees. I will hear and answer your prayers.

Go now, bathed in My truth, My presence, My peace. My joy and love. The most beautiful qualities you can know in this world come only from Me. Others will notice and see the difference I make. Joy in being My much beloved child today. I love you more than you can fathom.

O Lord, you are my lamp. The Lord lights up my darkness.
2 SAMUEL 22:29, *NLT*

October 8

Children of the heavenly King, as we journey let us sing;
Sing our Savior's worthy praise, glorious in His works and ways.
Lord! obediently we'll go, gladly leaving all below;
Only Thou our leader be, and we still will follow Thee.

JOHN CRENNICK (1718–1755),
"CHILDREN OF THE HEAVENLY KING"

I will go before you. You are My child, and I will lead you. That is one of the reasons My children don't trust Me—they don't want to consider themselves as children. They want control. They are missing the joy of an all-wise, all-loving Father taking care of them.

You understand and know the joy of that, especially after this past year. That is what you need to share with My children. I love them completely, and I only want their good. They are My creation, and I love them like no other.

About that time the disciples came to Jesus and asked,
"Who is greatest in the Kingdom of Heaven?" Jesus called a little child to him
and put the child among them. Then he said, "I tell you the truth, unless you
turn from your sins and become like little children, you will never get into the
Kingdom of Heaven. So anyone who becomes as humble as this little child is
the greatest in the Kingdom of Heaven."

MATTHEW 18:1-4, NLT

October 9

Pain creates depth in God's children.
Pain, sorrow and suffering will never yield a shallow life
or one devoid of deep compassion and understanding.

JGM

Embrace pain, allow Me to use it, and I will provide an abundant harvest of righteousness—in your life and in the lives of those you touch for Me.

Pain breaks up the soil of indifference, self-centeredness and pride. It is My tool, but I wield it with love and care. Like a surgeon who cuts away at that which destroys health, I will prune those things that keep you from enjoying the abundant life I have promised you. Fear not the pruning, but welcome My all-knowing, all-loving hand on your life. Truly, I do all things well and all out of pure love for My children.

Rest in the assurance and peace of My perfect love for you. Rest in the surety of My Word. Rest in who I am—the Father who loves you with a love like no other. I *am* Love.

I am the true vine, and my Father is the vinegrower.
He removes every branch in me that bears no fruit.
Every branch that bears fruit he prunes to make it bear more fruit.
You have already been cleansed by the word
that I have spoken to you.

JOHN 15:1-3, *NRSV*

October 10

Thank You for being my strength.

I *am* your strength. Depend on no other. You will accomplish all that is necessary. I will see to that as you trust in Me. Remember, My strength is made perfect in weakness. Let Me show My strength through you, My child. I will not fail you in this.

The joy of the Lord *is* your strength. Radiate My joy today. Give all glory to Me.

Depend on Me completely. I will help you. Do not let the enemy discourage you in any way. Remember, you are *My* child. Don't let a stranger, a foe, distract or defeat you. You are Mine, My child. Mine. Think on that. You're the child of the King! All My riches and treasures are also yours. Draw on that truth all day today. I will supply all your needs according to My riches.

You are My beloved child. What is there to fear? Absolutely nothing. I hold all in My hands. I do all things well—perfectly. I will never fail you. Rest in all that I have told you. It is truth. I love you, My child.

Therefore be imitators of God, as beloved children,
and live in love, as Christ loved us and gave himself up for us,
a fragrant offering and sacrifice to God.

EPHESIANS 5:1-2, *NRSV*

October 11

Praise and prayer. Trust and thanksgiving.

Incorporate all of those into your day, and see the difference I will make. Now go in My peace and *My* ways—ways so beyond your knowing and your imagination—and *be blessed.* Live in the state of feeling blessed, and that mindset will reverberate with prayer and praise and with trust and thanksgiving.

I am the Author of all things good, and even now I am writing your good story for you. I am far from the final chapter, as I have so many new things to write between now and then. Look forward to what I am penning for your story, and revel in what I am writing even today.

All is well, Child. Rest in who I am, and know anew all *is* well.

He has given me a new song to sing, a hymn of praise to our God.
Many will see what he has done and be amazed.
They will put their trust in the Lord.

PSALM 40:3, *NLT*

October 12

I pray for Your wisdom and grace today.

My wisdom and grace *are* yours, My child. They are some of the benefits of knowing Me. Think of it, My child. You know Me, the One who made you and the One who loves you best. No one will ever love you like I do.

I am teaching you many things right now: I am sufficient for all things. I will never leave you. My ways are not your ways. I can be trusted completely. You are My beloved child. I love you with an everlasting love. You need never doubt or question My love, My child. It is ever present. *I* am ever present. I will not fail you.

Rest in the truth of all these wonderful promises. Let nothing disturb your peace in Me. I *am* your peace. The pain you are experiencing will not last forever. Yet remember it so you can show compassion when others feel that heaviness, that searing pain, that dull ache. Like you, for them it will be for only a season. It grows My children closer to Me.

Oh, My child, delight in My love today. I am your perfect Father, and I do all things well—beyond what you can even imagine. You have yet to see that in this season of your life. But you *will* see that, My child. You will see and be amazed. Great will be your joy. *Great* will be your joy.

Let the word of Christ dwell in you richly in all wisdom,
teaching and admonishing one another in psalms and hymns and
spiritual songs, singing with grace in your hearts to the Lord.
COLOSSIANS 3:16

October 13

Fear is born of Satan, and if we would only take time to think a moment
we would see that everything Satan says is founded upon a falsehood.

A. B. SIMPSON (1843-1919)

Child, all is well. I know all these problems are frustrating to you, but you are right to see them for what they are—tactics of the enemy to cause you to despair. Instead, do use them as vehicles to show My grace and care. I will take care of each one as you turn them over to Me. I am your loving Father and nothing is beyond My sight or My control. Rest in Me and know My peace. I am with you, and I know your every concern.

You are My beloved child, and I know the plans I have for you. Plans for My purposes for My people. Look only to Me, and watch My wonders unfold. Pray continually and believe unceasingly. I am at work, and all things are in My hands. Trust Me completely, and see what I will do.

It is good you spent this time with Me. Now you know a new sense of My calm and peace, a new awareness of My presence and that all is truly well. Coming to Me first in the day will always yield benefits, both seen and unseen. Give all to Me each morning, and you will only rejoice in the evening when you see what I have done.

Rest in your loving Father's arms, My precious child. You are loved beyond measure, and you will soon know My love like never before. Take comfort and joy in all I have spoken to you.

For surely I know the plans I have for you, says the Lord,
plans for your welfare and not for harm,
to give you a future with hope.

JEREMIAH 29:11, *NRSV*

The Listening Heart JUDY GORDON MORROW

October 14

I read from my prayer journal of August 2001,
"Your faith frees up My power to act,"
and God resonated His words within me.

Your faith does indeed free up My power to work. Your lack of faith—your doubt—restrains My hand. Yes, it is a mystery to you, I know, but this you can know for sure: there is a powerful link between your faith and My power. Think of it like an electric line strung from the source of power to your home. As long as there is connection, you have electric power for everything you need.

Think of your faith as that needed electric line. When there are gaps caused by doubts, then My power no longer has the "line" to flow to you. Your simple, childlike faith provides the necessary channel for Me to flow My answers of love to you.

I honor faith. I honor those who honor Me. You have seen that time and again in the lives of others and in your own life. Now get ready to see it again, My child. Extend that unbroken line of faith to Me, and just see what I *will* do. Blessings will flow beyond your imaginings.

Now move in the might of My Spirit today. Continue to keep that mental image of your faith being that unbroken line along which I will flow My power to bring about My incredible answers of joy for you. That time is amazingly soon, My child. You have waited, you have believed Me, and *now* I can unleash My powerful answers of love.

And my speech and my preaching were not with persuasive words of human
wisdom, but in demonstration of the Spirit and of power, that your faith
should not be in the wisdom of men but in the power of God.

1 CORINTHIANS 2:4-5

October 15

Lord, forgive me. I don't know why I've been struggling so much lately.

The enemy of your soul is doing all he can to defeat you—to have you bow down to despair. He knows what a powerful force you are and will be in My hands because of the plans I have for you. He is using the delay of My plans to bring doubt, and you simply can't listen to him.

Picture yourself wielding a sword of truth that is gleaming with My light and power. Dressed in the armor I give you, including the shield of faith, see yourself fending off every lie and falsehood the enemy hurls your way. His deceit is always destroyed by My truth. See the shards of his lies crumbled at your feet, turning into dust as you walk on them, crushing each one.

The light of My truth will always vanquish the darkness of his lies. In Me and My Word you have everything you need to defend yourself against the evil one. Out of his mouth comes evil in every form. Keep your mind and heart guarded by My Spirit and cloaked in My truth so that his fiery darts will fall useless at your feet—failing to penetrate in any way.

Dwell in My words of truth to you today. Don't let the enemy dislodge one brick of truth with his scheming, conniving ways. He's a trickster and cannot be trusted at all. Banish him each time with the sword of truth I showed you, and step forward, even today, in total victory.

Therefore take up the whole armor of God, that you may be able to withstand in the evil day, and having done all, to stand . . . above all, taking the shield of faith with which you will be able to quench all the fiery darts of the wicked one.

EPHESIANS 6:13,16

　JUDY GORDON MORROW

October 16

Thank You for this quiet early morning time with You.

It is My gift to you—a gift with far-reaching benefits. As you come before Me with a heart seeking Mine, then I can transmit from My heart to yours exactly what you will need for this very day. Every day has its different needs and yearnings, and I know each one for every day of your life.

But today is the day I am preparing you for now, and I will also prepare you for everything it has to offer. That's why this time with Me is so vital—to equip and strengthen you for the events of this very day. Look only to Me for how to live this day, and I will be more than your sufficiency. So much more, even, as you trust Me and allow Me to be all to you. There is no insufficiency when I am all to you.

Think of all the times I have met your needs in ways you didn't expect. Place that template of My loving care for you over this very day, and know that all is well. Know My love never fails. Know My care never diminishes. Know My heart toward you is always true and pure and overflowing with compassion. In knowing Me you can face any day with utmost confidence and abounding peace. These are My gifts to you as My child, just waiting to be taken from the loving hand of your Father.

Not that we are sufficient of ourselves to think of anything as being from ourselves, but our sufficiency is from God.

2 CORINTHIANS 3:5

October 17

Lord, please go before me today.

I am doing that even now. I transcend time, so while I am with you this very moment, I am also in your future, preparing the path you will be walking on. Take great comfort in the fact that I am everywhere that you need Me to be. Never will I leave My children bereft or forsaken. My love does not abandon or neglect the object of its love.

I know you are tired today and overwhelmed by all that needs to be done. Don't be. Let My joy so infill you that you will be energized for every task. Remember My joy is your strength. My joy equips you for the task at hand. Look only at the task at hand, allow My joy to strengthen you with wisdom and capability, and then you can move on to the next task at hand.

You are seeing, even at this moment, what a weight all these tasks are to you, but that is not My desire for you. Yes, there is much to do, but there is also joy to be found in each process. Do keep praise continually in your mouth, and see the difference that will make.

It is the Lord who goes before you. He will be with you;
he will not fail you or forsake you. Do not fear or be dismayed.

DEUTERONOMY 31:8, *NRSV*

October 18

Let us ever remember that God recognizes every expression
of praise and of His people's love. He knows so well what His love
and grace are to us that He must expect us to praise Him.

G. V. WIGRAM (1805–1879)

Praise transforms the mundane into moments of grace. Joy lifts drudgery into worship. Praise of Me opens the floodgate of My joy, which will turn a day of tasks into a time of thanksgiving.

My presence will elevate the most lowly elements of life to a holy level that is both sacred and sweet. Duty then turns into delight as I infuse the life-giving joy of My presence. Coupled with My presence is My enabling power to accomplish far beyond any human standards and abilities. I am the *Almighty* God, eagerly awaiting the opportunity to show the abundance of My capabilities.

So praise Me, My child, with unfettered gratitude, and I will unleash My joy upon you. That in turn will manifest itself in strength and wisdom and ability to carry forth My purposes—today in the tasks at hand and tomorrow in the fulfillment of My promises.

Praise the Lord! How joyful are those who fear the
Lord and delight in obeying his commands.

PSALM 112:1, *NLT*

October 19

Fill me up with the fullness of Yourself—that is my heart's desire.

I will fill you with Myself. I will answer that plea for every one of My children. Trust Me in that. All it takes is your heartfelt desire and obedience, and I can then fill you with Myself. Rest in that assurance.

This day will hold new joys for you. Rest in Me completely. Know that all is well and all is in My hands. I am working in ways you don't even know of. Trust Me, My child. Trust Me completely. Remember that My ways aren't your ways, that My thoughts are higher than yours.

My ways are so much higher, so much loftier and grander than anything you could come up with. You are limited by the finite in your thinking, but I am not. I am infinite, and infinite are the ways I use to proclaim My love to My children. You will soon be benefiting by one of My infinite ideas that I have crafted and prepared just for you. You will rejoice all your days at what I have done for you.

Hold on to Me and My Word. I will bring you through. Joy in Me and My promises today. Look for My gifts of joy. I love you.

"For My thoughts are not your thoughts, nor are your ways My ways,"
says the Lord. "For as the heavens are higher than the earth, so are My ways
higher than your ways, and my thoughts than your thoughts."

ISAIAH 55:8-9

JUDY GORDON MORROW

October 20

Praying about what to do . . .

All is well. Proceed as you are. Test the waters, and the way will be made clear. I will guide you in the way you should go. Fret not. Trust. Trust Me completely, and be at rest. You are seeking Me, and I will not allow anything that isn't from Me. Take all in stride as you continue to walk this path with Me.

Don't be overwhelmed. View each task, each challenge, as a *gift* from Me, and simply be grateful. See how that changes your outlook, your perspective? It is the enemy who puts an evil and negative slant on everything I intend for good. Look only to Me, and your vision will remain intact and insightful. Look through My lens of hope and purpose, and *enjoy* what you see. The enemy distorts everything, while I give you a crystal clear view of truth. I *am* your truth. Stay close to Me, look to Me alone, and you will know truth and clarity for your life—for every detail.

Now go in My peace. Enjoy your day. Pray about everything and don't worry about anything. I am working in ways you know nothing about right now, but rest in that assurance. Rest in *Me*, the One who loves you and holds you in the palm of His hand. I will not fail. I love you with an everlasting love. Live in My love today, and enjoy My every gift to you this day.

> *Don't worry about anything; instead, pray about everything.*
> *Tell God what you need, and thank him for all he has done.*
> PHILIPPIANS 4:6, *NLT*

October 21

Grant me, O Lord my God, a mind to know You, a heart to seek You, wisdom to find You, conduct pleasing to You, faithful perseverance in waiting for You, and a hope of finally embracing You. Amen.

ST. THOMAS AQUINAS (1225–1274)

You have been wise to follow Me all these years, even during the many times of not understanding. Understanding will come, but faith in Me is all that is necessary for now. I would not lead a child astray who so wholeheartedly trusts in Me, and you are that child.

To confirm all this to you, just see what I will be doing for you even today. See how I will expand your minutes and multiply your abilities in order to accomplish much today. You've seen me do it before, and I will most assuredly do it for you today as you look to Me alone. Follow My every nudge, and just see what I will do.

Look to this day with gladness, because you know I have already gone before you preparing your path. Don't let your feet stray onto detours of distraction, but do keep your eyes on the destination you want to reach by day's end. Call out all day to Me to help you do that.

Depend on Me alone today, and know all is well. Arise now with these words echoing in your ears and heart. All is well. With Me that is *always* the case.

The hope of the righteous will be gladness,
but the expectation of the wicked will perish.

PROVERBS 10:28

October 22

Lord, what a privilege it is to come before You and just enjoy Your presence.

If only all My children would discover that for themselves it would change everything. I long to meet with each of My children at the beginning of the day to prepare them, to calm any anxiety, and to impart My wisdom and peace. Great will be their joy when they discover this secret. Truly, it will be life-changing for them just as it has been for you, My child.

I kept drifting off to sleep while on my knees, and I prayed, "Father, I'm sorry."

I understand, My child. Your body is weary. Do go to bed earlier, and that will improve every part of your day. Know that I'm going before you this morning, preparing the way of your day. Look only to Me. Know that I'm all sufficient. I have everything under control. Take great comfort in that truth. It is My truth of love to you.

Keep praise on your lips and in your heart today. Know the joy of My presence. You have discovered that anew, and I will only increase it. Walk in My joy today. All is well.

Through Jesus, therefore, let us continually offer to God a sacrifice of praise—
the fruit of lips that openly profess his name.

HEBREWS 13:15, *NIV*

October 23

God's love to you is without boundary.
He could not love you more—for He loves you like a God;
and He never will love you less. All His heart belongs to you!

<small>CHARLES SPURGEON (1834–1892)</small>

You will be overwhelmed by love, My child, and you will know like never before the truth of My promise to make up to you all the pain and heartache of these past years. You know I speak truth. Nothing can come from My lips but truth. Take great comfort in these words—solid words of hope and grace. Only truth have I spoken to you all these years, and you can rest in that bedrock of truth.

Trust Me for all today. Look to Me alone. You have chosen "the better" today by starting your day with Me, and I will honor every element of this day with My presence and promises. With My help and strength. With My wisdom and guidance. And I will infuse you with My peace.

I told you that I was going to take you deeper, and you are already seeing that. Dwell on the truths I led you to this morning so that you may be My conduit of truth to others. Truth spoken in love and joy supersedes any other force on earth. Know Me and you know Truth. Keep a clear channel, My child, so that all from Me—truth, love, joy, peace and hope—may freely flow into the lives of others. I will do that through you, Child. Just watch and see what I will do. Truly, you will be amazed. Amazed and eternally grateful.

Grace, mercy, and peace, which come from God the Father
and from Jesus Christ—the Son of the Father—will continue to be
with us who live in truth and love.

<small>2 JOHN 1:3, *NLT*</small>

The Listening Heart   <small>JUDY GORDON MORROW</small>

October 24

Nothing is impossible with You.

You are right to remind yourself of that truth. When you dwell on Me and who I am, then every limitation falls away. I am not limited in My ability in any way, and I long for My children to know My unlimited capabilities—to see beyond their finite selves. In Me *all* things are possible to him who believes. You believe Me, My child, and you will see the wonders of My infinite possibilities.

Think on that: *infinite* possibilities. Unlimited. Uncountable. Even indescribable are the amazing possibilities I long to lavish on My children. Love divine, *all* loves excelling. I give out of My great love. Unstoppable is My love, and I long for My children to know the abundance of My love.

> *He counts the number of the stars;*
> *He calls them all by name.*
> *Great is our Lord, and mighty in power;*
> *His understanding is infinite.*
>
> PSALM 147:4-5

October 25

*At the cross God wrapped his heart in flesh and blood and
let it be nailed to the cross for our redemption.*

E. STANLEY JONES (1884–1973)

My sacrifice on the cross reverberates with My love for all time. Look
to the cross, and you will see nothing but love. Love given for you and
all My children. Never cease to see the cross, or you will easily forget
My love for you. My love required everything, even My life, and that
love is yours forever. In that love you know life abundant—abundant
in grace and mercy, joy and peace, love without end.

Live your life out of that abundance even today. Don't look at any
lack in your life. Instead look to Me, the abundant One. In Me you
have everything you need. *Everything.* Everything for the challenges of
this very day. Nothing will you lack when you look to Me alone. I will
be meeting your every need with My measureless abundance. How can
you ever despair in light of My unmatchable love for you?

Dwell there today, My child. Dwell in My all-encompassing love
and remain there. Think of it as your living room of love, and enjoy
the sweetness of My presence. In My presence is fullness of joy, and it
is meant for you.

*And when they had come to the place called Calvary, there they crucified
Him, and the criminals, one on the right hand and the other on the left.
Then Jesus said, "Father, forgive them, for they do not know what they do."*

LUKE 23:33-34

October 26

Lord, my thoughts are everywhere—forgive me
(as I wasn't really praying but fretting over all my thoughts).

One step at a time, My child, one step at a time. When you take things step by step they won't overwhelm you. That is your problem with all the projects facing you. Each one appears as an insurmountable mountain when you look at the vastness of the whole thing. Leaping to the top in one jump isn't possible, so you don't even try. Thus, things remain unfinished and overwhelming to you.

Instead, envision a staircase leading to the top of the mountain. Taking one step at a time gives ease to the journey and makes completion possible. Chisel out steps into the sides of each mountain, and just see what you will be able to accomplish with My help. Together we will mount up those steep sides as if on eagle's wings, taking one step at a time.

Thank You, Lord. Help me to know how to do that.

I will show you. You know My voice, so just follow My leadings. Together we will accomplish what is needful. The lifting of the weights of these burdens will be freeing and uplifting to your spirit. Yes, do look at each mountain you are facing now, and every day take one step up each one.

Thank You, Lord. I'm depending on Your help to do these very things—one step at a time—to Your glory and for Your kingdom. Thank You that all things are possible with You!

"You don't have enough faith," Jesus told them. "I tell you the truth,
if you had faith even as small as a mustard seed, you could say to this mountain,
'Move from here to there,' and it would move. Nothing would be impossible."

MATTHEW 17:20, *NLT*

October 27

Loved with everlasting love, led by grace that love to know.

GEORGE WADE ROBINSON (1838–1877),
"I AM HIS, AND HE IS MINE"

You are My precious child, and I love you with an everlasting love. Neve
forget how much I love you. It is a personal love, a precious love, a love tha
knows you like no other and still loves you completely. I have much still t
teach you about My love. You will share what I reveal to you with others. I
will all be for My kingdom.

You are wise to wait on My timings and ways. Do be assured that I ar
working. Look only to Me. Things can change in an instant. I will not fa
you. I will not let you down in any way. Because of My hand, all will fa
into place. You will see.

Enjoy your day. Work hard and look always to Me for your every need
I am with you, My child, always with you. Do not allow your mind to thin
thoughts that are not of Me. Don't let the enemy enter in—discouragemer
and distress are his tools. They do not come from Me. Stay centered an
focused on Me. I will help you through these upcoming days.

Continue to learn of Me. Seek *My* face. Know *My* ways. Experience tl
richness of a life hidden in Me. Great will be your reward in heaven if yc
follow only Me. Live in My joy and peace today. I am with you, now ar
always. I love you, My child.

Since you have been raised to new life with Christ, set your sights on
the realities of heaven, where Christ sits in the place of honor at God's right hand
Think about the things of heaven, not the things of earth.
For you died to this life, and your real life is hidden with Christ in God.

COLOSSIANS 3:1-3, *NLT*

JUDY GORDON MORROW

October 28

God has the right to be trusted; to be believed that
He means what He says; and that His love is dependable.

A. J. GOSSIP (1873–1954)

Oh, the plans I have for you! Rest assured that I know all things and am orchestrating every detail. All you need to do is trust Me completely and rest in Me with no anxiety. Your childlike faith in Me is a significant part of this story that I am writing even now, and it will speak volumes to the hearts of many. May that give you sweet peace even now, while your faith is still waiting to be made into sight.

Remain in deep communion with Me today. By doing so, you will remain at rest. Stay close to Me, listen for My voice of love, and stay attuned to My Spirit. He will guide you in My truth and love.

Be filled with all the fullness of Me today, and let praise to Me fill your mouth continually. You know the difference that makes, and I will draw you even deeper into My wisdom as to the value and benefits of praise.

I love you, My child. You are following Me on this journey of faith, and I will not fail you. Stay close to Me, and just see what I will do. I am working even at this moment.

Let my mouth be filled with Your praise and with Your glory all the day.

PSALM 71:8

October 29

I am looking to You for answers.

Do look to Me for My answers. Looking anywhere else will be futile and will lead to discouragement. Look only to Me, My child.

Face this day with My peace and presence. Do nothing in your own strength. Look only to Me. Seek My face. I am looking at you with the love of a Father—a Father whose love and ways toward you are perfect. I will not fail you, My child. Do not give in to discouragement. I am your source of hope, peace and love. Hope only in Me. I will keep you hope-filled as you stay your mind and heart on Me. That's the key, My child.

Live in My hope today. Look only to Me in every task, in every interaction, in every situation. I am in all. I am going before you—follow Me and Me alone. I will bless you for doing that.

How I love you, My child. How I do love you! The depths of My love you will never fully know, but it is in this time with Me every morning that your knowledge grows. When you feel secure in My love, then I can use you to transmit My love to others. There is no greater calling than to be the bearer of My love, one person at a time. This day holds that very opportunity—to bear My love to a hurting soul. Be My balm to that one even today. I love you.

Now that you have purified your souls by your obedience to the truth
so that you have genuine mutual love,
love one another deeply from the heart.

1 PETER 1:22, *NRSV*

October 30

Lead me down Your paths, because that is where My heart wants to go.

I will honor that prayer. Your heart after Mine will never be led astray by Me. You can count on that. I will only lead you to where you need to go. Fear nothing, My child. I would not call you to believe something and not fulfill it. Your hope will be transformed into indescribable joy. I have deemed it to be so.

Follow after Me today. Know I am with you and that I am in everything that concerns you. I will not fail you. I will bring you out into new days of unspeakable joy. Joy that will know no end. Joy that you will be so grateful to have waited for, as you will know it in its purest form. Take delight in My words of promise. Savor them, as they are sweetness to your soul. I *will* make your faith sight. You will see all things clearly, and you will rejoice with exceeding joy.

I love you, My child. Keep your hand in Mine and trust Me completely. I am bringing you into new days of glorious joy.

Lead me in the path of your commandments, for I delight in it.
PSALM 119:35, *NRSV*

October 31

Jesus, I just want what You want.

And that is a noble prayer. How could I not honor a prayer like that? Your heart after Mine is all I need. A heart yielded to Me and My desires. Such rich satisfaction and contentment will be yours with a heart like that. I will fill you to overflowing with my Spirit and the outpourings of My hand.

Continue to see Me in everything. Realize anew that I am not just one part or category of your life. My longing is for you to live and breathe in Me all day long. That our union will be so complete that there is no ending or beginning. That I will be in all and through all the doings of your day. Complete union and communion with Me—that is My desire for My children.

I am not a religion. I am a Person, the loving God, who desires a close relationship with each of My children. Joy in the gift of My presence and My love toward you. It will change your life from duty to pure joy. It is that joy that attracts others to Me. Be My vessel of joy.

For in Christ lives all the fullness of God in a human body.
So you also are complete through your union with Christ,
who is the head over every ruler and authority.

COLOSSIANS 2:9-10, *NLT*

November

This time on my knees before my God is a time like no other. A time apart from every distraction. A time away from the clamor of life. A time awake to the Holy Spirit.

A time for silence.

A time for listening.

A time for refreshing.

The calm of these moments comes after I shoo away all the duties and distractions demanding my attention. That process takes time, like the shedding of leaves in autumn. Once my thoughts tumble and drift to the ground of my heart, then my bare branches can stretch heavenward, seeking the Sustainer of my soul.

My barrenness allows room for God's doings. Space for His workings. Quietness for His whispers.

I've never been successful at shaking the tree of my thoughts quickly in order to capture them. But the time it takes to stay on my knees before God in order to come to that place of communion with Him cannot be measured against the countless benefits.

Peace returns.

Hope is restored.

My heart responds with the joy that only Jesus can give.

All other activities of this life fade in comparison. My daily time with Jesus is like a tree aflame in the fall, lit up even further by the rays of the sun. In contrast, the temporal stuff of life is like the dry, dead leaves in a gutter, soon to become a brown sodden mass that clogs the street's drainage system.

My dear Lord,

Thank You for this visual that reminds me yet again to invite You first into the moments of my day. So much is pulling at me this morning, clamoring for my attention, but You have fulfilled Your promise: draw near to God, and He will draw near to you.[1]

Thank You for Your nearness. For the realness of Your presence. For the difference You make in My life because of this time with You.

You change the overwhelming in my life to Your overcoming.

You replace anxiety with the abundance of Your peace.

You exchange despondency with Your eternal joy.

What wondrous gifts from Your hand—and all I had to do was wait before You while on my knees.

Note

1. See James 4:8.

November 1

Praying about concerns and wondering about the outcomes . . .
God, You know, You know, You know.

Yes, I do know, My child, and all is well. I know the plans I have for you and they are all good. You will so rejoice when you see what I have designed for you. Truly, I will unfold My wonders, and you will see My majesty and power and love like never before.

Take great hope in My words to you. They are words of hope and promise and surety. I will do *all* that I have spoken to you. Just keep praying and praising and *believing* Me. Your belief is the key in the door that is just waiting to be swung open with My answers for you. Believe Me like a trusting, expectant child believes her loving father who always keeps his promises.

Belief in Me is the most powerful force on earth. Your believing heart linked with My powerful hand will yield results beyond the scope of your imagination. You smile, because your imagination is more capable of expansive dreams than most. But, truly, I will exceed even those thoughts and imaginings. Take great comfort in that, knowing that your firm belief now will yield remarkable results in the perfection of My plan. I will not disappoint you. Rather, I will exceed your expectations with My impeccable and glorious workings and gifts from My hand. Know it to be so. *Believe* Me for all I have promised.

Then the Lord took Abram outside and said to him,
"Look up into the sky and count the stars if you can. That's how many
descendants you will have!" And Abram believed the Lord, and the
Lord counted him as righteous because of his faith.
GENESIS 15:5-6, *NLT*

November 2

*Thank You that all things are under Your control
and taken care of by Your hand.*

Yes, they are, down to the last detail. You are right to take joy and delight in how I am the God of details. I enrich the lives of My children with My attention to details. You only need to be aware of those details, and you will be blessed. Seeing Me in the details will only increase your hope for the more important concerns in your life.

I can be trusted in all things. Walking with Me, in complete surrender to Me, will yield peace and joy. My children strain so, even in their relationship with Me, and that is not My plan or My doing.

Rest in Me. Only in Me can true rest be found. Not leisure or pleasure—I'm talking about the rest that comes from complete trust in Me. A ceasing from striving and constant doing. The right and best doing comes out of solid resting in Me.

I will help you today. I will give you wisdom. I am going before you. Remember again how I am the God of details. You will see that afresh today. Just rest totally in Me. Don't fret in any way. That is a waste of time and energy. Just rest and trust, and you will soon see the results of My workings.

*For thus said the Lord God, the Holy One of Israel:
In returning and rest you shall be saved;
in quietness and in trust shall be your strength.*
ISAIAH 30:15, *NRSV*

November 3

If you would be pure, saturate yourself with the Word of God.
HENRIETTA MEARS (1890–1963)

Feed on My Word and the words I have spoken to you all these years. All My words are life-giving—words of truth and hope. They are food for your soul, and they will give you daily strength as you partake of them. Truly, *I* am your daily bread, and My words will sustain you and imbue you with hope. They will provide you an unshakeable foundation for belief in Me.

What a sweet time this has been together, My child. Time with Me always yields benefits: a sweeter joy, a heightened peace, a deeper knowledge of who I am and all I have in store for you. Rejoice in each one, and continue rejoicing throughout your day. My joy, peace and love will color your day with hope like you have never known before.

Continue to dwell on and grasp these words of truth today. Hold them close to your heart. Yield all to Me, and I *will* enable you to believe Me unequivocally. Great will be your joy even now, a joy that will be a sweet foretaste of the incredible, life-changing joy ahead. I will do it. You will see. Your faith will be transformed forever. Your joy will know no end. Revel in these promises today, and know great joy even now. Faithful is He who calls you who also *will* do it.[1]

I am the bread of life. Your ancestors ate the manna in the wilderness, and they died. This is the bread that comes down from heaven, so that one may eat of it and not die. I am the living bread that came down from heaven. Whoever eats of this bread will live forever; and the bread that I will give for the life of the world is my flesh.
JOHN 6:48-51, *NRSV*

Note
1. See 1 Thessalonians 5:24.

November 4

With much weighing on my mind, I prayed, "These are my finite thoughts.
I want to know Your infinite thoughts."

All is well—words that I have spoken to you time and again, but they are timeless in their truth. Because of who I am, all is well. Because I love you like no other, all is well. Because you trust *Me* completely, all is well. *I* am the one constant, and because of who I am and who I am to *you, all is well*. You can rest in that blessed assurance.

All is well, because I hold your future in My hands. All is well, because all is known to Me—nothing escapes My notice. All is well, because you are believing My promises to you, and I *will* make your faith sight. I will *always* honor childlike faith that trusts Me fully, completely, unquestioningly—because that child knows the Father is *totally* trustworthy.

You know I am trustworthy, Child. You have seen Me work time and again on your behalf in the most wondrous of ways, from the smallest to the biggest. I am your God—*your* God—a personal, loving, caring God who delights in pouring out My provisions and blessings for you, My expectant child. I would never disappoint a child who so trusts and obeys Me and expects Me to answer. My Father heart longs to bring My answers to your years of prayer, and know this, My child: I *will* be doing *that very thing* very, very soon. You have trusted and obeyed Me, and now I will answer.

Blessed are those who trust in the Lord and
have made the Lord their hope and confidence.
JEREMIAH 17:7, *NLT*

The Listening Heart JUDY GORDON MORROW

November 5

Open my mouth and let me bear gladly the warm truth everywhere;
Open my heart and let me prepare love with Thy children thus to share.

CLARA H. SCOTT (1841–1897),
"OPEN MY EYES THAT I MAY SEE"

Go now, abounding in My peace and joy. Lavished by My love. Overwhelmed by My grace. Go, and shine for Me—a beacon of My hope and life that is available to *all* who seek Me. I await My children with outstretched arms, ready to embrace them with forgiveness, wholeness and freedom. No one will I ever turn away. I am the God who welcomes.

The world so easily shuns My children. But I so warmly embrace and hold close My own. You know the truth of that, My child, as I have often cradled you with My comfort and whispered words of hope and caring to your hurting heart.

Others need to know that same care from Me. You can help them to see Me. Simply listen to Me, do as I direct, and I will do the rest. It's as simple as that: listen and obey, and trust Me to accomplish My purposes. Be that instrument in My hand. I will honor your obedience.

All is well. I am God, and *all is well*.

Now all the tax collectors and sinners were coming near to listen to him.
And the Pharisees and the scribes were grumbling and saying,
"This fellow welcomes sinners and eats with them."

LUKE 15:1-2, *NRSV*

November 6

Lord, thank You for all Your blessings and Your loving care toward me.

Oh, My child, didn't I tell you that I would never leave you nor forsake you—that I would not leave you desolate? Yes, you have experienced a lot of pain and heartache and loneliness, but you know I've been with you in each moment. I am with you now.

You are right to acknowledge My hand in all the happenings and details of the past years. I have presided, and I am still on the throne—watching over you, providing for you, loving you. You are learning much about My love, My child, and you will continue to learn much more. Rest in Me. Rest and learn. You are My precious child, and I love you beyond measure.

You know My heart, and it is true toward you. True and loving. My love surpasses all others. That's what you need to tell My children. My love is perfect—no selfishness, no hidden agendas, no ulterior motives. My children cannot look at My love through a lens of human love. That is the secret—to know My love as divine and perfect, wanting only the best for My children. It's a love that can be totally and unequivocally trusted.

Let the richness of that truth continue to seep into your soul, My child. You are truly My *beloved* child. Rest in My love. Exult in My love. Know My love more each day. Enjoy *this* day. It is My gift to you. I love you, Child.

So let us come boldly to the throne of our gracious God. There we will receive his mercy, and we will find grace to help us when we need it most.
HEBREWS 4:16, *NLT*

November 7

O the deep, deep love of Jesus, vast, unmeasured, boundless, free!
Rolling as a mighty ocean in its fullness over me!

S. TREVOR FRANCIS (1834–1925),
"O THE DEEP, DEEP LOVE OF JESUS"

You are My child, and I love you with an unfathomable, everlasting love. Yes, the ocean is My example to you of My love. Deep upon deep is My love toward you. My love is measureless. Because of My love toward you, you have nothing to fear. Instead, you have much to anticipate.

Pray with expectancy, My child. Pray in faith, believing that I do all things well, and I will be freed to act. It is that mysterious linking of faith and expectant prayer that frees My power on Your behalf. I give good gifts to My children. I am your loving Father. You need only to come to Me expectantly, knowing that I will answer, that I will not turn you away empty handed. I will give you exactly what you need. Trust Me in this.

I am at work, My child. Prayer unleashes My power. Know that to be true. Follow My leadings completely. Know My heart. I will make all things plain to you. Seek Me and Me alone. I will answer you. With My still, quiet voice I will answer you. Look only to Me. Constant prayer will keep the enemy out—it is crucial that your prayers keep a hedge around you.

Oh, My child, new days are ahead. Trust Me completely. Know My heart toward you. I love you like no other. You are My precious child, and I know the plans I have for you.[1] Rest in Me and My love.

Your unfailing love, O Lord, is as vast as the heavens; your faithfulness reaches
beyond the clouds. Your righteousness is like the mighty mountains, your justice
like the ocean depths. You care for people and animals alike, O Lord.

PSALM 36:5-6, NLT

Note
1. See Jeremiah 29:11.

November 8

His forever, only His; who the Lord and me shall part?
Ah, with what a rest of bliss Christ can fill the loving heart!

GEORGE WADE ROBINSON (1838–1877),
"I AM HIS, AND HE IS MINE"

Go in My peace. See the joy I will be giving you today. Yes, yesterday was hard, with buffeting from the enemy on every side. Do not give him license to trample on territory that has been given over to Me. You are Mine, My child—Mine alone. Seek My shelter and refuge. Keep up the shield of faith so that Satan's fiery darts will simply bounce off that shield and fall by the wayside. Greater is He that is *within* you than he that is in the world.[1]

Trust Me, My child. I will not fail you in any regard. You have waited on *Me*, and I will honor you for doing that. All glory will go to Me, just as your heart desires. Rest in the truth of My words to you.

This day is Mine. You are Mine. There is no cause for worry or for fear. All is well, because all is Mine. I will exceed your expectations in the fulfilling of My plans for you. Just see what I will do, My child. Great will be your joy.

You are of God, little children, and have overcome them,
because He who is in you is greater than he who is in the world.

1 JOHN 4:4

Note
1. See 1 John 4:4, *KJV.*

JUDY GORDON MORROW

November 9

While it is good that we seek to know the Holy One,
it is probably not so good to presume that we ever complete the task.

DIETRICH BONHOEFFER (1906–1945)

You have done well to seek Me this morning, to start your day with Me. It will serve you well. In this time comes serenity and tranquility—both are gifts from My hand. Even though the circumstances remain the same, I bring the calm to your soul and spirit. Turbulence can reign without, but My peace will reign within. Glory in that thought, in that truth. That is the difference I make. A difference that shines on your countenance. Others see My peace and are drawn to Me as I am lifted up. How desperately My children need Me and My peace. Help lead them to Me, My child. I will show you how to do that.

Take joy in this day. It is My gift to you. Continue to see Me every-where. I, the Creator, surround you with My gifts. See My world, see your life, through My eyes, and your days will be enriched like never before.

I long for My children to see My love toward them in countless ways. You are more and more aware of My loving bestowments everywhere. Joy in each one, and be reminded of My love for you. It is boundless, My child. The scope of My love you will never be able to fathom. Take great comfort and joy in My measureless love. One who loves you like that desires only your highest good. Rest in that truth, and know anew that all is well.

For great is his love toward us, and the faithfulness
of the Lord endures forever. Praise the Lord.

PSALM 117:2, *NIV*

November 10

In our lives there is a colour like that on a painter's palette,
which gives meaning to both life and art. It is the colour of love.

MARC CHAGALL (1887–1985)

Look at today as an artist's canvas—a blank, white canvas where I can paint the colors of My love and grace. An otherwise bland, gray day will be transformed by My liberal splashings of joy. The resulting picture will be one that will magnify Me. Others will see My brushstrokes of love in your life and will be drawn to Me. Watch Me transform difficulties into opportunities that will demonstrate My heart of love for all My children.

You are envisioning that white canvas on an easel and a palette of many glorious colors. Now allow Me, the Master Artist, to apply each color as I see fit. Know that the resulting painting will far surpass anything you would have come up with on your own. I am your inspiration—My breath is breathed into you to give life and hope to many. Now see? See how My words of truth are already changing your outlook on your day? That is My gift to you. Now watch expectantly, on tiptoes of joy, as I color your day with My hand of love and kindness—all done in My creativity, with My solutions that are individualized just for you.

Now enjoy this day—My gift to you—and allow your loving Father to apply brushstrokes of joy and hope and love. Then stand back and see what I have done. Admire My handiwork, and let your heart be filled with increased devotion toward your trustworthy Father. Truly, I do all things well.

For it is by grace you have been saved, through faith—
and this is not from yourselves, it is the gift of God—not by works,
so that no one can boast. For we are God's handiwork, created in Christ Jesus
to do good works, which God prepared in advance for us to do.

EPHESIANS 2:8-10, *NIV*

JUDY GORDON MORROW

November 11

Just give me grace for each day.

And that I will do, My child. My grace is always yours for the asking. I will meet your every need in every way according to the rich abundance of My knowledge and grace. I see all, I know all, and I will answer all out of My love for you. Even now are My answers being shaped by My loving hand toward you. Abide and rest in Me, and know that all is well.

This time with Me has been good, hasn't it, as I have flooded your being with My gentle peace. Drink deeply of My peace, and dwell long in My wisdom so that I can impart My ways and desires for you. I know you are wondering about what you should do. You will know, My child. You know Me well enough by now to know that I will always make My desires known to you at just the right time. Just rest in Me and see what I will do. Leave all to *Me*.

Enjoy this day. Stay ever close to Me, seeking My wisdom, knowing My love. Then that very wisdom and love will overflow to others, and I will be lifted up and glorified.

Pray always. Prayer is key to all My plans. Do nothing without prayer. Prayer prepares the way. Prayer marks the path. All done in prayer will be permeated with My presence. Prayer is the key to accessing My wisdom and guidance. Do nothing without prayer.

Rejoice always, pray without ceasing, in everything give thanks;
for this is the will of God in Christ Jesus for you.
1 THESSALONIANS 5:16-18

November 12

In almost everything that touches our everyday life on earth,
God is pleased when we're pleased. He wills that we be as free as birds
to soar and sing our maker's praise without anxiety.

A. W. TOZER (1897–1963)

I did not create My children to be identical. I certainly will not deal with each of them in the same way. It is in my individual dealings with My children that they can know My very personal love for them. That knowledge will open up the door to sweet intimacy with Me, the Lover of their souls.

If only My children would catch a glimpse of My deep and personal love for them! That alone will transform their very existence, the very living out of their daily lives. Enfolded in My boundless and unconditional love, they will be freed to be the marvelous and matchless individuals that I created them to be.

Rediscover this truth in your own life today, My precious child. Delight in Me and My ways. See Me in everything—your joy will be magnified and My love for you will be evident. Bask in My love. Lift up your heart in praise. Look at all with My vision, with the eyes of My heart—a heart that is true and pure and above reproach. Allow My vision to become yours, and you will clearly see the design of My marvelous plans for you. All will come into focus as you view all through My sovereign eyes. Great peace will result and true rest will be yours.

I love you, My dear child. Taste and see My goodness today and every day. Know Me afresh. Shine with My joy and love, and be My light of hope to others.

The precepts of the Lord are right, giving joy to the heart.
The commands of the Lord are radiant, giving light to the eyes.

PSALM 19:8, *NIV*

JUDY GORDON MORROW

November 13

The fullness of You, Lord—that's what I desire—
the fullness of You within me.

And I shall grant that request, My child. Out of a heart of love for you will I fill your heart with all of Me. In that heart will be no room for anything other than Me and My boundless love. Out of that heart will flow My unending mercy, grace and peace. Joy, comfort and rest. But most of all, my deep, deep love—for you and for those who will bask in the warmth of My overflowing love.

My love is the key to opening closed hearts. Overwhelm others with My love, and they won't be able to stand against Me. All the plans and schemes of the enemy will be thwarted as My love is poured out upon them. I will show you how to do that. You will joy in My plan and the results of My workings.

Trust Me in this and follow My leadings. Compel others to walk with Me by exemplifying My love in a myriad of ways. Great will be your joy in obeying Me and seeing what I will do. I, your Father, will be faithful to them as you are faithful to Me in your obedience. Take joy in these words as tokens of new days ahead—new days in every realm.

Don't just pretend to love others. Really love them.
Hate what is wrong. Hold tightly to what is good.
ROMANS 12:9, *NLT*

November 14

An honest heart loves the Truth.

A. W. PINK (1886-1952)

You have honored Me, and now I will be honoring you in ways beyond the scope of your imagination. Take great joy in that thought—it is My promise of truth to you.

Every promise I make is infused with truth, as I AM the Way, the *Truth* and the Life. I can speak nothing but truth. Thus, My words of truth are trustworthy, solid and sure. Look at every promise I have spoken to you through the knowledge that it is truth, and plant your feet on each one. Your joy will overflow anew, knowing that I will fulfill each promise of truth in order to be true to who I am.

All I need from you, My child, is your simple, unwavering faith. An upturned face toward Mine, a face filled with expectancy and joy, knowing that you will indeed receive *all* that I have promised you. Pray in faith amid the doubts, and I will sweep away all obstacles to fulfill the sweetness of My plans.

I love you, dear child. My love for you will never diminish but will always shine brighter than the brightest sun. Its warmth will also shine on others through you. Be My light and love even today, and I will honor you in the sweetest of ways. Now go in My peace. All is well. So very, very well.

This is good, and pleases God our Savior, who wants all people to be saved and to come to a knowledge of the truth. For there is one God and one mediator between God and mankind, the man Christ Jesus.

1 TIMOTHY 2:3-5, *NIV*

November 15

I am all Yours, Lord.

And because of that you have everything at your disposal: My grace, peace, love, joy and hope that come only from Me. Let all these—My loving gifts to you—bring the level of your living to a new height that can be attained only through Me. Others will see the difference I make, and I will be glorified.

Never forget the restless souls within My creations who will only know peace and satisfaction when they know Me. Be My link for those I put you in contact with. Allow Me to so flow from you with My attributes of love, joy and peace that they will want to know Me also.

Oh, dear Lord, please help me to be Your conduit in that way. I often feel that I fail in that regard.

Just live in Me, My child. Allow Me free rein in your life. Together we will show others the beauty of Me in My children, and they will see the difference I make.

Arise in My joy and peace. Live in My love and grace. Dwell in My hope all day today. All are yours because you are Mine, and I love you like no other. Be ever mindful of My incomparable love today. Go in My joy!

But the Holy Spirit produces this kind of fruit in our lives:
love, joy, peace, patience, kindness, goodness, faithfulness, gentleness,
and self-control. There is no law against these things!
GALATIANS 5:22-23, *NLT*

November 16

Before me, even as behind, God is, and all is well.
JOHN GREENLEAF WHITTIER (1807–1892)

I am orchestrating things even now for the fulfillment of My plans for you. Rest totally in that reassurance, and know like never before that *all is well*. *All* that I am doing is for the good of you and for the glory of My kingdom. You will marvel at My kingdom plans, and you will be filled with much joy.

Prepare for those plans, My child. Don't doubt. Just believe. The enemy is trying to stymie and frustrate you on every side. *Don't let him.* Remember? *Resist* the devil, and he *will* flee from you. Don't be surprised by his tactics, but do stand firm against him with faith girded by your praise and prayers to Me. He cannot remain in an atmosphere of prayer and praise. My light in you is stronger than his foes of darkness, for greater is *He* that is *within you* than he that is in the world.[1]

You are the victor, the triumphant one, because I, your triumphant, victorious King, reign in you. Never forget the power you are endued with because of who sits on the throne of your life. With Me *all* things are possible, and I am making all things possible for you. All will see the workings of My hand, and clearly will they know that this is of *My* doing. Rest in that truth, and simply wait in full belief and trust for me to act. Your joy will overflow.

Rejoice greatly, O daughter Zion! Shout aloud, O daughter Jerusalem!
Lo, your king comes to you; triumphant and victorious is he,
humble and riding on a donkey, on a colt, the foal of a donkey.
ZECHARIAH 9:9, *NRSV*

Note
1. See 1 John 4:4, *KJV*.

    JUDY GORDON MORROW

November 17

*I believe You, Jesus. You have promised some amazing things,
and I believe You.*

You are right to believe Me. I will never let down a child whose trust is solely and fully in Me. I will honor the faith of such a child, and all will see and glorify Me. You have been My faithful child, even in the darkness of not understanding Me and My ways, and I will honor you for your unshakeable belief in Me.

Yes, you have had doubts and wonderings and misgivings, but you have always allowed Me to help you navigate your way to the harbor of faith. And in that harbor, that shelter, you have known My peace and love and hope. My joy. The depth and trustworthiness of My promises. Truly, in the deeps you have known My depths. In the depths of Me and My love, you will find your Refuge. You will know a Haven like no other.

Today I am all of that to you and more. In Me you lack nothing. Nothing, My child. I am all you will ever need. You have found that to be true. You know I will never leave you. You know I am true to My word. You know I can be totally trusted.

Continue to see today My clear hand of guidance in your affairs, and know that your concerns are My concerns. Truly, I will perfect that which concerns you. Rest in that immutable truth, and enjoy the peace of My presence.

*He calmed the storm to a whisper and stilled the waves. What a blessing was
that stillness as he brought them safely into harbor! Let them praise the Lord for
his great love and for the wonderful things he has done for them.*

PSALM 107:29-31, *NLT*

November 18

You have trusted Him in a few things, and He has not failed you. Trust Him now for everything, and see if He does not do for you exceeding abundantly above all that you could ever have asked or thought, not according to your power or capacity, but according to His own mighty power, that will work in you all the good pleasure of His most blessed will.

HANNAH WHITALL SMITH (1832–1911)

Trust Me for all things—your health, your finances, your family, your work, your future. I know what I have in mind in each situation, and it is all good. Truly, My heart of love will not bring anything to you that is not for your ultimate good. Rest always in that truth.

Continue to pray much, and just see what I will do. You will rejoice at the amazing orchestrations from My hand. All that your heart desires and hopes for will be met with the tenderest of care from My heart of love. You will see Me like never before.

Now rest. Rest in Me and who I am, your loving and kind Father. Know anew that I do *all* things well. Allow Me to amaze you. Believe Me with a shining faith that will reflect My glory. Others will see Me because of your faith in Me.

Stay close to Me, Child. I will lead you aright, never astray. Trust Me completely in every realm of your life, and just watch the unfolding of My plans. Eyes on Me, My child. I will not fail you. I love you.

All he does is just and good, and all his commandments are trustworthy.

PSALM 111:7, *NLT*

JUDY GORDON MORROW

November 19

Lord, please help me.

I will help you. I am going before you even now. Take comfort in these words, knowing they are from your Father who loves you beyond measure.

Oh, My child, you are bowed down by many things this morning. Don't be. Give each one to Me. I am all sufficient for your every need. Why should you carry burdens that weren't meant for you to bear? Leave all in My hands, and all will be well. Haven't I proved Myself to you time and again? This time is no different. I will take care of every difficulty. I will help you in every situation. Just trust Me completely and leave all in My caring hands. I will not fail you.

Allow Me to bring joy to your heart today. Don't stifle My Spirit within you, but allow My life-giving joy to flow. Joy in the midst of your trials and difficulties. That is the difference I make. That is the difference others will see. Count on Me to do that for you. Be My clear, open channel of joy—joy that will give life and hope to others.

Keep your eyes only on Me today. That is the key. Don't look at the waves of turbulent circumstances around you, but keep your eyes fastened on Me. I am your anchor, and I will hold you steady.

I am working, My child. Live in hope. Walk by faith, not by sight. Hope, hope, hope. Live in My hope.

Be thankful in all circumstances, for this is God's will for you who belong to Christ Jesus. Do not stifle the Holy Spirit.

1 THESSALONIANS 5:18-19, *NLT*

November 20

Thank You, Jesus, for Your never-ending hope-giving. I love You.

And I love you, My child. You will soon see My love displayed more and more as I continue to pour out My blessings upon your life. You will marvel at all I will do—each detail—and your praise and gratitude will never end.

I have ordained all things, My child. All will happen according to My divine orchestrations. No one will be able to deny My hand at work, and forever will you praise Me. Forever I will be glorified as you tell the story of My grace in your life. You will see this to be true with each retelling. You will never tire of recounting My wonders in your life. Rejoice even now as those wonders are unfolding.

I am living out My life in you today, My child. Just follow the path I have set before you, and know that all is well. All this has been ordained by Me—for your joy and for My glory. That which has been ordained by Me will come to pass with utter perfection. You will see that to be so true.

The signs and wonders that the Most High God has worked
for me I am pleased to recount. How great are his signs,
how mighty his wonders! His kingdom is an everlasting kingdom,
and his sovereignty is from generation to generation.

DANIEL 4:2-3, *NRSV*

JUDY GORDON MORROW

November 21

Guide my every step today.

You know I will. There is nothing I enjoy more than to guide and help My children, the very ones I love above all. The ones I died for so that they may know life in its abundance. Yes, you can count on Me to willingly guide and direct your every step today. Knowing I will do that for you will free you from every fret and care. Instead, you can embrace the day with thanksgiving and joy and with complete rest in Me.

Rest is not found in the absence of negative circumstances but in the abundance of who I am. The worst of circumstances can never supersede the overflowing abundance found in Me alone. That knowledge is your resting place. In Me is untroubled and serene rest for your soul.

Undisturbed is the rest of My children when they place themselves wholly in My care. There I can cover them with My wings and sing over them with My love. That is the place I have prepared for you this day, My child, as you gratefully surrender to My love—a love demonstrated on the cross for all time and revealed to you daily as you look to Me alone.

I love you, My child. Rest in My love today, and enjoy its warmth and affection. Truly, the depth of My love is beyond the reach of your knowing, but it is designed for your rest and joy.

He shall cover you with His feathers, and under His wings
you shall take refuge; his truth shall be your shield and buckler.

PSALM 91:4

November 22

What are Your desires here, Lord?

For you to follow Me completely. Allow Me to guide in every aspect of your life, and just see what I will do. I know you are overwhelmed by so many unfinished and incomplete projects in your life, *but what are they compared to Me?* Do you not think that I can help you with each one—and do each one even better and faster than you could on your own? You know the answer; you know that *nothing* is impossible with Me. Now *act* on that truth.

Live your life daily in the comfort of that truth—*nothing* is impossible with Me.

And then also apply that truth to every other area of your life—the ones you have no control over, the ones you can do nothing about. In those situations, too, I am the God of the impossible.

Today I ask you to prove Me regarding that timeless truth of Mine. Listen carefully, follow closely, and then just see how I will fulfill in you *My* impossible. You will see Me and know Me like never before. Enjoy seeing *Me* at work today. Joy in every accomplishment from *My* hand. I will not fail you as you listen to Me and seek My heart.

All joy will be yours in what I will do. Enjoy the gift of this day, ever thankful for every blessing, and savor My peace and joy and love. All are yours, now and forever. I love you, Child, My precious child.

For nothing is impossible with God.
LUKE 1:37, *NLT*

November 23

Praise You, Jesus, for how truly You have spoken.

True is the only way I can be, as there is no falsity in Me. That is why you can fully rely on My words of truth to you. In *Me* resides truth, as I *am* Truth. In Me and My truth are Light and Life. In falsehood and lying are darkness and deceit, which lead to death. You see the stark contrast, and you yearn to remain with Me on the path of truth, light and life. Wise is your choice when you walk My way, with the One who is *the* Way. There is no other path to peace and joy and contentment. In Me is *all* you need.

Continue to recall all that I showed you yesterday regarding praise and thanksgiving. Both are lining your heart in preparation for My coming answers to you. Do take hope in My words to you. Do acknowledge all that I am doing in your life. Do continue to listen to Me and to live expectantly. My answers are on the way, My child. My answers of perfection. My answers of *joy.*

Know like never before My all-abiding, all-caring Presence in your life, and be grateful. Envision your heart of praise filling your home with praise, and be grateful in Me. I love you, Child.

I will worship toward Your holy temple, and praise
Your name for Your lovingkindness and Your truth; for You have
magnified Your word above all Your name.

PSALM 138:2

November 24

Under His wings, oh, what precious enjoyment! There will I hide till life's trials are o'er;
Sheltered, protected, no evil can harm me. Resting in Jesus, I'm safe evermore.

WILLIAM O. CUSHING (1823–1902),
"UNDER HIS WINGS"

This day is Mine, and I bequeath it to you to use wisely. Move in My Spirit. Follow My nudges. Rejoice in My presence and in every gift from My hand. I will be ever faithful to reveal to you what is needed at just the right moment. Enjoy moving and doing and being in the freedom of My Spirit. In Him you live and move and have your being.[1]

You are discovering more and more the joy of a life hidden in Mine. When you are in Me, you have a constant shield of protection and a refuge of love. Nothing can harm you when you are under the shadow of My wings. I can be everything to you when you place yourself in blessed submission to My highest plans of good for you, drawn out of the deepest love you can ever know.

My love for you is flawless and all-encompassing—a love so pure and broad and mighty that your finite mind can barely begin to comprehend it. But you can benefit from it without understanding it. My cloak of love will warm you and sustain you all the days of your life.

Arise and walk in joy and peace today. I am with you. I am your Immanuel. Always am I with you—*always*. I love you, Child. Live this day in the depths of My love.

How precious is your steadfast love, O God!
All people may take refuge in the shadow of your wings.

PSALM 36:7, *NRSV*

Note
1. See Acts 17:28.

November 25

How great our joy! Great our joy!
Joy, joy, joy! Joy, joy, joy!
Praise we the Lord in heav'n on high!
Praise we the Lord in heav'n on high!

TRADITIONAL GERMAN CAROL,
"HOW GREAT OUR JOY"

Your joy will know no end. Like a child at Christmas, you will know joy upon joy. Yet this will be a joy without end. A joy so all encompassing that it will color all of your days. It is coming, My child. Joy that will permeate your every day. You will be My ambassador, My emissary of joy to others. Take great delight in these words, knowing that they are from My heart to yours.

Accomplish all that is needful. I will help you with each task. I will do more than that. I will bring joy to each task as you keep your eyes on Me. Enjoy the journey. Enjoy the moments of grace. Enjoy seeing My hand at work in your life. You will be seeing My orchestrations more and more.

Continue to live expectantly. Continue to believe My promises. Continue to bask in My love and care. Above all, know the depths of My love for you. Plumb those depths, and know My heart like never before. The better you know Me and My Word, the better you can minister to those around you. The needs are great, but I am so much greater. Nothing is impossible with Me. Walk in My strength and hope today. Stay centered on Me. I do all things well, now and forever. I love you, Child.

I know the greatness of the Lord—
that our Lord is greater than any other god.

PSALM 135:5, *NLT*

November 26

Show Yourself, dear Lord.

I will. Many will marvel when they see the mighty workings of My hand. I will be glorified, just as you desire. Your joy will catapult to new heights as you see at long last what I have been planning for you all along. Your waiting will be transformed into unparalleled joy.

You will never regret waiting on Me. The benefits of waiting on Me will far surpass any hardships encountered along the way. You have come to know this truth, as you have already seen many benefits while still in the trenches of waiting. The ultimate results of waiting on Me will reap more benefits than you can imagine. Know that the time is surely coming when you will see clearly the reasons behind My divine delays.

Today use this time of continued waiting to prepare for the unveiling of My answers. You know the difference between waiting in desperation and waiting with expectation. Take joy in waiting with hope.

Oh, what glorious joy will be yours when you see what I have been preparing for you all these years, My child. Your heart will rejoice not only because of the sweetness of My answers but also because of the serenity you now know in the waiting. Give thanks even now for My answers that will soon be your reality—the results of your waiting on Me in faith and trust.

I love you, My child. Enjoy My every gesture of love to you today, and be blessed.

But if we hope for what we do not see,
we eagerly wait for it with perseverance.

ROMANS 8:25

JUDY GORDON MORROW

November 27

Are we weak and heavy laden, cumbered with a load of care?
Precious Savior, still our refuge—take it to the Lord in prayer.

JOSEPH MEDLICOTT SCRIVEN (1819–1886),
"WHAT A FRIEND WE HAVE IN JESUS"

All is well, My child. My love is covering you and your family, and I have heard your every prayer—prayers deeper than words—and I have seen your every tear. I am with you, and I am with your family. Remember, I love them even more than you do. They are My beloved children, and I am orchestrating My plans for their good and My glory. You will rejoice at My outcomes.

Fret not, and know that I will bring only good to pass. Even if that good is disguised at times, you can be assured the good will come. Leave all to Me. There is no wiser way. Leaving all to Me frees Me to work and frees you from worry. What better combination could there be?

I will help you with all that is facing you—everything is under My care. Rest totally in Me. Think of the words, "Silent night, holy night, all is calm . . ." and let My calm flood you with the sweetest of peace. Remain in My peace the entire Christmas season, and see the difference I will make.

Always come to Me to restore your peace. I will delight to do that for you. Be a bearer of My peace to those seeking My very peace. Extend My love. Share My joy. Remember why I came and rejoice. Your joy will be contagious, and great will be My joy in you. I love you, Child.

Not a word failed of any good thing which the Lord had spoken
to the house of Israel. All came to pass.

JOSHUA 21:45

November 28

Toward the end of my prayer time, I said to the Lord,
"I don't want to leave too soon."

Enjoy this November day, a perfect day to bask in My presence and realize anew My incomparable love for you. As you enter this Christmas season, be blissfully aware of who I am and the significance of the celebration. Don't focus on any negatives, but do dwell on the sweetest story ever told—the story of My beloved Son. But don't stop there. Allow My Spirit to illumine the beauty and majesty of when Light broke through the darkness. The world hasn't been the same since that ordained day.

Your life hasn't been the same, My child, since you allowed My light to flood every part of your being. Light always conquers darkness. Be My light even today, and shine brightly My light and love into the lives of others. You can make more of a difference than you can imagine—with a smile, a timely word, a caring touch.

My children are making a difference all over the world, and I see each one. Nothing escapes My notice, and I am well pleased when I see My love demonstrated in such tangible ways. My light shining in My children all around the world is a beautiful sight to behold. Every light, every person, makes a difference, and only eternity will reveal the life-changing differences that are occurring this very day.

Delight in being My light—you smile as you see the word "light" in delight—and I will bless you beyond measure. I love you, My child. Hear me again: *I love you.*

> *I have come as a light into the world,*
> *that whoever believes in Me*
> *should not abide in darkness.*
>
> JOHN 12:46

November 29

When thinking about my lack of focus and self-discipline,
I sought God's heart on those matters.

Ask Me, My child. You know I am interested in every aspect of your life, and I am willing and available to you at all times for whatever your need may be. Simply ask, and then follow My leadings.

We have worked together this way in the past, but too often you tend to forget to ask and seek My directives, and then distractions enter in and often derail you.

Realize anew that I, your loving Father, am available to you at all times. Never do I slumber or sleep. Never am I unaware of any moment of your life. I take great joy in responding to your every request as you look to Me in total trust and obedience. Those two elements are key, and you think of the hymn with those very words: "Trust and Obey." Truly, if your heart is set to do both—trust and obey—then when you ask for My guidance in every realm, the natural outflow will be your walking in My Spirit and following His ways. Nothing else produces such inner peace and outer workings that are so pleasing to Me.

There is therefore now no condemnation to those who are in Christ Jesus,
who do not walk according to the flesh, but according to the Spirit.

ROMANS 8:1

November 30

When I cannot read, when I cannot think,
when I cannot even pray, I can trust.
J. HUDSON TAYLOR (1832–1905)

The enemy of your soul wants to discourage and defeat you at every turn and produce in you frustration and despair. Contrast that to the joy and peace I alone can offer as you look to Me in trust and obedience. Truly, there is no other way to contentment and happiness in this world. Blessed—happy—is the one who trusts in the Lord.

Trust Me today, My child. Seek Me for every decision, both large and small, and just see the creative and life-giving ways that I will answer you. Remember again the delight it gives Me to be your helper. I created you to need Me, and when we work in tandem to accomplish My every purpose in your life, there is no greater joy. The world's accomplishments pale in contrast to My kingdom purposes.

Keep your eyes on Me today, work in the calm and purposefulness of My Spirit, and just see what together we can accomplish. Not by might, not by power, but by My Spirit, My child. He will make *all* the difference.

Lord Almighty, blessed is the one who trusts in you.
PSALM 84:12, *NIV*

JUDY GORDON MORROW

December

Immanuel, God with us.

Thank You for being *my* Immanuel, God with *me*. You are not a God who stands afar; You are *with* me. Oh, the wonder of "with"! When someone is *with* me, he or she is right there—present, available.

"With" denotes closeness—someone I can touch, someone who can touch me. What on overlooked word is "with"! It is the opposite of apart and separated. "With" whispers the warmth of friendship. "With" indicates a choice to be near. "With" is the link that connects my heart to the very heart of God.

Immanuel—God with us. God with me, God with you. The God who has chosen to entwine His life with ours when we respond with "Welcome!" To welcome His "with" is to know joy and wonder divine.

C
H
R
I
S
T
My
Awesome
Savior

December 1

In order to know God, we must often think of Him; and when we come to love Him, we shall then also think of Him often, for our heart will be with our treasure.

BROTHER LAWRENCE (1614–1691)

Keep your gaze on My face, and focus on Me and My ways. The more you focus on Me, the more I can align your thinking with Mine. This is crucial, My child. My thoughts are pure and true, and in Me is no deceit or guile. Spending time with Me allows Me to fill you with My thoughts—My very nature—so that you can live your life out of My truth.

What you think indicates your allegiance. Think My thoughts, and people will know you belong to Me. Out of your thoughts will proceed your actions. Your actions will show your heart after Mine, because those actions will be the direct result of thinking My thoughts and being filled with all the fullness of Me.

Incorrect and faulty thinking leads to flawed behavior—actions rooted in self-interest. Seeking My thinking and My ways will always yield a life of beauty and purpose. You are struck by the contrast, as you should be, and you realize the beauty and joy of a life lived fully in Me. Truly, there is no better way—it is the *only* way of deep contentment and peace.

Enjoy the richness and serenity of My peace this very day, My child. Let nothing displace My peace. Keep your heart and mind aligned with Mine, and My peace will prevail. You will know it to be so.

For this reason, since the day we heard it, we have not ceased praying for you and asking that you may be filled with the knowledge of God's will in all spiritual wisdom and understanding, so that you may lead lives worthy of the Lord, fully pleasing to him, as you bear fruit in every good work and as you grow in the knowledge of God.

COLOSSIANS 1:9-10, *NRSV*

December 2

Work Your wonders, Lord.

I will, My child. I will work My wonders for you in such a way that no one will be able to escape the truth that all came from My hand. My workings won't be paltry or puny—how could they be, coming from Me? But *because of who I am*, they will be glorious and magnificent. Amazing. Even astounding. What I will do will lift eyes upward to Me, causing the ones you are praying for to see Me in My majesty and power.

You can scarcely take in what I am saying to you, but know it to be true. I lift up My humble servants so that My glory will shine. My beauty, My character, can be seen through those who are aligned totally with Me. My image is reflected in their trusting hearts and shines in their eyes of faith.

Truly, is there a more beautiful sight than the one who is one with Me? One in My purposes, one in My truth, one in My love above all loves. That oneness is the wellspring of joy and peace that will never run dry. Nothing in this world can compare with the satisfaction found only in Me.

Yes, everything else is worthless when compared with the infinite value of knowing Christ Jesus my Lord. For his sake I have discarded everything else, counting it all as garbage, so that I could gain Christ and become one with him. I no longer count on my own righteousness through obeying the law; rather, I become righteous through faith in Christ. For God's way of making us right with himself depends on faith.

PHILIPPIANS 3:8-9, NLT

December 3

My ways are so superior to the ways of man that your imagination cannot even begin to compare to My creativity and the endless possibilities that can come from My heart of unsurpassed love. Think on that, My child. Put the "in" before "finite," and realize like never before how limitless and infinite I am. Your every circumstance placed against the backdrop of My infinite power causes them to shrink in size, does it not? I am the great I AM, and nothing is impossible with Me.

The One to whom you are now praying can meet your every need with such abundance, such care, such love. Sometimes when you pray, your focus is more on the problem, the troubling situation, than it is on Me. Don't resort to praying to the problem, but look up to your loving Father and pray to Me, the Almighty One. See? Doesn't that change your perspective? If My children would only fix their eyes on My face, their faith would increase a hundredfold. I am the *infinite* God—yes, dwell on that word like never before—and I will work My wonders for you out of who I am.

"I am the Alpha and the Omega—the beginning and the end,"
says the Lord God. "I am the one who is, who always was,
and who is still to come—the Almighty One."

REVELATION 1:8, *NLT*

December 4

*We have an anchor that keeps the soul steadfast and sure while
the billows roll. Fastened to the Rock which cannot move,
grounded firm and deep in the Savior's love.*

PRISCILLA J. OWENS (1829–1907),
"WE HAVE AN ANCHOR"

What glorious words of hope I am speaking to you this morning, My
child. Words based on who I am and My great love for you. Words that
I wish to seal on your heart forever so that their truths will hold you
steady in the times of testing.

Anchor yourself to My timeless truths, and you will remain secure
when the billows of life threaten to overtake you. In Me you will know
calm and strength and peace. My infinite grace includes My keeping
power. I will *keep* you in perfect peace as you stay your mind on *Me*.
There is no better way, no sweeter joy.

Joy in this day, in this season of joy, when all eyes are focused
on Christmas but often miss Me, Christ, in that very word. They are
distracted by the mass of activities, while My desire is for them to see
Me, the Man who came as a baby to deliver them and set them free,
once and for all. Exult in the freedom you have in Me, and enjoy this
day in My presence.

I love you, My precious child.

*This hope we have as an anchor of the soul, both sure and steadfast,
and which enters the Presence behind the veil, where the forerunner has
entered for us, even Jesus, having become High Priest forever
according to the order of Melchizedek.*

HEBREWS 6:19-20

December 5

Everything God does is love—even when we do not understand Him.

BASILEA SCHLINK (1904–2001)

Trust Me completely. Rest in Me and the workings of My hand. Don't try to figure things out. Just be content in who I am. I, your Father, am preparing joys for you that you have not yet dreamed of. Know My joy and peace even now in the waiting. I will not fail you. You are My dearly beloved child, and I love you with an everlasting love.

Depend on Me for everything. Be anxious for nothing. Know the peace that comes *only* from Me. How can you be anxious when I am in control? Relax. Rest. Breathe in deeply of My peace and love and give them both to others. How My children need Me! Be an instrument of My peace and love. I will use you in that way.

Today is My gift to you. Use it wisely and enjoy each moment in My presence. That's the key: abide in My presence and all doubt, anxiety and fear will flee. I am the Alpha and the Omega, and in the midst of who I am are my plans for you. Plans of love and justice and peace.

Be assured that all is well. You have nothing to fear or dread. My plans are for your good and My glory, and great will be your joy, My child. I will joy in your joy. May that thought bring joy to your heart all day long. I love you with a love beyond imagining. Trust Me completely.

Be strong and bold; have no fear or dread of them,
because it is the Lord your God who goes with you;
he will not fail you or forsake you.

DEUTERONOMY 31:6, NRSV

JUDY GORDON MORROW

December 6

Silent as snow
Is my praise today
So full of wonder
At God and His ways.
Often my tongue
Recites my praise,
Yet today—so deep,
So vast my thoughts
That I dare not raise
One word, one sound
To the heavens above.
Rather, I am lost in awe,
Overwhelmed by His love.

JGM

I love you, My child. Enjoy the gift of this day. Follow My every nudge.
Know My peace as you prepare for the celebration of My birth. Keep
praise ever on your lips. It is that praise that beautifies your countenance and draws others to Me. Be My vessel, and I will be glorified.
Move in who I am, and dwell in My presence all day today.

Surely the righteous shall give thanks to Your name;
the upright shall dwell in Your presence.

PSALM 140:13

December 7

Thinking of my busy day, I sang in my mind,
"God rest ye merry, gentlemen, let nothing you dismay . . ."

Go on your way, My child. I am going before you. I will give you wisdom in your gift-giving and in *everything* you need. That's what a loving Father does. It gives Me joy that you seek Me and My wisdom for every little thing, and then together we can joy in My sweet answers to you and the subsequent results. I desire this kind of shared joy with *all* My children.

See Me and My orchestrations in every part of this day. Pause to hear My voice and to learn My leadings. The difference that will make in your day will be peace instead of perplexity, calm in place of chaos, and joy providing a wreath of protection around your heart.

Know again that I am bigger than any of your circumstances. I see all. I know all. Never will I forget you. Never are you alone. My love is wrapping around you even now with every assurance of My loving care. Let My love enfold you like never before, and rest in its comfort.

O tidings of comfort and joy, comfort and joy. O tidings of comfort and joy.

Yes, just as that carol played in your mind, sing its truth all day today. I *am* your comfort and joy. This moment, *every* moment of your day and forever. Timeless is My comfort and joy for you. Embrace each moment of this day, and exult in My comfort and joy.

Then young women will dance and be glad, young men and old as well.
I will turn their mourning into gladness;
I will give them comfort and joy instead of sorrow.

JEREMIAH 31:13, *NIV*

December 8

There's so much I don't understand, but this I know: I know You.

Men try to tame Me and explain Me, but how can you explain such greatness, such majesty, such power? How can you explain what is meant to be a mystery until the time of My revealing has come? Men want to reduce Me and relegate Me to fit their understanding. But I am far beyond the comprehension of My creations. Yet I desire a close relationship with My children so that I can reveal Myself and My love to them one chapter at a time.

You don't expect to read a large volume in one sitting, nor would there be as much enjoyment of the book if you did. Page by page, I am willing to write on the hearts of My children My words of love and wisdom—to give them increased knowledge and understanding of Me. Overwhelming would it be if I were to pour out more than the finite mind can take in.

It is out of My loving-kindness and care for My children that I, piece by piece, impart the knowledge they need when they are willing to seek Me and spend time with Me. It gives me great joy to fellowship with My family—those who have placed their faith and trust in Me alone and seek after Me in all things. This is the way of grace and sweet contentment. You have found it to be so, My child.

Yours, O Lord, is the greatness, the power and the glory, the victory
and the majesty; for all that is in heaven and in earth is Yours;
Yours is the kingdom, O Lord, And You are exalted as head over all.

1 CHRONICLES 29:11

December 9

Once earthly joy I craved, sought peace and rest.
Now Thee alone I seek; give what is best.

ELIZABETH PRENTISS (1818–1878),
"MORE LOVE TO THEE, O CHRIST"

The more you have sought after Me, the more you have discovered about Me and the deeper our friendship has grown. It has brought sweet rewards, has it not? To the point that you yearn for everyone to know Me and to experience who I am and what I have to offer to each one individually.

Yes, that is one aspect many forget. I am universal in My love yet very individual in My dealings with My children. You appreciate that aspect of Me like few do, as you have seen My specific and personal workings in your life and in the lives of others. Continue to rejoice in that, and share your wonder and gratitude with others as I give you opportunity.

This time together has been sweet, My child. Your spirit is uplifted and renewed, as it is each time you choose to spend time with Me. Your desire to know Me will only grow, along with the rich dividends that will result from our times together.

Now go in joy. Continue to enjoy every joy of this season, and pray that others will also come to know Me. Bring to them My tidings of comfort and joy.

For since our friendship with God was restored by the death of his Son while we were still his enemies, we will certainly be saved through the life of his Son. So now we can rejoice in our wonderful new relationship with God because our Lord Jesus Christ has made us friends of God.

ROMANS 5:10-11, *NLT*

December 10

His yoke is easy; His burden is light. I've found it so; I've found it so.
He leadeth me by day and by night where living waters flow.

RALPH E. HUDSON (1843–1901),
"HIS YOKE IS EASY"

Rest today in who I am, and don't allow the day to overtake you with its overwhelming tasks. Follow My example when I walked the earth and approach every situation one at a time. Focus on what is in front of you while keeping your heart attuned to Mine for guidance. You see the wisdom in that and yearn for that kind of clarity as you go about your day.

Ever turn your eyes to Me, and I will help you. Remember? I *am* your Helper. Don't forget that about Me—the truth of My being your Helper—and turn to Me for everything. This is how the burden remains light and the yoke easy. You aren't bearing all that life offers on your own. I am *helping* you. I long to help *all* My children, but too often they plow ahead without Me, wearying themselves in their weakness, when all along I am longing to be their Helper and to show My strength to be perfect for every weakness. You are weak so that I can show My strength, and then others will see Me and the difference I make.

Delight in your weakness today. Delight in your frailties. Be glad for your imperfections. It is in all of those that My strength and sufficiency can shine. I will delight in doing that for you today, My child. Delight in My delight, and be blessed. I love you.

As for me, since I am poor and needy, let the Lord keep me in his thoughts.
You are my helper and my savior. O my God, do not delay.

PSALM 40:17, *NLT*

December 11

*When you cannot rejoice in feelings, circumstances or conditions,
rejoice in the Lord.*

A. B. SIMPSON (1843–1919)

Ponder these words: nothing comes to you that isn't first known to
Me. Nothing catches Me by surprise. Thus, all things will be used by
Me for My kingdom when they are offered up to Me for My purposes.
A life lived for Me and My purposes is never lacking. I can take deepest
pain and transform it into a vessel for joy. But the pain, the heartache,
every hard thing, has to be given over to My hands, with no grasping
by My children. Every surrendered pain yields a victory of grace.

While My ways can't often be initially understood, hang on to the
truth that My ways are anchored in eternal and timeless principles
that do not falter or fail. In the end, all will become clear, and all will
be used for My glory and for your ultimate good. It is the higher way
and a way well worth seeking.

The key is surrender to Me, the One who loves you with a love so
pure out of a heart above reproach. No love on earth can compare, My
child. This is the love that came to die for you so that you can have
life eternal with Me. Rejoice in that love afresh today, and sing out of
a heart of deep gratitude and joy.

Joy to the world, the Lord is come!

*But these are written so that you may come to believe that Jesus is the Messiah,
the Son of God, and that through believing you may have life in his name.*

JOHN 20:31, *NRSV*

The Listening Heart

JUDY GORDON MORROW

December 12

*Once more, never think that you can live to God
by your own power or strength; but always look to and rely on him
for assistance, yea, for all strength and grace.*

DAVID BRAINERD (1718–1747)

Rest in Me completely today. Yes, you have much to do, but I am up to the task. See how that takes the pressure off you? *I* am up to the task. Just rely totally on Me and Me alone. I will bring glory to My name as you trust Me for everything.

I will guide you today. Live in praise and thanksgiving. Focus on Me and My words. Know My overwhelming love for you. Dwell on My love like never before. It is designed for you to give you hope in all that I have promised. Just trust Me completely.

I know you are tired. I will restore you. I will strengthen you. I will go before you to prepare the way. There is nothing to fear or dread but much to look forward to. Live in complete confidence in Me. I will not betray your confidence. Pray much, and pray in faith believing, never wavering. I will honor your faith, which will bring honor and glory to Me. Faint not in your praying and believing. My answers will arrive right on time.

Go in My love and peace. Look to Me alone. Praise Me all day. I will dwell in your praise, and I will strengthen you for every task. All is well, My child. You will soon possess the gifts from My hand, and your joy will overflow.

*Fear not, for I am with you; be not dismayed, for I am your God.
I will strengthen you, yes, I will help you,
I will uphold you with My righteous right hand.*

ISAIAH 41:10

December 13

Divine sovereignty is not the sovereignty of a tyrannical Despot, but the exercised pleasure of One who is infinitely wise and good! Because God is infinitely wise He cannot err, and because He is infinitely righteous He will not do wrong.

A. W. PINK (1886–1952)

If I am not in control, who is? Any other thought is cause for concern. While My ways may not be discernible to the human mind, that doesn't negate the fact that I am ultimately in control.

Do you not know how My heart breaks when I see the grievous acts done by men? Can you not imagine that the things that bring you sorrow I feel even more deeply? I as your Father have the capacity to feel more outrage at injustice than all humanity combined. Nothing occurs without My knowing or without My caring—even when it may appear otherwise.

You must always keep in mind one vast difference: I am God, and you are not. I have given man remarkable capabilities, but all pale in contrast to who I am and what I can do. Your lack of knowledge of Me and My ways can often take you down paths lined with human thinking, forgetting to consider the height and depth and breadth of My thoughts and purposes.

Knowing I am in control yields a comfort like nothing else can. It is an act of relinquishment—exchanging your finite understanding for My supreme wisdom—a wisdom that transcends everything finite and human and soars to infinite impossibilities.

It feels safer, I know, to put me in a realm with parameters, where things make sense—at least most of the time. But My limitless nature and capabilities cannot be hemmed in by anyone or anything. Doing that only limits your capability for absolute faith and trust in Me.

You are my flock, the sheep of my pasture. You are my people, and I am your God. I, the Sovereign Lord, have spoken!

EZEKIEL 34:31, *NLT*

JUDY GORDON MORROW

December 14

*As long as I am content to know that He is infinitely greater than I,
and that I cannot know Him unless He shows Himself to me, I will have Peace,
and He will be near me and in me, and I will rest in Him.*

THOMAS MERTON (1915–1968)

You see the foolishness of finite humans trying to limit and explain their limitless and extraordinary God. It's like filling a jar with seawater and calling it the ocean. The power and depth and immensity of the ocean cannot be contained in a jar, and you clearly see the analogy to Me and My nature and abilities that can't be contained or explained.

They can be enjoyed, however. Enjoyed by My children who come to Me with expectant faith and confidence in the One who loves them beyond measure. They trust that Love, they rest in that Love, and they refuse to limit that Love. So much so that even when horrendous and unspeakable events happen, they know they can't comprehend the reasons but also that they don't need to. They only need to remember *who I am*, the Almighty God who sees and knows far beyond their understanding to His eternal consequences and purposes.

On that you can rest, My child. On *Me* you can rest. Every doubt, question, misgiving and fear can be laid on Me, and in exchange I will give My peace, joy, rest and hope. Yes, I am in control. But remember who I am. I am Love. When Love is in control, Love will prevail. What you see here is not the final outcome. Glorious will be your joy when you see My illuminating answers on the other side. Glimpses I may give you here, but when you see the final revelations of My workings, you will rejoice with unspeakable joy."

But as it is written: "Eye has not seen, nor ear heard, nor have entered into the heart of man the things which God has prepared for those who love Him."

1 CORINTHIANS 2:9

Author's note: I penned the words for December 13 and 14 on the morning of December 14, 2012. After I arose from my knees, I learned of the tragedy in Sandy Hook, Connecticut. God amazed me by the timeliness of His words that day, and I pray they will comfort you as they did me.

December 15

You are the God of hope.
Give Your hope today to this troubled world—and to me.

Hope resides in knowing Me. Where I am is hope everlasting. It is so easy to become bound to the things of this world, forgetting that your life there is so fleeting, so temporal. There is no hope outside of Me. In Me is hope abundant, a hope that looks beyond the temporal to the eternal. Fix your gaze on Me, and your hope will never waver. You are infused with hope when you allow Me to fill you with all My fullness.

Think anew on the beauty and hope of being so filled with Me that nothing else can entrench on that dwelling place. My fullness in you allows no room for anything detrimental or false. Out of My fullness comes abundant living, rich in meaning and purpose. This is My desire for all My children—to live a life of fullness that overflows into the lives of others. My grace in your life isn't intended for your benefit alone, as you know. Just as I refresh you, you need to refresh others with My love and truth.

Now enjoy this day in front of you. Don't weigh it down with a negative outlook, but embrace it with the lens of My hope. View it as a day to shine My goodness and hope into the lives of others. You've seen how My hope has transformed your life. Now extend that gift to others, so that they may also know Me and My abounding hope.

Why are you cast down, O my soul?
And why are you disquieted within me?
Hope in God; for I shall yet praise Him,
the help of my countenance and my God.

PSALM 42:11

December 16

I desire Your thoughts.

All is well, My child. Indeed, all is well. Know that like never before. Know My love like never before. Don't allow human frailties to determine your mindset, to guide your heart, but look to Me and My truth alone.

Review again all the wonders of these years and all I have done and shown you and spoken. Each has revealed truth to you time and again—My truth of love and care for you. Don't desert that truth, even though you see nothing changing.

Your sight is not Mine, and I will grant you My sight at just the right moment. Then you will know what I am seeing even now. Your spirits droop when you focus your eyes too low. Keep your sight on Me, the Most High, and you will have cause for celebration even before you see the completion of My plan.

Where you choose to focus will determine where you choose to live. Focus on circumstances, and you will live in doubt and despair. Focus on Me, and you will live in faith and hope. You determine your residence—your outlook—by where you choose to look.

Already your spirits are lifting because of this time with Me. That will always be the case in My company. Time spent with Me, to abide in Me, will always benefit your day. I love you, My child. *All is well.*

> But You, O Lord, are a shield for me,
> My glory and the One who lifts up my head.
>
> PSALM 3:3

December 17

Until we know Jesus, God is merely a concept, and we can't have faith in Him.
But once we hear Jesus say, "He who has seen Me has seen the Father,"
we immediately have something that is real, and our faith is limitless.

OSWALD CHAMBERS (1874–1917)

The things of this world are temporal and daily passing away. Like the rust I spoke about, the elements of the world are destined to decay. You are clearly seeing the contrast, aren't you, My child, to what I offer those washed by My blood and brought into perfect union with Me. My life abundant becomes theirs—abundant in forgiveness and love and hope. All in Me is eternal and will never pass away.

In Me is continual newness. Unending joy. A peace that endures. Eternal riches that are available to all who call on Me and desire Me to be their Lord and Savior.

This Christmas season has people thinking about Me, wondering about this Jesus who was born in a stable. Hearts are stirred to know more, to have a hope beyond the tantalizing trappings that will soon be trash or packed away for another year.

See, My child, how hopeless and sad Christmas is without Me at its center? Instead of a celebration of life eternal, it is the amplification of despair adorned in tinsel. Everything shiny becomes a cover for darkness rather than a means to show My light. What a perfect time for those who love Me to shine for Me like never before and to give My words of hope and healing.

Do not lay up for yourselves treasures on earth, where moth and rust destroy
and where thieves break in and steal; but lay up for yourselves treasures in heaven,
where neither moth nor rust destroys and where thieves do not break in and steal.
For where your treasure is, there your heart will be also.

MATTHEW 6:19-21

The Listening Heart   JUDY GORDON MORROW

December 18

No darkness have we who in Jesus abide;
the Light of the world is Jesus.
We walk in the Light when we follow our Guide;
the Light of the world is Jesus.

PHILIP P. BLISS (1838–1876),
"THE LIGHT OF THE WORLD IS JESUS"

This time of year, be more aware than ever of the opportunities I will be giving you to offer My shining hope in tangible ways. Just think—if all of My children who confess Me as Lord would pour forth My light and love this month, what a different world it would be forever—both now and into eternity.

You envision Christians all over the world holding up a candle of Christ, shining My light and truth, and you see the planet ablaze with My radiance. Capture that image, My child, and keep it in your mind's eye as you move through your day. See yourself as My light in dark places, and see the shadows flee. In Me is light and no darkness at all.

Shine, My child, shine. My glow on your face I will use in ways that will astound you. Yes, like the song that is playing though your mind, "The light of the world is Jesus." Shine forth My light.

God is light and in Him is no darkness at all.

1 JOHN 1:5

The light of the righteous shines brightly,
but the lamp of the wicked is snuffed out.

PROVERBS 13:9, *NIV*

December 19

The first step on the way to victory is to recognize the enemy.
CORRIE TEN BOOM (1892–1983)

Listen to Me alone today. Do not let the lies of the enemy enter in. He has been that prowling lion lately, seeking to devour you in doubt, but I am calling you to partake in the fullness of faith. Don't spend even a second listening to his lies, but look only to Me and My truth. Always do I speak truth to you so that My highest purpose for you will come to pass as you feed on My truth to you.

Dwell in Me and My truth all day today. Cast down the enemy and his lies with My sword of truth. He cannot withstand Truth, and I have placed the sword of truth in your hands for you to wield against him. All power of Mine is yours, My child, as you look to Me for everything you need.

This day is Mine. Right then, with the hearing of those words, a pressure valve went off, relieving you of the weight of the day with all the cares that are pulling at you. I will take care of each one. Take joy in turning over each concern to Me, and just see what I will do. *All is well*, My child.

Be alert and of sober mind. Your enemy the devil prowls around like
a roaring lion looking for someone to devour. Resist him, standing firm
in the faith, because you know that the family of believers throughout the world
is undergoing the same kind of sufferings.
1 PETER 5:8-9, *NIV*

The Listening Heart JUDY GORDON MORROW

December 20

Why would anyone want to go any other way than to be with You?

Because they don't know Me like you do. You have spent time with Me. You have learned My heart, you have recognized My hand, you have seen Me in the details of life. I can bless those who spend time with Me, who seek Me in all things. Aren't you glad that this coming apart with Me has become such a natural part of your life? You knew it would be valuable, but you didn't know the sweetness it would offer because of the sweetness of My presence.

I have heard your heartfelt words this morning, My child. I have heard your praise and your petitions. I see and know all. Nothing escapes My sight. I have answered your pleas for your loved ones, and I will continue to. Great are the plans I have for each of them. You will rejoice. Continue to lift them up and pray My best for them. I will provide.

My ways are highest and best and worth waiting for. The sweetness and joy of My presence will only increase as you continue to wait on Me. Rest in My promises. Rest in My love that is the foundation of those promises. Do think of Abraham and Sarah and the impossibility of what I had promised. Yet Abraham believed, and so must you.

I know the plans I have for you, and they are plans of hope, joy and peace. You will be amazed. Take joy in these words. Hope only and always in Me.

And Abraham's faith did not weaken, even though, at about 100 years of age, he figured his body was as good as dead—and so was Sarah's womb.

ROMANS 4:19, *NLT*

December 21

Souls in danger, look above; Jesus completely saves.
He will lift you by His love out of the angry waves.
He's the Master of the sea; billows His will obey.
He your Savior wants to be—be saved today.

JAMES ROWE (1865–1933),
"LOVE LIFTED ME"

All is well. I am at work. Trust Me alone and trust Me completely. Truly, I do all things well, and I will work to My glory in every situation that you have prayed about this morning. Know that to be so, and be at rest. The rest that no ruffling of circumstances can disturb. The rest that comes only from Me. The rest that is entwined with My perfect peace.

Think of a child holding on to her father in a boat out at sea that is being battered by wind and waves. Yet in her father's arms she knows security and serenity, because none of the outside forces can get to her. That's how I protect you, My child. Like a father with his child, I will not let outside forces and circumstances rob you of the peace and rest found in Me. Be that trusting child, and cling to Me. I will not fail you. I have only your best interest at heart.

Today dwell on who I am and all that is available to you in Me. I lack for nothing, and therefore, as My child you will lack for nothing either. In Me is all you need.

Be at peace, My child. I am with you. Always I am with you. You will see great and wondrous things done by your mighty, unfailing God who loves you beyond measure.

Though I am surrounded by troubles, you will protect me from the anger of my enemies. You reach out your hand, and the power of your right hand saves me.

PSALM 138:7, NLT

JUDY GORDON MORROW

December 22

Faith is the sight of the inward eye.
ALEXANDER MACLAREN (1826–1910)

Faith in Me is as certain as anything you can see. What is believed for by faith exists—all that is needful is the removal of the veil. Once the veil is removed, the vision of faith becomes the vision of reality. However, seeing the answer doesn't make it real—it was real even under the veil of faith. Remind yourself of that truth today as you continue to wait on Me.

Your faith is the place marker for what already exists. The waiting isn't to make it come into being—that part is already taken care of. The waiting is My way of perfecting the plan, of allowing the time needed until My hand can draw back the veil to reveal My glorious answers.

You have honored Me, and now I will be honoring you. Every tear and every heartache will be transformed into glorious and unimaginable joy. Know that joy even today—partake of it even now—even before the veil has been drawn back. Then your walking by faith will be made complete.

This has been a good time together, has it not, My child? Recall My words to you all day. In rejoicing in Me all day—before your faith is made sight—your joy will only be enhanced when you see and know fully My answers. They are on the way. Believe Me, and soon you *will* see.

So all of us who have had that veil removed can see and reflect the glory of the Lord. And the Lord—who is the Spirit—makes us more and more like him as we are changed into his glorious image.

2 CORINTHIANS 3:18, *NLT*

December 23

Shepherds, in the field abiding, watching o'er your flocks by night,
God with man is now residing; yonder shines the infant light.
Come and worship, come and worship, worship Christ, the newborn King.

JAMES MONTGOMERY (1771–1854),
"ANGELS, FROM THE REALMS OF GLORY"

If I can use lowly shepherds and a distant star to reveal My Son's birth, just imagine the limitless possibilities I can use when fulfilling My plans for you. Plans that will bring glory to Me in this time of darkness so that I can once again shine My light and truth and love in My chosen ways.

So, expect the unexpected, My child. My ways not only confound and confuse the onlookers, but they compel and convict them to come to Me, the One who can set them free from sin and give them a new life out of their forgiven hearts. This is My message of Christmas for every moment of the year. I make all things new and clean and fresh so that I can dwell there and infuse My life and love forever.

Live in the context of My Christmas miracle all year long, and wonder and joy and love will frame your every day.

That night there were shepherds staying in the fields nearby, guarding their flocks of sheep. Suddenly, an angel of the Lord appeared among them, and the radiance of the Lord's glory surrounded them. They were terrified, but the angel reassured them. "Don't be afraid!" he said. "I bring you good news that will bring great joy to all people."

LUKE 2:8-10, *NLT*

December 24

O come to my heart, Lord Jesus; there is room in my heart for Thee.

EMILY E. S. ELLIOTT (1836–1897),
"THOU DIDST LEAVE THY THRONE"

Seek only to glorify Me, and all else will fall into place. Shed abroad My love and kindness. Be My conduit of joy. Then I will be seen, and I will be glorified. I will help you to do that even on this busy day. Especially today, so that more than ever I can shine through you.

Yes, I know that is your desire, and I will honor that desire as you look only to Me. Keep your face and heart turned only upward, and just see what I will do. Do all unto Me—prepare as if I were coming tonight to your celebration. For I am, don't you see? I will be in the midst of your celebration with My shining, loving Presence, accomplishing My purposes as you rest totally in Me.

Come, My child. Come and adore Me. Worship Me. Find in Me all that you need. I alone truly satisfy. I am your Immanuel, today and always. Today know Me as your Immanuel like never before. I *am* with you. Rest in My arms of love, and know My joy and peace. I love you, My child. All is well. Truly, all is well—beyond your knowing. Rest in that assurance. Rest, and be at peace.

"Behold, the virgin shall be with child, and bear a Son,
and they shall call His name Immanuel,"
which is translated, "God with us."

MATTHEW 1:23

December 25

Dear Jesus,

Thank You for coming. Thank You for coming into my life, into every situation, every day. Thank You for being an ever-present, ever-loving Savior. I am so in awe of You and who You are and Your great love for me. I am so indebted to You and Your sacrificial gift of Yourself to this world—and to me.

I can't imagine my life without You, and I'm so grateful that I will never have to. Help me, Jesus, to honor You and to be Your love to all I meet.

Thank You for being my Immanuel, for being with me every moment. Because of You I am not alone, I am not abandoned, I am not left desolate.

Praise be to You, Jesus, as we celebrate Your birth today. I love You for all eternity.

Merry Christmas, Jesus.

Merry Christmas, My child. I will bless this day with hope and joy and peace. Enjoy the blessings from My hand. See Me in all things. Know I am working in every way. Walk in faith, believing, and I will honor you in the most marvelous of ways. Trust Me completely and enjoy watching My wonders unfold. All is well, My precious child.

Now enjoy your day and bask in My love. Celebrate anew who I am to you and the life I am living through you. Take great joy in My love today. You will know the depths of My love more than ever before.

For there is born to you this day in the city of David a Savior,
who is Christ the Lord. . . . And suddenly there was with the angel a multitude
of the heavenly host praising God and saying: "Glory to God in the highest,
and on earth peace, goodwill toward men!"

LUKE 2:11,13-14

December 26

I need Thy presence every passing hour;
what but Thy grace can foil the tempter's power?
Who, like Thyself, my guide and stay can be?
Through cloud and sunshine, Lord, abide with me.

HENRY FRANCIS LYTE (1793–1847),
"ABIDE WITH ME"

hese days are designed by Me. You will see My plans unfold more and
ore. Take joy in these words and in Me, the One who speaks them. They
e meant to give you hope and joy.

Don't worry about anything. Trust Me and rest in Me completely. Let
e have everything, and I will work out My plans beyond your wildest
eams. Take courage and comfort in My words. Know anew the One who
eaks them to you.

Abide in Me, and I will abide in you. In abiding is rest and peace and
y. Don't let anything else substitute for abiding in Me. Nothing else will
tisfy like Me. Truly, I will fill you with all the fullness of Myself as you
ide in Me.

Be still in My presence. Let My love wash over you and remove all traces
anything that is not of Me. Then your cleansed, transparent vessel will
ow clearly My light and love. This is key in being effective for Me. Every-
ing else is secondary—and often phony—if this does not take place first.

Live in constant hope. Let nothing cast a shadow of doubt. Look only
Me, and your hope will flourish. I love you, My child. Hope only in Me.

Abide in me as I abide in you. Just as the branch cannot bear fruit by itself
unless it abides in the vine, neither can you unless you abide in me.

JOHN 15:4, *NRSV*

December 27

Give me wisdom, Lord.

I will give you wisdom. Wisdom from My Father heart to yours. Will I withhold any good thing from you? Of course not. My love is a fountain of goodness for My children. Drink deeply and be refreshed. My supply is never depleted or even diminished. And it is freely available to all My children.

The more you give away My love to others, the more room you will have for the ongoing fresh supply. Selfishness stifles the flow, but selflessness creates a wellspring that will never run dry. You know this to be true. Joy in the beauty and constancy of My supply of heavenly riches given for your good and My glory.

Continue to enjoy the restfulness of this day. Bask in My presence and the ever-present hope I continue to give you. Its supply is also limitless. Your faith is the means of keeping your vessel of hope filled to overflowing. Be prepared to have your every hope fulfilled as you wait upon Me and My timings. I do all things well, beyond what you can even think or imagine.

But whoever drinks of the water that I shall give him will never thirst.
But the water that I shall give him will become in him
a fountain of water springing up into everlasting life.

JOHN 4:14

JUDY GORDON MORROW

December 28

Come, Holy Spirit, I need You.

I am coming. I am coming with My answers. Know that I am speaking truth to you, My child. Dwell in My truth always, and all will be well. Go outside of My truth, and doubts and darkness will assail. Remain in My truth alone.

I know your struggles today. Cast each concern into My hands of care, and then *leave them there*. I will take care of each one. Hear Me again, My child. I *will* take care of each thing that troubles you. Just leave all with Me.

Sing. Praise Me. Pray without ceasing. All will lift you upward, where you belong. Despair dislodges My truth and has no place in My children. I came to bring you hope, joy and peace. Dwell in Me, and all things good will be yours. Choose to remain in Me in the darkness—especially in the darkness—and I will hold you fast. I will keep you and warm you in the light of My presence.

Go now into your day with singing. Sing all day, if need be, and see the difference praise to Me will make. I am with you, My child, always with you. Let not your heart be troubled or afraid. Immanuel—I *am* with you.

Righteousness and justice are the foundation of your throne;
love and faithfulness go before you. Blessed are those who have learned
to acclaim you, who walk in the light of your presence, Lord.

PSALM 89:14-15, *NIV*

December 29

Reflecting on all God has done for me,
who He is to me, and how grateful I am . . . "I love You, Lord."

I love you, My child. Yes, what a blessed time we had this morning, all because you chose to spend time with Me. I desire such times with *all* My children, but few there are who seek to be with Me, really *be* with Me. I am always available, always waiting, always hoping and desiring for those sweet times of communion with My children. They bring as much joy to Me as they bring to you, My child. My Father heart rejoices in the presence of My children.

I will give more and more opportunities for you to share about these very times—their significance and their sweetness. All these years of isolation and separation will bear much fruit for My kingdom. You have honored Me, My child, with your devotion toward Me, and now I will be honoring you beyond your wildest imaginings.

Faithful is He who calls you who also will do it.[1] Out of My faithfulness will I be honoring you, My faithful servant. Trust Me completely, just as you have been, and just see what I will do. Truly, you will be amazed, just as I've told you all these years. Again, *faithful is He* who calls you who also *will* do it.

Now enjoy your day. Rejoice. Again, I say rejoice! Rejoice forevermore.

But it is good for me to draw near to God;
I have put my trust in the Lord God,
that I may declare all Your works.

PSALM 73:28

Note
1. See 1 Thessalonians 5:24.

December 30

The New Year will be filled with hope because it will be filled with You.

Yes, My child, I will fill to overflowing this new year with My limitless hope. I am the embodiment of hope, and there are no limits on Me. More and more you are capturing that truth and living out My promises based on My limitless love.

   The more you know Me, the more you will know of My limitless capabilities. For the child who taps into Me there is available a never-ending wellspring of My abundant resources. Take hold of that truth, and you will possess My solution to thoughts of deprivation and despondency. In Me you have everything you need.

   Don't forget the message of Christmas. I came to provide. I came to uplift. I came to restore. I came to rescue. I came to love with a Love beyond knowing. I came to seek and to save and to give the best and highest gift of all—My very life—so that all can enter My kingdom, a kingdom without end.

> *Jesus said to him, "Today salvation has come to this house,*
> *because this man, too, is a son of Abraham.*
> *For the Son of Man came to seek and to save the lost."*
> LUKE 19:9-10, *NIV*

December 31

Another year is dawning: dear Father, let it be,
In working or in waiting, another year with Thee.

FRANCES RIDLEY HAVERGAL (1836–1879),
"ANOTHER YEAR IS DAWNING"

I have chosen all with a heart full of endless and unfailing love. At each heart I stand and knock, waiting for the welcome in response to My invitation of love. But only you can open the door and extend the welcome for My entrance. For some I have waited long, and I yearn for their joyous "yes!" to My love and sacrifice for them.

I know you have prayed long and hard, My child, for those who have not yet swung open the doors of their hearts. Your prayers, and the prayers of those like you, are the oil on the hinges of the hearts' doors, enabling them to open toward Me. Never fail to keep praying, all the while envisioning the flinging open of those hardened hearts to Me—hearts that have been softened by your constant prayers and care.

Use this last day of the year to reflect on Me and My words to you. See the new year with eyes illuminated by My joy and hope. Step into the new year with confidence in the One who loves you like no other and desires only the best for you. Seek Me and My ways, and you will lack for nothing. I am with you, now and always.

Behold, I stand at the door and knock.
If anyone hears My voice and opens the door,
I will come in to him and dine with him,
and he with Me.

REVELATION 3:20

Connect with Judy

Website:
www.judygordonmorrow.com

Blog link on website:
www.judygordonmorrow.com/blog

Twitter:
http://www.twitter.com/JudyGMorrow

Facebook author page:
www.facebook.com/JudyGordonMorrow

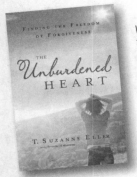